A Walk around the Pond

Gilbert Waldbauer

A Walk around the Pond

Insects in and over the Water

Harvard University Press

Cambridge, Massachusetts, London, England · 2006

Illustrations by Meredith Waterstraat

Title page illustration:
Recently emerged from a river, an adult mayfly, dragonfly,
and damselfly cling to a cattail plant.

LIBRARY OF CONGRESS CATALOGING-IN-PUBLICATION DATA

Waldbauer, Gilbert.

   A walk around the pond : insects in and over the water /
Gilbert Waldbauer.

      p. cm.

   Includes bibliographical references.

   ISBN 0-674-02211-4 (alk. paper)

   1. Insects.   2. Pond animals.   I. Title.

   QL463.W25 2006

   695.7—dc22   2005044737

To Phyllis Cooper,
dearest friend and unrelenting but constructive critic
of my writing

Dragonflies mating in the "wheel" position,
a method of insemination unique in the animal kingdom

Contents

A First Look

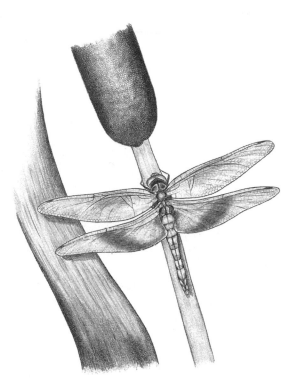

*This dragonfly will dash from its perch to snatch
an insect, its next meal, from the air*

As you walk around a pond early on a bright summer day, you will hear and see many entrancing things. You will probably see barn swallows swooping low over the water as they snatch insects from the air. If you are lucky, you will hear the rattling call of a kingfisher as it plunges into the water to grab a fish, and maybe be startled by the deep bellow of a bullfrog. Looking over the water, you may be delighted by dragonflies, their wings flashing in the sun as they fly in swift pursuit of mosquitoes and other small insects. You may also see another kind of dragonfly dart out from its perch on a cattail to catch passing insects, just as does the willow flycatcher nesting in a shrubby willow growing on the bank. On the surface and not far from shore, you'll probably see a small group of shiny, black beetles twirl and gyrate around each other. Their common and scientific names, whirligigs and *Gyrinidae,* describe their seemingly frenzied behavior. Beneath the surface of the pond is a busy community of life teeming with plants and animals—including the immature forms of the dragonflies and whirligig beetles. You can get an amazingly clear view of life below the surface of a pond by looking down into a shallow area through a glass-bottomed bucket with its bottom a few inches beneath the distorting ripples and reflections on the surface. (You can make one by cutting out the bottom of a plastic bucket, leaving a half-inch flange to which you attach a circular piece of glass on the inside with a watertight seal of silicone aquarium cement.) You may see fish and perhaps a turtle passing by, but by looking closely you will also see many different kinds of insects: among them a water scorpion (an insect despite its misleading name) clings to a plant as it waits for a passing insect, its next meal; a sleek, streamlined water beetle swims smoothly and gracefully between the plants; on the bottom, almost covered with silt, lurks a predatory dragonfly nymph; a caddisfly larva, protected by a portable, tubelike case it made of sand grains bound together with silk, nibbles on the leaves of a pondweed.

Insects are almost always the most numerous and diverse inhabitants of freshwater habitats. In North America alone there are about 10,000 aquatic and semiaquatic species with diverse ecological roles. Among them are not only plant feeders and predators such as those we have just met, but also scavengers and others that filter tiny microorganisms from the water. Although they are greatly outnumbered by the 84,000 North American species of land-dwelling insects, they outnumber the birds that occur in America north of Mexico by a factor of 10, and, more to the point, they greatly outnumber the other major groups of animals in North American freshwater habitats: in all only 790 fish, 155 frogs, toads, and salamanders, and 800 crustaceans (crayfish, crabs, and their relatives).

Where did all of these insects—both land-dwelling and aquatic—come from? The fossil record, although incomplete, tells us that the insects are an ancient lineage, preceding the dinosaurs, birds, and mammals by almost 200 million years. About 400 million years ago, the first insects-to-be were making the gradual transition from the water, where life began, to the land—probably via moist organic debris at the edges of ponds.

The oldest known fossil of an aquatic insect, a mayfly, was found in sedimentary rock about 320 million years old. There are surely older aquatic insects, but their fossils have yet to be uncovered by paleontologists. The known fossil record is not yet complete enough to tell us whether the aquatic insects evolved from ancestors that stayed behind in the water or from land-dwelling insects that went back into the water to take advantage of the many unexploited opportunities offered by freshwater habitats. But as P. J. Gullan and P. S. Cranston wrote, the nature of the aquatic insects' respiratory system—clearly adapted to function on land—indicates that a return to the water by land-dwelling insects is the more likely scenario.

The water-dwelling ancestors of the insects "breathed" by absorbing, probably through gills, the life-sustaining oxygen dissolved in the water—much as do present-day crustaceans such as the crabs and lobsters of the sea and the crayfish of fresh water. As in crustaceans, the oxygen was distributed to all the cells and tissues of the body by the blood, more precisely by the blood's blue, oxygen-carrying hemocyanin, functionally an equivalent of the hemoglobin in the red blood cells of vertebrates. But insects do it differently. They have a complex, branching, network of air-filled tubes, tracheae (windpipes) that conduct air that enters the body through the spiracles (air holes) to all the tissues and cells of the body.

If we hypothesize that the aquatic insects are descended from ancestors that never left the water, we are obliged to explain away evidence to the contrary, the indisputable fact that all of them—even those that have gills—have spiracles and a tracheal system, which are clearly adaptations for living on land. James Marden and Michael Thomas postulated that the tracheal system may have evolved not in land dwellers but rather in semi-aquatic insects that lived on the water surface. But they were, nevertheless, evolving a way to take oxygen directly from the air. Hemocyanin is presumably unnecessary if oxygen is not transported by the blood, and, as is to be expected, it is absent from most insects. It does persist in the blood of silverfish, the most primitive of the insects, and recently it was found to be present and functional in the blood of a stonefly by Silke Hagner-Holler and coauthors.

Insects have taken advantage of the many yet-to-be exploited opportunities offered by aquatic habitats. They have conquered the physical challenges of this environment, and have also adapted to each other and to the other creatures and plants that live in the water. In this way, complex, integrated aquatic communities of living things came into being. Together with their physical environments, these communities constitute the diverse ecosystems of the many different freshwater habitats. Mayflies, dragonflies, beetles, flies such as mosquitoes, and even a few parasitic wasps are among the insects that are at home in these habitats, which are many and varied—including mountain streams, great rivers, tranquil ponds, wave-swept lakes, temporary rain puddles, the water trapped in cavities in trees, water in the pitfall traps of insect-eating pitcher plants, and even the water in your birdbath.

But how did land-dwelling insects conquer the water? How do aquatic insects get the oxygen without which they cannot live? How do they move around in the water, a much denser medium than air? How did they become specialists equipped to live in only certain kinds of habitats, from roaring mountain streams to tranquil ponds? How do they manage to efficiently utilize different sorts of foods: plants, other insects, and even the microscopic life that swarms in the water? The answer is, of course, that natural selection, the driving force of evolution, molded them to become what they are.

In the following pages I consider the various ways that insects have evolved for coping with the new challenges that came with living in these many different aquatic habitats. Some aquatic insects have gills, as do fish, to absorb dissolved oxygen from the water. Others have evolved various methods of obtaining oxygen directly from the atmosphere: among them, long tubes—"snorkels"—that extend to the surface, bubbles of air obtained at the surface and used as a scuba diver uses her air tank, or even sharp air tubes that pierce air-filled hollows in plants. The ways in which aquatic insects move through the water range from paddling with oarlike legs to rocket propulsion. They utilize all available foods. A few feed on aquatic plants; some eat land-dwelling insects that fall onto the surface; many prey on aquatic insects or even small fish and tadpoles; and others feed like baleen whales, straining minute floating organisms from the water. As we will see, these methods for coping with life in the water are not as simple as they may seem. They require a great many anatomical, physiological, and behavioral modifications that are often complex and radical— and always interesting.

Who's Who in the Water

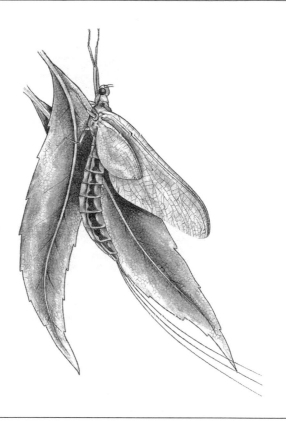

*Recently emerged from a river,
an adult mayfly clings to a willow leaf*

It was in Beardsley Park in Bridgeport, Connecticut, that I, a budding naturalist, first became acquainted with aquatic insects. I found them in the quiet coves of Bunnell's Pond, an impoundment of the Pequonnock River, which flows south through the city to Long Island Sound. By the time I was a junior in high school, I had collected them, kept them in an aquarium, and had learned their names from Frank Lutz's *Field Book of Insects*. But almost everyone I knew was indifferent to—if not oblivious of—almost all terrestrial and aquatic insects except for the very few that bit, stung, or otherwise pestered them.

But before going on, I will say a little about what insects are. Like their relatives the spiders, centipedes, millipedes, and lobsters and crabs, insects have segmented bodies and paired, jointed legs. The body segments of insects form three body regions: a 5-segmented head (the segmentation is visible only in the embryo); a 3-segmented thorax bearing 3 pairs of legs and, in most adult insects, 2 pairs of wings; and a legless 10- or 11-segmented abdomen that bears the genitalia.

The land-dwelling adults of some aquatic insects just can't be ignored. But few have even noticed the aquatic immature stages, which live in streams, rivers, ponds, and lakes. We have all swatted mosquitoes, but few of us have seen the larvae swimming in their aquatic birthplace. In the Midwest, huge piles of adult mayflies are removed with snowplows from under city lights. But the immatures go unnoticed as they burrow in the mud of lakes or the backwaters of rivers.

Aquatic insects are an ecologically important and varied lot that represent 11 of the 31 orders (major groups) of insects—indicating that in evolutionary time there were at least 11 independent invasions of the water from the land. Some, such as mayflies, dragonflies, and mosquitoes, are aquatic as immatures and land dwellers as adults. Some species of beetles and true bugs (insects of the order Hemiptera, usually just called bugs) are strictly aquatic in the immature stage but in adulthood are amphibious, living both in the water and on land.

The lives of insects are best understood in the context of their metamorphosis, defined as a significant change in form and behavior from the immature to the adult stage. Metamorphosis is a fundamental influence on the life styles of all insects. Among the aquatic insects, mayflies, dragonflies, stoneflies, and bugs all undergo a gradual metamorphosis with only three life stages: the egg; the nymph, the growing stage; and the adult, or reproductive stage. Wings gradually develop externally as nymphs grow and molt several times but are not fully formed and flight-worthy until after the last molt, the molt to the adult stage. In immature land-dwelling insects with gradual metamorphosis, nymphs generally closely resemble adults in appearance, choice of food, and other behaviors. Even a tiny grasshopper or praying mantis just out of the egg looks like its parents except for the absence of wings. But nymphal aquatic insects differ from adults in appearance and behavior because of their conspicuous gills and several other adaptations to aquatic life. Among the aquatic insects with gradual metamorphosis, only true bugs (members of the order Hemiptera) are similar in life style and appearance in the nymphal and adult stages, both of which are at home in the water.

Most insects undergo a complete metamorphosis, which includes four developmental stages: the egg; the wingless larva, the growing stage; the pupa, or transformation stage, in which the larva metamorphoses to the final stage, the reproductive adult stage; the adult usually has wings, which developed internally during the pupal stage. Complete metamorphosis allows larvae and adults to follow different evolutionary paths, to specialize so as to accommodate their different roles. Among the aquatic insects, mosquitoes are a good example. The legless larvae are eating machines that almost constantly strain small particles of food from the water. Their role is to eat, survive, and grow. But the winged adults are sex machines devoted to reproduction. The females of some species obtain protein to produce eggs by sucking blood from animals, but males do not bite; they just suck nectar from flowers.

Among the insects that have complete metamorphosis and are aquatic as immatures are all of the alderflies and dobsonflies, virtually all of the caddisflies, one small group related to the aphidlions and antlions (order Neuroptera), and some of the beetles, moths, flies, and wasps. Complete metamorphosis is an evolutionarily more successful strategy for survival than gradual metamorphosis—at least as judged by numbers of extant species. Of the 900,000 currently known insects only 135,000, or 15 percent, have gradual metamorphosis, but 765,000, 85 percent, have complete metamorphosis.

Mayflies (Order Ephemeroptera)

Nymphs of mayflies and other aquatic insects with gradual metamorphosis are sometimes more aptly and engagingly called naiads. In ancient Greek mythology, the nymphs are among the many minor divinities of nature, but naiads are the particular nymphs of lakes, rivers, and ponds. As tempted as I am to call them naiads, I will call them nymphs, the more commonly used term. Nymphs of the world's 2,000 mayflies have three, occasionally only two, long, thin tails and a row of fringed or platelike gills along each side of the abdomen. They are variously adapted to live in rivers; fast-flowing, rocky streams; or the standing waters of lakes, ponds, weed-choked backwaters of rivers, and bogs; or even in temporary ponds. Some burrow in or sprawl on muddy bottoms, others cling to water plants or, in fast-flowing streams, to a stone with legs and a suction disk formed by their overlapping platelike gills. A few are predators, but the great majority feed on particles of organic debris and algae. Often exceedingly abundant, mayfly nymphs are important intermediaries in aquatic food chains. They eat organisms too small for larger animals to eat, thereby becoming "packages of food" big enough to be profitably eaten by larger animals such as fish and large insects.

Full-grown nymphs float to the surface and there molt to the adult stage, standing on the surface film briefly before flying off. At rest, mayflies hold their wings above the back like butterflies. Among the insects, they are highly unusual—but not unique—in that males have two "penises" and females two "vaginas." Another peculiarity is that they are the only insects with two adult stages. A newly emerged adult flies to a perch on shore and then undergoes a final molt to the definitive adult stage. Adults cannot feed and usually live for only a day, hence the scientific name of their order, Ephemeroptera, derived from two Greek roots meaning for a day, and wing.

Dragonflies and Damselflies (Order Odonata)

The almost 5,000 species of dragonflies and damselflies are all predators both as nymphs and as adults. Adult odonates (a term including both dragonflies and damselflies), have long, thin abdomens, are often brightly colored, and are conspicuous as they gracefully swoop and course through the air. Both damselflies and dragonflies have long, rather narrow wings, but at rest dragonflies hold them out to the sides like the wings of an airplane, while most damselflies hold them together and raised above the body, just as do butterflies.

Damselfly nymphs are long and slender and have three large, conspicuous, leaflike gills at the end of the abdomen. But dragonfly nymphs are robust, wide-bodied, and have internal gills in the rectum—more about this strange arrangement later. Except for a few Hawaiian damselfly nymphs that live in very moist terrestrial microhabitats, odonate nymphs are aquatic. They live in streams, lakes, ponds, swamps, bogs, and even brackish estuaries. In fast-flowing streams, they may cling to stones, and in other habitats cling to aquatic plants, lurk in debris, or burrow in the bottom. They have a strange and unique way—to be explained later—of grasping their prey. Full-grown odonate nymphs crawl to land and cling to a tree trunk or some other support as they molt to the adult stage, leaving behind a light-colored, ghostlike husk, the molted skin.

Stoneflies (Order Plecoptera)

Stoneflies are aptly named. The nymphs of most species cling to or burrow under stones in cold streams or at the wave-swept shores of cold lakes. A very few live on land at the tops of cold, wet mountains in Patagonia and New Zealand. Stanley Jewett discovered that both nymphs and wingless adults of a probably unique species live permanently in the depths of Lake Tahoe. The 2,000 known species of stoneflies have gradual metamorphosis, but their wings, and those of all the following orders, are of an evolutionarily advanced style that, unlike those of mayflies and dragonflies, the most primitive of the winged insects, can be folded down against the body; an arrangement that inspired the scientific name of the order, formed from the Greek roots meaning folded and wing.

The ability to fold their wings was a hugely important evolutionary step that opened up many new opportunities for insects, both aquatics and land dwellers. Because they can get their unwieldy wings out of the way, they can exploit the many cracks and crevices of the environment. They can, for example, live under bark or a rock, burrow in the soil, or inhabit the stems, leaves, or roots of plants. The fact that there are only 7,000 species with the primitive style of wings, but about 800,000 with wings that can be folded, leaves no doubt that this was a watershed evolutionary step.

Many stonefly nymphs live in the same habitats as mayfly nymphs, but have much longer antennae, only two long tails, and their gills are clusters of filaments that are usually at the bases of the three pairs of legs on the thorax. Some of them feed mainly on algae or plant debris, but others use their long, sickle-shaped mandibles to prey on insects. Full-grown nymphs swim to shore, crawl out of the water, and then are likely to cling to tree trunks or bridge abutments to molt. Nymphs of a few species become adult in winter, and may have to crawl over snow to find a suitable place to molt. Adults differ from adult mayflies not only in folding the wings but also in having much longer antennae and only two tails. Most are awkward aerialists; in some species the males are short-winged and cannot fly; and in others both sexes are incapable of flying. Some adults do not feed; others drink honeydew, the sugary excrement of aphids; and some eat leaves, rotting wood, or algae that encrust bark.

True Bugs (Order Hemiptera)

The true bugs have piercing-sucking mouthparts and front wings with a leathery basal half and a membranous tip—hence the ordinal name, from the Greek roots for half and wing. With 50,000 known species, they are by far the most numerous of the insects with gradual metamorphosis. Most are terrestrial, but those of 12 of the 44 families (subdivisions of an order) in North America are aquatic. Among the most common are the water striders, marsh treaders, water boatmen, backswimmers, creeping water bugs, giant water bugs, and water scorpions. With the exception of most water boatmen, all are predators that feed mainly on insects and may even attack small fish and tadpoles.

True bugs differ from other aquatic insects with gradual metamorphosis in that adults and nymphs are similar in appearance, are aquatic, eat the same food, behave similarly in the water, and must come to the surface for air. The adults are generally winged and can disperse to other bodies of water. They occupy a variety of aquatic habitats, even salt ponds and hot springs. Their habits are varied. Some, the water striders and marsh treaders, live on the surface; others, such as the water scorpions and creeping water bugs, cling to water plants; and many, such as the water boatmen, backswimmers, and giant water bugs, are good swimmers with legs broadened into oars by flattening or by a fringe of stiff hairs.

Dobsonflies, Fishflies, and Alderflies (Order Megaloptera)

The dobsonflies and their relatives, the alderflies and fishflies, are the most primitive of the insects with complete metamorphosis. The dobsonfly, the giant of the North American aquatic insects, is about 3 inches long and has an impressive wingspan of over 6 inches. Females have relatively short mandibles, but the male's are very long, slender, curved, and sharply pointed. Neither sex feeds during the adult stage, and Elsie Klots says that the male's jaws are of little use other than for holding the female during mating. But I know from personal experience that they can give a painful nip if you happen to brush against one. My encounter with an adult dobsonfly resting on foliage near a stream was a memorable experience.

The dobsonflies and their relatives, all of them aquatic, are a group of only 300 species. Their ordinal name comes from the Greek roots for giant and wing. But not all are as large as dobsonflies; the smoky alderfly, for example, is only 0.6 inch long. Some live in fast-flowing streams, while others prefer rivers, lakes, ponds, or swamps.

They live under stones in fast-flowing streams, may grow to a length of over 3 inches, and all feed on insects and other invertebrates. They obtain oxygen through a row of long, filamentous gills along each side of the abdomen. Bass love to eat them. Consequently, anglers use them as bait, searching for them by turning over stones in streams. Full-grown larvae crawl ashore, pupate under a stone or log, and emerge as adults after about 2 weeks.

Dobsonfly larvae are commonly called hellgrammites and sometimes conniption bugs, gator fleas, or gogglegoys—all American folk names of unknown origin.

Spongillaflies (Order Neuroptera)

Among the nearly 5,000 species in the order Neuroptera (from Greek roots meaning veined and wing) are the familiar land-dwelling aphid-eating lacewings; the mantispids, parasites in spider egg sacs; and antlions, which dig pits to trap their prey. Only the spongillaflies (family Sisyridae), with just 30 species worldwide, six of them in North America, are aquatic. As larvae, all are parasites in the bodies of freshwater sponges, which are often attached to dead wood in slow-running streams. The small young larvae absorb sufficient oxygen through their skin, but the older and larger ones have gills to meet their greater need for oxygen. Mature larvae come ashore to pupate in silken cocoons spun on nearby objects. After 5 or 6 days, the adults emerge and feed on pollen and probably small insects, according to the entomologist Harley Brown.

It is now well established that sponges are animals, but James Needham, one of the great authorities on aquatic insects, wrote that early in the nineteenth century, the spongillafly, "an inno-cent victim," was dragged into a controversy between French and British entomologists. A French scientist maintained that sponges are animals because he had found "in the sponge body numerous fine filaments that moved to and fro." A British en-tomologist thought they were plants, arguing—falsely, it turns out—that the filaments seen by the Frenchman were actually hairs on the bodies of spongillaflies.

Beetles (Order Coleoptera)

The 300,000 known beetles constitute about a quarter of the 1,200,000 presently known species of animals. Adult Coleop-tera (from Greek roots meaning sheath and wing) have thick, hardened, opaque front wings not used in flight but serving as wing covers, or elytra, sheaths of armor that cover most of the thorax and usually all of the abdomen. Less than 2 percent of the beetles are aquatic. But even this small fraction amounts to 5,000 species, one of the largest groups of aquatic insects. The members of at least 15 of the 112 families of beetles are ei-ther all aquatic or include from a few to many aquatic species, which as larvae are always aquatic, as are the majority of adults, although they can and do fly. Beetles live in virtually all bodies of water, including hot springs, water-filled cavities in trees, and even salt ponds and the seas. With the exception noted be-low, larvae come ashore to pupate in the soil.

The predaceous diving beetles (family Dytiscidae), which include the largest of the aquatic beetles, are predators both as larvae (water tigers) and as sleek, fast-swimming adults. Groups of shiny black whirligig beetles (family Gyrinidae) gyrate wildly on the surface as they scavenge insects that fall onto the water, but the larvae are fierce predators that hunt on the bottom. A few of the Hydrophilidae, water scavenger beetles, live in dung, but the great majority are aquatic. Adults, competent swimmers, are mainly scavengers, but most larvae are predators. A few riffle beetles (family Elmidae) live in ponds or lakes, but most of these tiny plant eaters crawl on the bottom or on plants in cold, fast-flowing streams. The behavior of the beetles of the family Haliplidae is described by their common name, crawling water beetles. They feed on algae and other plants, and are often found in masses of vegetation. Almost all the herbivorous leaf beetles (family Chrysomelidae) are land dwellers; a mere handful, species of *Donacia* and *Haemonia*, feed on aquatic plants and are unusual because the larvae tap hollow spaces in these plants to obtain air. They pupate under water in airtight silken cocoons attached to plants and filled with air from the plant.

Caddisflies (Order Trichoptera)

Caddisfly larvae are aquatic and live in ponds, lakes, rivers, or brooks, except for a few land-dwelling species in Europe and Oregon. Many build and live in portable cases open at both ends, which, depending on the species and habitat, differ in architecture and building materials. Bound together with silk, cases are made of various mineral or plant materials—or even tiny clam or snail shells. A case may be shaped like a cylindrical tube, a tube square in cross-section, a cone, a log cabin, or a snail shell. (In his classic entomology textbook, John Henry Comstock noted that one of the last type was at first thought to be a real snail.) Most case-making larvae are omnivores that eat algae, small bits of plant material, and small invertebrates such as insects and worms. Some caddisflies of rivers and streams build stationary silken or stone-walled shelters and spin nets of silk attached to nearby stones. At intervals the larvae leave their shelters briefly to eat small organisms caught in their net.

Both caddisfly larvae and pupae have gills, and do not come to the surface for air. Unlike nearly all other aquatic insects, they do not spend the pupal stage on land. Some pupate in a silken cocoon, but case makers pupate in their case after anchoring it and closing off both openings with silk or a pebble, but leaving small openings for water circulation. The pupae, unlike those of most other insects, are active. When ready to molt to the adult stage, they leave the cocoon or case, and, in running water, swim to the surface, molt there, and immediately fly off. In still water, they molt after swimming to the shore or climbing up a plant or some other object protruding from the water.

Adults of the 5,000 known caddisflies are mothlike, and the wings are covered with hairs, which gives this order its scientific name, Trichoptera, from Greek roots for hairy and wing. Most are nocturnal, often come to lights at night, drink water and nectar, and may survive for several weeks.

Moths and Butterflies (Order Lepidoptera)

The moths and butterflies that constitute the order Lepidoptera number almost 120,000 species, but only about 450, all moths, are associated with water as caterpillars; about 90 of them are fully aquatic and the others are semiaquatic and live on wet shores or on plants protruding above the water. Caterpillars and pupae of the aquatic species absorb dissolved oxygen from the water through gills or the skin. Like terrestrial caterpillars, they are plant feeders, eating the leaves or burrowing in the stems or roots of aquatic plants. Some live in portable cases made of bits of leaf fastened together with silk or in a piece of a hollow plant stem. Some pupate in cocoons attached to plants well below the surface and filled with air from holes bitten into the plant's stem.

After the moths pupate, the adults leave the water to find mates and reproduce. If you hold an adult—of any moth— by its wings, a colored "powder" rubs off on your fingers. It consists of almost microscopic scales that cover the wings the way shingles overlap on a roof. The ordinal name comes from Greek roots meaning scale and wing. Losing or damaging its cover of scales would probably doom a moth. They give the wing its color and pattern, in many moths the camouflage that protects them from predators, and in flight they are aerodynamically important because they smooth the flow of air over the wings. In his beautifully illustrated book *Insects of the World*, Walter Linsenmaier described how the adult moth escapes from the water. When the moth sheds its pupal skin, "air is stowed under the wings as though in a diving bell, and lifts the insect to the surface." Its track is briefly visible in the water as a streak of wax particles "brushed off the wing during the swift ascent." This coating of wax waterproofs the moth and keeps it dry until "it reaches the surface, crawls ashore, and unfolds its delicate wings."

Mosquitoes and Other Flies (Order Diptera)

Mention flies, and most people picture a house fly, which many think of as "the fly," but adult flies—including the aquatic ones, about half of the 150,000 known species of flies—are extremely varied in appearance and behavior. Consider, for example, a small, delicate, blood-sucking mosquito; an innocuous, long-legged crane fly, sometimes mistaken for a gigantic mosquito; a nectar-drinking drone fly, a convincing mimic of a honey bee; or the large, stout-bodied, blood-sucking horse flies such as the "greenies" that plague bathers on New Jersey beaches. Flies are virtually unique, because they have only front wings. The hind wings have become small, gyroscopic sense organs that stabilize flight by informing the insect if it yaws, pitches, or rolls. Diptera, the ordinal name of the flies, comes from the Greek roots for two and wings.

"The flies living today," wrote Harold Oldroyd in his book on the natural history of flies, "can with fair certainty be looked upon as two evolutionary lines." The first, and presumably more primitive, includes crane flies, mosquitoes, black flies, and the various families of midges and gnats. Many of the female flies of this line suck blood from humans and other animals. "The second line leads on to the house-fly and bluebottle" and includes also fruit flies, hover flies, and robber flies. A great many species of the first line are aquatic in the larval stage, among them all mosquitoes and black flies, and many of the crane flies and midges. Those of the second line, except for some horse flies, snipe flies, and just a few others, are overwhelmingly land dwellers.

Aquatic fly larvae live in almost any body of water that persists for at least a few weeks, including salt ponds, hot springs, and rot cavities in trees; and mosquito larvae will even live in a beer can or a discarded tire. The larvae of one unusual species of shore fly (family Ephydridae) live in pools of crude oil. Most burrow in bottom sediments, feeding on detritus or small animals; others burrow in the leaves, stems, or roots of aquatic plants. Many, such as mosquito larvae, strain small particles of food from the water. Some have gills or absorb dissolved oxygen through the skin, and others come to the surface for air. Mature larvae of some species, such as horse flies and hover flies, leave the water to pupate, while others, such as mosquitoes and black flies, pupate in the water. Pupae of Oldroyd's "second line" of flies are encased by an ovoid, cocoon-like structure. This is the puparium, the darkened and hardened skin of the last of the three larval stages, which is not split and shed, as are those of the other stages, although the pupa has separated its body from it.

Wasps (Order Hymenoptera)

Incredibly tiny parasitic wasps, "fairyflies," each one small enough to perch on the head of a pin along with several companions, swim through the water of ponds. They are adult females searching for victims—the eggs of backswimmers, damselflies, predaceous diving beetles—that will be shelter and food for their parasitic larval offspring. With their piercing ovipositors (egg-laying organs) they insert one or more eggs into each of many host eggs, up to 50 into one egg of a large predaceous diving beetle. The larvae eat the yolk, pupate in the shell of the host egg, and emerge into the water as adults that absorb dissolved oxygen through their skin. These wasps, family Mymaridae, mate under the water, or standing on the surface film, or clinging to an aquatic plant protruding from the water. In Europe and Asia, females of a considerably larger parasitic wasp *(Agriotypus)* dive into the water to attach eggs to the body of a case-building caddisfly.

These parasites are a tiny minority of an order of well over 100,000 species, the Hymenoptera (from the Greek roots for membrane and wing), which also includes the more familiar wasps, as well as the ants and bees, neither of which are parasitic. Of the thousands of parasitic wasps in North America, only 51 are aquatic. They are pioneers that, to avoid the fierce competition for terrestrial hosts, have overcome the problems of living in the water to take advantage of the unexploited resources it offers.

Broadly speaking, there are two kinds of wasps, parasites and predators. A few of the thousands of predaceous wasps are noticed by many, notably the yellowjackets, often mistaken for bees, that in late summer and early autumn show up to participate in picnics. Predaceous wasps hunt for insects or spiders to feed to the larvae in their nests. In North America, only one predaceous wasp is aquatic. The females dive into the water to capture aquatic spiders.

Spiders (Class Arachnida, Order Araneae)

Spiders are not insects, although the two groups are related. Insects have six legs and two antennae, are often winged, and among them eat both plant and animal matter; spiders have

eight legs and no antennae, are never winged, and are all predators that eat mainly insects. Of the 30,000 known spiders, a few
are semiaquatic, but Rod and Ken Preston-Mafham wrote in
their fascinating book on spiders that there is only one truly
aquatic spider in the world, because "no spider has developed
the ability to 'breathe' underwater using a gill or via diffusion,
as has happened with numerous insects, particularly in their
larval stages." Read on to see how one spider manages to get air
under the water.

The large, handsome, semiaquatic fishing spiders will hunt
at some distance from the water but more often "adopt a waiting stance at the water's edge." They seek prey by running over
the water's surface like a water strider, but sometimes go under
the water briefly, usually preying on insects but taking the occasional small vertebrate. The research of Horst Bleckmann and
Thomas Lotz showed that they take notice of surface waves to
detect and locate small fish. They can, for example, pinpoint
from 7 inches away the center of the concentric rings of ripples
caused by a fish touching the water surface.

But the unique European water spider *Argyroneta aquatica*,
the world's only truly aquatic spider, has, wrote the Preston-
Mafhams, "developed a far more high-tech approach, which
enables it to live a comfortable underwater life on a permanent
basis—it constructs a diving bell." *Argyroneta* makes its diving
bell by spinning an airtight sheet of silk moored to underwater
plants and then filling it with air by making repeated trips to
the surface for bubbles of air that it releases under the silken
sheet, which becomes dome-shaped when it is fully inflated.
The spider lives comfortably in its air-filled diving bell but

leaps out to pounce on passing insects or even small tadpoles or fish.

The approximately 25,000 insects that live in water for part or most of their lives are variously adapted to survive in a wide variety of aquatic habitats—indeed, almost any body of water. We will next look at some of the more unusual aquatic habitats and the insects that live in them.

Where They Live

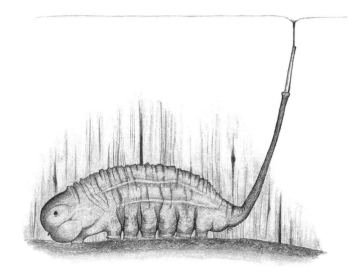

A rat-tailed maggot, the larva of a bumble bee–mimicking hover fly, with its air tube extended to the surface of the water

Running waters start in highlands. Trickles meld to form little rills that join to form brooks that come together to form fast-flowing streams that, merging with other streams, flow on as a large river that wanders slowly across its flood plain. As water makes its way down to the sea, its attributes are progressively changing. Its oxygen content and the velocity of the current decrease, but its temperature, the load of silt it carries, and usually its depth increase. Each of its many different habitats offers its own opportunities and challenges, and each is inhabited by its own mix of insects that are evolutionarily adapted to cope with it.

The great majority of aquatic insects inhabit fresh water, not only rivers and streams, but also lakes, ponds, and temporary puddles. Some of the insects that live in lakes will be found in the various microhabitats of warm, shallow bays with aquatic plants rooted in the bottom; others in the dark, cold depths with silty bottoms devoid of plants; and yet others at the turbulent shores where, as Matthew Arnold wrote, there are "pebbles which waves draw back and fling." We will come to these "conventional" habitats in other chapters. But insects have succeeded in colonizing virtually all aquatic habitats, and, as we will now see, some live in very unusual places where we might not expect to find them.

Among them are some species that live in water held by plants: in water-filled cavities in trees, the pitfall traps of insect-eating pitcher plants, cupped leaves, hollow stems, and the like. In tropical forests they live in water trapped in the crowns of plants—bromeliads, relatives of the pineapple and Spanish moss—that cling to the branches of trees high above the ground. Water-filled cavities in trees, known as tree holes or rot cavities, are microcosms, little worlds unto themselves. Well, not always so little; some may contain several gallons of water.

Every aquatic habitat, even the smallest, consists of a variety of different microhabitats, each one inhabited by insects adapted to prosper in it. A flooded cavity in a tree, for example, is shared by a variety of insects, some that cling to its walls, some that swim in the open water, others that lurk in the organic debris at the bottom. A tree hole is likely to be inhabited by hordes of bacteria and other microorganisms and a smaller variety of larger creatures: mainly mosquitoes, other flies, beetles, and mites (relatives of spiders and ticks) in the North Temperate Zone, and in the New World tropics also by the nymphs of dragonflies, "giant" damselflies, and even tadpoles and small frogs. These creatures eat each other, the decomposing leaves and the few dead insects that fall or are blown into the tree hole, and also the bacteria and fungi that do the decomposing. They also feed on one-celled algae, other microorganisms, and tiny particles of detritus that they filter from the water.

In 1974, Norman Fashing of William and Mary College published an article on a new species of aquatic mite that he had collected at several sites in the eastern United States. This tiny mite, barely visible to the naked eye, lives only in water-filled tree holes and feeds on the mass of decomposing leaves and other organic matter at the bottom of the hole. In winter, or when a tree hole goes dry, the mites survive by burrowing into the moist debris and becoming quiescent. These infinitesimal and wingless creatures are, of course, incapable of moving from one tree hole to another under their own power. They overcome this difficulty by hitching a ride on a flying tree hole dweller—in this case a hover fly—that will, if it survives the trip, transport the mite to another tree hole, perhaps to a distant one.

These hover flies, two species of the genus *Mallota* (they have no common name) are among the largest (almost an inch long), handsomest, and most interesting members of the tree hole community in eastern North America. After Fashing found his mites clinging to the bodies of these flies, he stopped at the University of Illinois to consult me as an "expert" on hover flies. I was one of less than a dozen North American entomologists who were working on these flies (family Syrphidae), a small frog in a very small puddle.

*Mallota*s survive the winter as larvae hibernating in tree holes. In spring they crawl out of the hole to molt to the pupal stage in the soil, and about 2 weeks later transform to the adult stage. My former graduate student Chris Maier and I found that these flies visit flowers for nectar and pollen in the morning but in the heat of the afternoon retreat to the shade of the forest. Males patrol flowering shrubs in the morning and pounce on and mate with feeding females. In the forest, they defend territories around tree holes against males of their own species and, ever driven by the pressing compulsion to be succeeded by offspring, mate with females that come to lay eggs there. The adults soon die, but larvae hatch within a few days and feed on the detritus at the bottom of the hole. By late summer, found Maier, they are fully grown and go into diapause, a quiescent state similar to hibernation, in preparation for winter.

In spring, mites—they are just hitchhikers, not parasites—climb on board a newly emerged adult *Mallota*, cling tightly to its body, and when the searching fly enters another tree hole, get off and join other members of their species or, if the hole is unoccupied by their kind, found a new colony. Fashing discovered that in the spring, when adult *Mallota*s are busy flying from tree to tree—when the "bus service" is good—the mites transform to a life stage with legs anatomically specialized for hitching rides and holding on. As I said, the mite will survive only if the fly survives. Fortunately for the mites, the flies' chances for survival are enhanced because these flies trick birds into not attacking and eating them, as I will explain later.

Mosquitoes, because some are an aggravating nuisance and some transmit diseases such as malaria and West Nile fever, are the most studied and best known of the aquatic insects. Many mosquitoes, including some transmitters of disease, live in water-filled tree holes in the larval stage. In the southern United States, and in many other parts of the world, larvae of the infamous yellow fever mosquito *(Aedes aegypti)* occasionally inhabit tree holes, probably their ancestral habitat, but are now most often found in artificial containers—which are often more numerous than tree holes—even abandoned tires, but especially barrels and other containers made of wood.

The geographically widespread eastern tree hole mosquito (*Aedes triseriatus*) is a nuisance wherever it occurs, but is particularly important in the north central states, because it transmits the LaCrosse virus to people from chipmunks and other small rodents. Named for the area in Wisconsin where it was first found, this virus causes a disease that is usually mild, but in children may involve the central nervous system and rarely cause a fatal encephalitis, inflammation of the brain.

In cold climates where the water in tree holes freezes, these mosquitoes survive the winter only as diapausing eggs in the tree holes. Even though they have yet to take a blood meal from an infected animal or even a healthy one, adults that originate from the overwintered eggs contain the virus and are capable of transmitting it to humans and rodents by "biting." But how is it possible for them to have the virus if they were not contaminated with it by drinking the blood of an infected animal? This is not a trivial question. The answer is essential to understanding how this virus persists in the environment and how it is transmitted.

An obvious possibility is that mothers pass the virus on to their offspring through the egg, what medical entomologists call transovarial transmission. It was then, in the 1970s, well known that ticks pass on viruses through the egg, but the conventional wisdom of medical entomology was that mosquitoes cannot. Fortunately, there was a graduate student at the University of Wisconsin who was still too inexperienced to know and be hampered by this misleading bit of conventional wisdom. Douglass Watts and his collaborators demonstrated that eastern tree hole mosquitoes do indeed pass on the LaCrosse virus in their eggs. It was later discovered that the virus can also be transmitted venereally, from one sex to the other during mating.

🦟 A spectacular giant damselfly of Central and South America has the scientific name *Megaloprepus,* which, translated from its Greek roots, means conspicuous giant. With a body as much as 5.3 inches long and a wing span of up to 7.4 inches, it is the largest—but not the heaviest—of all the living odonates. It is a striking and hard-to-miss member of forest communities because of its size, its distinctive manner of flight, and its conspicuous wings, patterned with bright blue. (The wing of a related species is so attractive that, as D. C. Geijskes noted, it has been used as a nose plug ornament by at least one member of the Kofan Indian tribe of western Colombia.) In 1923, Philip Calvert described these damselflies on the wing:

> When flying the four wings are spread quite far apart, fore and hind wing of the same side far apart, body horizontal. Flight slow enough so that the movements of each separate wing can be seen—insect consequently moves slowly but can dodge. Mr. Barnes compared the movements of the wings to that of a windmill, but the revolving movements are lacking; I should say the effect produced by the wings is more like that of a jumping-jack with moveable arms and legs pulled by one string, rather slowly, but, of course, at regular intervals.

A well-known and accomplished student of the ecology and behavior of damselflies, Ola Fincke of the University of Oklahoma, wrote in 1992 that giant damselflies, rather than feeding on flying insects as do most damselflies and dragonflies, specialize in catching web-building spiders, a behavior shared by only a few other damselflies. These insects, wrote Fincke, "are highly skilled at locating and catching spider prey . . . on two occasions I watched as [a species of giant damselfly] darted to the leaf litter and came up with an unlucky spider that tried to avoid capture by dropping from its web."

While most odonate nymphs inhabit streams, lakes, or ponds, the giant damselflies and their few relatives live in small bodies of water held in various parts of plants. Giant damselflies occupy water-filled tree holes in the trunks or branches of trees. Tree holes in the wet tropics harbor a diverse community of animals, among them predators such as giant damselfly and dragonfly nymphs and even a mosquito larva that eats mainly other mosquito larvae. The most abundant and ubiquitous prey in these tree holes is mosquito larvae. There are also larval midges, in some tree holes hover fly larvae and tadpoles, and always smaller nymphs of their own species for the cannibalistic damselfly nymphs to eat. Damselfly nymphs in tree holes with narrow, slit-like entrances are spared the unwelcome gastronomic attention of dragonfly nymphs, because adult dragonflies, which can hold their wings only out to the side like an airplane, cannot enter to lay eggs. But adult damselflies can pass through such narrow entrances to lay their eggs, because they hold their wings together over the body, almost like a butterfly.

In an article published in 1996, Fincke reported her observation that although giant damselfly nymphs do not stake out and defend feeding territories, they do fight with each other. An aggressive and escalating encounter begins when two nymphs approach within about 2 inches of each other. At first they raise and vibrate the three leaf-like gills at the end of the abdomen; they next swing the abdomen from side to side in a wide arc; then they repeatedly strike out with their long, well-armed lower lips; and, finally, one nymph grabs the other with its lower lip and the other tries to pull away and retreat.

Fully grown nymphs molt to the adult stage in the early morning. As Fincke wrote, they "climb out of the tree holes and may [crawl] as far as several [yards] before emerging, usually on the tree trunk. Newly emerged giant damselflies can fly within 1–2 hours after emergence and disperse widely from the tree hole habitat. Males require 3 weeks to become sexually mature, whereas females require about 5 weeks."

In 1901, Professor John B. Smith of the Department of Economic Entomology at Rutgers University in New Jersey published the first report of the previously unknown pitcher plant mosquito, now known as *Wyeomyia smithii:*

> My good friend J. Turner Brakeley wrote me in the late summer that, in looking at the contents of some pitcher plant leaves he had found mosquito larvae in abundance in the water they contained . . . Late in November I spent three days with Mr. Brakeley at Lahaway [New Jersey], and one of our walks was into a huckleberry and wild cranberry swamp where pitcher plants were abundant . . . The interesting point was that in every leaf examined there were wrigglers [mosquito larvae] varying in size from an eighth to a quarter of an inch in length.

Specimens were sent to the eminent insect taxonomist Daniel Coquillett. He recognized them as a new species and named it *Aedes smithii* after John Smith. Not long thereafter, *smithii* was taken out of the genus *Aedes* and placed in the new, recently recognized genus *Wyeomyia*.

Pitcher plants are among the 538 known species of carnivorous plants on earth. Some carnivorous plants trap insects on sticky tentacles, and some catch them in "snap traps"; but pitcher plants drown them in water that partially fills their pitfall traps, which are modified vaselike leaves. The trapped insects die and are digested and assimilated, supplying these plants, which grow on soil deficient in minerals, with nutrients without which they could not survive.

The water in the pitfall trap of the common pitcher plant of eastern North America is, according to Thomas Givnish, host to a miniature ecosystem of organisms that are not digested by the plant and whose nutritional foundation is the insects that are trapped by the plant and die. This ecosystem includes, among other organisms, many different kinds of bacteria and other microorganisms, tiny crustaceans, and three species of flies. The most famous of the flies, the pitcher plant mosquitoes, swim actively and eat microorganisms they filter from the water. The larvae of a flesh fly feed mainly on recently drowned insects at the surface of the water, and the larvae of a midge feed on the accumulation of decomposing insects in the bottom of the pitcher. These fly larvae, the so-called infauna of the pitcher, are thought to aid the plant's digestion.

In Borneo, certain ants have a unique relationship with a vinelike, climbing pitcher plant whose vaselike traps hang from tendrils at the tips of the leaves. The ants are housed in the hollow tendrils and feed on trapped insects that they hijack from the pitcher. C. M. Clarke and R. L. Kitching of the University of New England in Australia were amazed to see these ants swimming in the fluid of the pitchers searching for large trapped insects. "They swam to all parts of the pitcher, either at the surface of the fluid or below it. They remained submerged for up to 30 seconds . . . When a prey item was located, it was grasped in the mandibles and hauled from the liquid (sometimes with the assistance of more ants, depending on the size of the prey)." Clarke and Kitching found that the fluid in pitchers overloaded with large prey putrefied, killing the animals that normally live in the pitcher (the infauna) and thereby disrupting the pitcher's digestive system. They believe that the pitcher plant, the ants, and the infauna are in a three-way mutually beneficial association. The plant provides the ants with food and a domicile, the infauna enhances the pitcher's digestive system by breaking down the prey, and the ants, by removing excess prey, prevent putrefaction from killing the infauna.

Egg-laying katydids pave the way for communities of aquatic insects that live in the cylindrical internodes, hollow compartments, of bamboo stalks in Peruvian forests. If you have ever handled a bamboo fishing pole, you know that these compartments have no openings to the outside world; they are tightly sealed. So how do insects get into the internodes? According to Jerry Louton and his coworkers, the wall of the internode is breached by female katydids that insert eggs into the developing, still-soft stalks by piercing the walls of a compartment with their ovipositor. Eventually, adjacent, slot-like punctures coalesce to form large openings that may be further widened by other creatures passing in and out.

The internodes, about a foot long and with a maximum inside diameter of about 2 inches, hold at most about 11 ounces of water, which is secreted by the plant and fills about the bottom quarter of an internode. The water is occupied by insects, mainly mosquito larvae of several species, but there may also be others, among them the larvae of biting midges and hover flies, and nymphal pinwheel damselflies, the commonest and probably most important aquatic predators in the internodes. The dry upper area of the internodes may harbor cockroaches, katydids, bugs, beetles, ants, and even small frogs or snakes.

The flight of the pinwheel, or helicopter, damselflies is very unusual, and is graphically described by Mary Beebe and C. William Beebe in a charming book that recounts their adventures in South America in 1908 and 1909. "Spinning through the aisles made by the giant columns of tree trunks, were curious translucent pin-wheels." They did not realize that these things were damselflies until they caught one in a butterfly net. "The movement of the long, narrow wings, with a spot of white at the tips was, to the eye, a circular revolving whirl, with the needle-sized body trailing behind. The white spots revolved rapidly, while the rest of the wings became a mere gray haze." This damselfly revealed its kinship to Ola Fincke's giant damselflies by its habit of feeding on spiders. "From under leaves or from the heart of widespread webs, good-sized spiders were snatched. A momentary juggling with the strong legs, a single nip, and the spider minus its abdomen dropped to the [ground]."

In the coastal waters of the Atlantic, Indian, and Pacific Oceans—and even hundreds of miles offshore—water striders of the genus *Halobates* skate on the waves. They are among the few hundred insect species that live in or on the seas. But why have so few of the 900,000 known insects invaded this vast environment? The seas, after all, cover about two thirds of the globe and, mostly in the coastal shallows, offer multitudes of opportunities for an animal such as an insect to make a living—as ecologists would put it, they offer a multitude of ecological niches. Certainly, insects are not barred from the seas because they are not capable of evolving ways of coping with their salinity. After all, a few do live in or on the seas, and others live happily in inland lakes 10 times as salty. Another explanation, one that seems plausible, is that there is virtually no "room" for insects in the seas, because almost all of its ecological niches have been preempted by the crustaceans, which got there first—not only many species of shrimps, lobsters, and crabs, but also at least 30,000 other kinds of crustaceans such as sand fleas, barnacles, and parasitic fish lice.

The five species of oceanic water striders, like their freshwater relatives, are predators, but as Nils Andersen and John Polhemus said, "One of the puzzling questions about the open ocean species of *Halobates* is what they eat." Among the scientific observations of the 1873–1876 H.M.S. *Challenger* expedition is that water striders were seen feeding on floating dead jellyfish such as the Portuguese man-o'-war. More recently, however, Lanna Cheng found that captive oceanic water striders would not feed on jellyfish of any sort, but that they did feed on larval fish and minute crustaceans trapped in the water's surface film.

Not unexpectedly, none of the oceanic water striders has wings. They would probably be of little or no use, not worth the energy it takes to develop and maintain them. These insects have no need to disperse between separate bodies of water as do the freshwater species. If one bit of ocean surface is more accommodating to them than another, then there is always a good chance that they will be carried there by the wind, the waves, and the tide. Because they have gradual metamorphosis, as do all the other true bugs, the nymphs are as capable of riding the waves as are the adults, and of course there is no immobile and vulnerable pupal stage. But where do the adults lay their eggs? It seems that they glue them to any available floating object—probably usually seaweed, but Andersen and Polhemus report 100,000 or more *Halobates* eggs on a small piece of floating cork, and hundreds of them attached to the tail feathers of a noddy, a ternlike sea bird that rests by floating on the surface.

Most aquatic midges live in fresh water as larvae and are land-dwelling and winged as adults. But some unusual species, about 70 of them according to Dietrich Neumann, are marine—most of them restricted to the intertidal zone, the area between the limits of the lowest and highest tides. One of these species, *Clunio marinus,* wrote Raili Koskinen, inhabits rocky shores along the Atlantic and North Sea coasts from Spain to above the Arctic Circle in Norway.

Clunio larvae live on the bottom, feeding on algae, microorganisms, and bits of organic debris. They are covered by the sea except during the spring tides of the lunar month, at the time of the full and new moon, when the water retreats the farthest from the shore. It is only then, when the sea bottom is most exposed, that the adults emerge from the pupal skin, the winged males on their own and the wingless females only with the aid of a male. He peels back a female's pupal skin and may mate with her before she is completely uncovered. It is with good reason that *Clunio* has been dubbed the 1-hour midge. Mating and egg laying must be accomplished in a big hurry, because the tide begins to come in almost immediately after it has receded, and the area where *Clunio* lives, at the seaward end of the exposed bottom, is very soon again covered by water. Males survive for an hour or less but during that brief period may inseminate two or three females. Females mate only once, immediately lay a jelly-like mass of eggs, and die shortly thereafter.

Clunio can synchronize its life cycle with the spring tides only because it can "predict" when they will occur. This is made possible by an "internal clock" that counts off about 2 weeks, the interval between spring tides. Another clock counts off the hours, and at the right moment triggers all individuals to emerge from the pupa at almost precisely the same moment. Emerging with the crowd maximizes an individual's chance of finding a mate and having offspring that will perpetuate his or her genes in future generations.

There is nothing unusual about internal clocks. All organisms, both plants and animals, seem to have them, even humans. We become conscious of our internal clock when we suffer from jet lag after a long overseas flight. When we arrive at our destination we feel discomfort because our internal clock tells us that, for example, it is time to go to sleep, while the sun and activity around us says that it is time to get up.

It has been known for many years that insects have internal clocks. The results of observations and experiments done in the 1930s, summarized by Stanley Beck in *Insect Photoperiodism*, can be explained only if insects have internal clocks. For example, crickets that become active just after sunset and then become quiescent at sunrise maintain a corresponding rhythm of activity if subjected to constant darkness in the laboratory. For decades, the "clock works" were unknown. The clock was a "black box" whose inner mechanism was not understood. But beginning in the 1970s, biologists began—slowly at first— to pry open the black box. Now, however, with our new understanding of molecular genetics, experiments with the laboratory fruit fly *(Drosophila)*, summarized by Michael Young and Steve Kay, have identified a set of genes that constitute a "light-responsive molecular clock," one that is set by light.

Just as the 1-hour midge lives close to shore in the intertidal zone, most marine insects live in coastal habitats such as beaches, mangrove swamps, coral reefs, tide pools, or wave-formed beach pools. Included among these insects are shore bugs, water boatmen, beetles, horse fly larvae, and even case-making caddisfly larvae. But the only saltwater insects that most people are likely to be familiar with—usually all too familiar— are salt marsh mosquitoes. Various species occur in much of the world, from the tropics to the temperate zones. In eastern North America, a few species, mainly *Aedes solicitans,* are plentiful in the salt marshes behind the barrier islands, actually wave-formed sand bars, that stretch down the Atlantic coast from New Jersey to Florida and along the Gulf Coast to southern Texas.

During their larval stage, they live in temporary pools of brackish or salt water in the marshes. When they mature to the winged adult stage, the males—which do not feed on blood— tend to stay in or near the marshes, while the females fly off in search of an animal from which they can suck the blood that provides the nutrients they need to develop eggs. They may find an unwilling donor nearby, but sometimes migrate en masse for considerable distances. Thomas Headlee reported that in New Jersey they often move 35 to 40 miles inland and have on occasion appeared as much as 100 miles away from the marshes where they originated.

Female salt marsh mosquitoes, William Horsfall reported, will feed avidly on any available animal including humans, often people sunning and swimming at nearby beaches. The bite of a mosquito is in itself not always immediately painful, but, as we have all found to our discomfort, the site of the bite soon swells and becomes painful and itchy, a response to an anti-clotting agent that the mosquito injects into its victim.

William Downes and I learned how horrible an encounter with salt marsh mosquitoes can be while collecting insects in Texas in 1960. We camped on a debris-littered beach on the Bolivar Peninsula a few miles east of where the Texas Highway Department's ferry to Galveston docks. As darkness approached and we sat around our fire of driftwood, we saw what we at first took to be a great cloud of smoke arising from the marsh behind us. But it was not smoke. It was a swarm of hundreds of millions, perhaps billions, of mosquitoes coming towards us on the breeze. When they arrived—accompanied by hordes of hungry, gorging swallows, dragonflies, and even bats—they made life absolutely miserable. Most were deterred by our repellent, but hundreds hovered within inches of our faces and some bit viciously despite the repellent. Had we not sheltered in our screened tent, we might well have been drained of blood during the night. The next morning, the mosquitoes had settled down in the grass at the edge of the beach. The previous afternoon we had walked through that grass with impunity, but that morning scores of the hungry mosquitoes bit our ankles and drove us away if we so much as stepped into the grass.

Commenting on a manuscript version of this book, Ann Downer-Hazell of Harvard University Press wrote: "The 'smoke' cloud of mosquitoes anecdote is something out of a horror film. But great—I love it. Once my husband and I were sitting inside a cabin in Maine watching a ball of mosquitoes mill around just outside. I wondered aloud why they were expending their energy in what looked like milling around and my husband replied, 'They're trying to figure out how to cut glass.'" Mosquitoes are persistent, but not that persistent.

Attempts to control salt marsh mosquitoes have included draining marshes and drenching them with insecticides, thereby damaging the marsh ecosystem—no small matter, because salt marshes are winter refuges for huge flocks of migrating ducks and geese and indispensable nurseries for the young of many marine animals, including blue crabs, shrimp, flounder, sea bass, bluefish, and others that are important in the human diet. There are alternatives to destroying the marshes. The most promising is to help and encourage native predators of mosquito larvae that already inhabit salt marshes. Among them are the little killifish, or mummichogs, that live in permanent pools in the marsh. Mosquito larvae do not survive in these pools because the fish eat them, but they thrive in temporary tidal pools not inhabited by killifish. In the 1930s, engineers, apparently not aware of the ecological importance of marshes, tried to control salt marsh mosquitoes by draining the marshes with a rectilinear grid of straight, regularly spaced ditches. But there is a much better way that preserves the marsh. In Cape May

County, New Jersey, for example, marshes are ditched with discrimination rather than pointless geometric regularity, not to drain them, but to connect temporary tidal pools with permanent pools so that killifish from the latter can invade the temporary pools and devour the mosquito larvae.

Swimming and diving in salt water does not protect marine birds and mammals from parasitic insects. Colonial auks, cormorants, and other seagoing birds that nest on the same sea cliffs every year are ambushed when they return to their nest sites in the spring by blood-sucking ticks and fleas, landlubbers that stay behind on the cliffs when the birds leave to return to the sea for the winter. But there are also truly seagoing parasitic insects: lice that are permanent residents of the feathers or fur of marine birds or mammals.

There are two groups of lice. The piercing-sucking lice (Anoplura) parasitize only mammals and suck their blood. The biting lice (Mallophaga), most of which parasitize birds, have chewing mouthparts and feed on feathers and dander, although some may also bite the host's skin and lap up oozing blood. Penguins, auks, puffins, petrels, albatrosses, and probably all marine birds are parasitized by biting lice. Most of them live among the feathers, but a few species of one genus live in the throat pouch of pelicans, clinging to its inner wall so tenaciously that they are not swallowed and not ejected with the excess water that is engulfed when a fish is caught.

In an article by M. D. Murray, there is a photograph of an entomologist stealthily sneaking up behind an elephant seal to look for lice on its hind flippers. If I had seen this photograph before May 22, 1992, I might have done the same thing. On that day Steven Bailey and I were birding at Año Nuevo State Park on the Pacific coast near San Jose, California. Very early in the morning we had seen rare black swifts zooming through the air near caves in the sea cliffs, but later in the day we saw several huge male elephant seals that had hauled themselves onto the beach. Elephant seals are "hair seals." But only sparsely clothed with hair, they are insulated from the cold water not by their pelage but by a thick layer of blubber. "The lice on a hair seal," wrote Murray, "are immersed in water whenever the seal goes to sea and thus lead a truly marine existence." The other group of seals, the "fur seals," have a luxurious coat of fur that traps an air blanket which keeps them warm. Their lice live in this layer of air and are thus not truly aquatic. The lice on both hair and fur seals can feed on blood while their host is at sea but can mate, reproduce, and move from parent seals to offspring only when the seals come ashore to mate and bear their young.

🦟 If there is an unoccupied ecological niche, an unexploited opportunity to wrest a living from the environment, it is virtually certain that some insect or other creature will move in and make it her bailiwick. Coping with the challenges and opportunities of a new niche probably requires new and perhaps unique anatomical, physiological, and behavioral adaptations. Nevertheless, insects have been supremely successful at seizing virtually any and all opportunities. Aquatic insects have made themselves at home in some very strange and seemingly inhospitable habitats: lakes and ponds many times as salty as sea water; hot springs reaching a temperature of 130° Fahrenheit, and even pools of crude oil.

Salt lakes and ponds vary in their salt content. Some have less or no more than the 3.5 percent content of ocean water, while others are much saltier. Those that are not too salty may be inhabited by a few species of true bugs, caddisflies, beetles, and flies, but the salt content of the Dead Sea in Israel and Jordan, from 26 to 35 percent at different places, is too great for living things other than bacteria to survive. Fish washed into it from rivers die instantly. The Great Salt Lake of Utah, with a salinity of from 11 percent to 28 percent, is a little friendlier to living things. No fish or other vertebrates can survive in it, but it is home to just a few invertebrates, mainly brine shrimps and some kinds of brine flies. Brine shrimp eggs harvested from the Great Salt Lake are sold in pet shops. Aquarists hatch them and feed the larval shrimps to tropical fish. The larvae of brine flies, noted Willis Wirth, wriggle everywhere in the water, probably feeding on bacteria and algae. The adults and puparia can be astonishingly and profusely abundant.

In 1912, J. M. Aldrich reported that the small puparia of this fly wash up on shores in such astronomical numbers—he estimated 370 million flies per mile of beach—that Indians collected them for food. He quoted from a letter written by William Brewer of Yale University in 1863 about brine flies in Mono Lake, California:

> They drift up in heaps along the shore, and *hundreds of bushels* could be collected! They only grow at certain seasons of the year, and then Indians come from far and near to gather them for food. The worms are dried in the sun, the shell [puparium] rubbed off by hand, when a yellowish kernel [the pupa] remains, like a small yellowish grain of rice. This is oily, very nu-

tritious, and not unpleasant to the taste, and, under the name of *koo-chah-bee* (so pronounced), forms a very important article of food . . . My guide, an old hunter there, told me that everything fattens in the season of *koo-chah-bee;* that ducks get very fat, but their flesh tastes unpleasantly from it, and the Indians get fat and sleek.

When passenger trains of the Southern Pacific were about to pass near the Great Salt Lake, recounted Aldrich, the conductors rushed through the train shutting the windows "on account of the salt-flies," which would "come into open car windows by myriads." He also noted that on some summer evenings so many of them congregated on the railroad tracks that the tracks became slick enough to stall freight trains.

Some organisms are amazingly tolerant of the high temperatures of the water in hot springs found in volcanically active areas such as Iceland and Yellowstone National Park in Wyoming. Some bacteria can survive temperatures greater than 203°F, only 9 degrees below the boiling point of water at sea level; blue-green "algae" (cyanobacteria), somewhat less than 165°F; green algae and fungi, a bit less than 140°F; and insects and other multicellular animals, as much as 130°F. Water temperature varies from one hot spring to another, and where the temperature is down to a "cool" 130°F or lower, increasingly complex communities of organisms may exist.

Rodger Mitchell, a zoologist at Ohio State University, proposed a plausible evolutionary route by which organisms adapted to live in hot water might have evolved. "The origins of the blue-green algae of hot springs are uncertain, but the snails and flies that eat the algae, and the mites parasitic on the flies, seem to have evolved from species that lived in water-margin habitats. The wet shores of water margins are regularly warmed up to 40°C [104°F] by the sun."

There have been many ecological and entomological studies of thermal springs in Yellowstone National Park. These bodies of water are an interesting enticement to ecologists, because they are microcosms. As Nicholas Collins and his coworkers put it, "they are natural systems with distinct boundaries and they function largely independently of their surroundings." They are inhabited by only a few heat-tolerant species of bacteria, algae, and arthropods (insects and their kin) that are very different from those of surrounding ecological communities. Therefore, these very limited ecosystems, which can be considered to be models for larger and more complex ecosystems, are relatively easy to "dissect" and study in the hope of finding principles that apply to all ecosystems.

Collins examined the community of organisms in a small spring with a water temperature of about 104°F, well above temperatures that are lethal to most insects after an exposure of 1 hour or somewhat more: 100°F for cockroaches and fleas, 97°F for a fly, and for mayfly nymphs from streams and ponds, 70°F and 104°F respectively.

The nutritional foundation of the food chain in this hot spring is a floating, mucilaginous mat of bacteria and blue-green algae that grow well only above 104°F. They are eaten by larvae of a species of shore fly that is in the same family as the brine flies. But these larvae grow best at a temperature below 104°F, between 77°F and 95°F, temperatures that occur only at the edge of the outflow from the spring and in patches of the mat around which the flow of hot water has been diverted by unusually thick bumps in the mat. Thomas Brock and Louise Brock watched adult shore flies go under water in a bubble of air to feed on algae. The bubble keeps the fly dry and probably also insulates it from water hotter than it can tolerate.

A tiny mite parasitizes the adult flies and eats their eggs. As soon as the mites hatch from the egg, they station themselves on the mat and jump onto passing adult flies and, as Norman Fashing told me, they probably feed by sucking the flies' body fluids. After the molt to its next stage, the mite becomes a predator that wanders over the algal mat eating shore fly eggs. Another predator, an adult long-legged fly (family Dolichopodidae), wanders over the hot mat and feeds upon the eggs and larvae of the shore fly. It would be killed by the heat if it did not keep cool by holding its body well above the mat with its stilt-like legs.

For many years, petroleum technologists knew that maggots live in pools of waste crude oil in the oil fields of California, but it was not until the end of the nineteenth century that this amazing fact became known to entomologists. Oil, of course, is not water, but it is a liquid medium that can be conquered, in part, by behavioral adaptations much like those of insects that live in water. In 1930, the entomologist W. H. Thorpe published what is still the most comprehensive account of the behavior and natural history of the "oil fly" *(Helaeomyia petrolei)*. In considering how this fly evolved the ability to survive in a substance deadly to all other insects, Thorpe wrote, "It is obvious that the evolution of a species involving such a revolutionary change of habit can hardly have taken place since man began to exploit the natural resources of the country; there must have been natural seepages of petroleum on the surface of the ground available throughout a long period."

Oil fly larvae squirm through the viscous oil by undulating their bodies and obtain atmospheric oxygen by periodically thrusting the spiracles at the hind end of the body above the surface of the oil. The maggots' digestive system is full of oil from front to back. They get no nourishment from it and are protected from its toxicity by a thin membrane that separates the oil from the lining of the digestive system. These maggots are scavengers that feed on insects that become trapped in the sticky oil. While watching oil fly maggots through a low-power microscope, Thorpe observed that if "a piece of a small caterpillar was thrown into the oil they would quickly cluster around it and could be watched devouring it greedily. If the food was first coloured with some non-toxic stain . . . it could easily be seen in the mid gut shortly after the commencement of feeding." The adult flies, which, as far as Thorpe could determine, lay their eggs at the edge of the pool, walk upon the surface of the oil, which would trap any other insect the moment it came in contact with the oil—but only the fly's feet are protected from the ensnaring power of the sticky oil. If the oil happens to come in contact with any other part of its body the fly is at once trapped in the oil with no hope of escape. Thorpe did not know why the flies are not trapped by the sticky oil. He guessed that they were protected by unknown glandular secretions from hairs on their feet.

Life in the water is impossible unless an organism has some way to obtain oxygen, the essential gas of life for all organisms, with the exception of certain (anaerobic) bacteria. In all animals, including humans, insects, and even the lowliest worms, oxygen is an indispensable element in the metabolism of nutrients—carbohydrates, fats, proteins—which releases the energy that sustains life and fuels activities such as walking, swimming, and flying. We next consider some of the many different and sometimes unusual or even bizarre means of respiration used by aquatic insects.

The Breath of Life

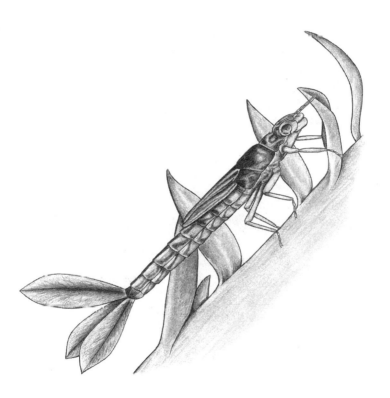

*A damselfly nymph rests on an aquatic plant
as the leaflike gills at the end of its abdomen
absorb dissolved oxygen from the water*

Early in the earth's history, beginning about 4.5 billion years ago, there was almost no oxygen in the atmosphere. Nevertheless, there was life, anaerobic bacteria, which did not require oxygen and would actually have been poisoned by it. (Some of these bacteria, which then dominated the earth, still occur in swamp muck, decaying matter, sewage, and other environments with little or no atmospheric oxygen, although many others are now adapted to well-oxygenated environments, where they are often numerous.) But about 3 billion years ago, photosynthetic bacteria appeared and began to release oxygen, a byproduct of photosynthesis, into the atmosphere. Other photosynthetic organisms followed, including the multitude of green plants that now grow all around us. Most paleobotanists think that green plants moved onto land about 400 million years ago, but Daniel Heckman and his coauthors say that it may have been 700 million years ago. In either case, the oxygen content of the atmosphere gradually increased to its present level of about 21 percent in a mixture with 78 percent nitrogen and small quantities of carbon dioxide and other gases.

If you watch the insects in a pond for a while, you will notice that predaceous diving beetles periodically swim to the surface for a "breath" of air but that water scorpions and dragonfly nymphs do not. All animals that live in the water must have access to the oxygen in the air and get it in one way or another. Fish, for example, have gills that absorb dissolved atmospheric oxygen from the water; but dolphins and whales must come to the surface for a breath of air. And so it is with insects. Of the three insects you just saw in the pond, the dragonfly nymphs obtain oxygen as do fish, but the others, the beetle and the water scorpion, get oxygen directly from the atmosphere in two different ways that I will soon explain.

Some aquatic insects live on top of the water, not in it, among them the gyrating whirligig beetles and two true bugs, the fleet-footed water striders and the plodding marsh treaders that walk on the surface film as they search for prey. Surrounded by air, these surface dwellers do not need the special adaptations for obtaining oxygen that are universal among insects that live *in* the water. Most aquatic insects have gills that absorb atmospheric oxygen dissolved in the water. But many, according to Sir Vincent Wigglesworth, a pioneering insect physiologist, have ways—actually several different ones—of obtaining oxygen directly from the atmosphere.

Most aquatic insects that get their oxygen directly from the atmosphere—backswimmers, diving beetles, mosquito larvae, and many others—must rise to the surface periodically for a fresh "breath" of air. I will come to them later. But a few other more or less sedentary aquatic insects, such as the various species of water scorpions and rat-tailed maggots, have long air tubes, "snorkels," that extend to the surface, making it possible for these insects to remain submerged indefinitely. As the aquatic ecologist H. B. N. Hynes points out, insects with snorkels must live in shallows where their air tubes can reach the surface. Only insects with gills can survive in depths where they are far removed from the atmosphere. But that is not to say that insects with gills do not live in shallow water.

The common water scorpions have at the end of the abdomen a very thin air tube that, in some species, is almost as long as the body. They cling to aquatic vegetation and, with the air tube thrust up to the surface, wait in ambush or crawl slowly and stealthily, searching for prey that they will seize with their formidable grasping front legs and then suck dry with their piercing-sucking beak.

One of the rat-tailed maggots, the larva of the honey bee–mimicking drone fly *(Eristalis tenax),* lives in polluted fluids that contain little or no oxygen—such as the liquid in decaying carcasses, in sewage, or in fermenting vegetation. (The drone fly, a native of Eurasia, has spread throughout the world, following in the wake of the construction of sewage disposal plants.) The maggot, named for the long, thin air tube—which looks like a rat's tail—at its posterior end, rests on the bottom and seldom moves as it ingests decaying matter. The telescoping air tube with two spiracles at its tip can be retracted or extended to much more than the length of the body to reach the surface. But only with suction can air be drawn down through such a long, thin tube. The suction is provided by an interesting modification of the tracheal system described by the Swedish entomologist Gustav Alsterberg. Parts of the large tracheal tubes are greatly enlarged to form air sacs that can be alternately deflated and inflated as muscles of the body contract and relax, applying and releasing pressure on the blood that fills the body cavity and surrounds the air sacs. As the pressure is relaxed, the air sacs become inflated and air is drawn down the tube; as pressure is applied, they are compressed and air is exhaled.

Other insects, be they aquatic or land-dwelling, have comparable air sacs through which air is inhaled and exhaled—much as in our lungs—but, unlike our lungs, they do not aerate the blood. They do, however, forcibly ventilate the tracheal system and in that way bring more oxygen to the muscles and other organs than would unaided diffusion. As you may recall if you took physics in high school, gases diffuse from areas of high concentration to areas of low concentration. Accordingly, oxygen diffuses from the atmosphere into the tracheae, where its concentration is low because the insect is using it up. (Carbon dioxide, which is constantly produced by an insect's metabolism, is toxic and must be eliminated from the body; it diffuses in the opposite direction.) But because diffusion alone cannot supply enough oxygen to sustain vigorous activities such as running or flying, most insects have evolved respiratory mechanisms much like that of the rat-tailed maggot.

In 1932, Gottfried Fraenkel investigated the respiratory movements of grasshoppers, showing that they exhaled when muscles compressed the abdomen, thereby increasing blood pressure and compressing the tracheae, and that they inhaled when the pressure was released and the abdomen expanded, and the tracheae sprang back to their usual shape. He found that during inhalation the two pairs of spiracles on the thorax are open and the eight pairs of abdominal spiracles are closed. During exhalation, the thoracic spiracles are closed and the abdominal spiracles are open. In this way, a directed stream of air is forced through the tracheae. Seventy-one years later, Mark Westneat and several collaborators used a synchrotron, which accelerates and polarizes subatomic particles, to produce an x-ray beam that they used to make videos of the tracheae of living, "breathing" insects—crickets, beetles, and ants—thereby confirming only a part of Fraenkel's discoveries: that the contraction of muscles increases blood pressure and thereby compresses the tracheae.

All insects that come to the surface for air, whether or not they have air tubes, have the problem of penetrating the surface film of the water to expose their spiracles to the air. But what is the surface film, and how can we demonstrate to ourselves that it is a real barrier, at least for very small animals such as insects? In contact with air, the water surface behaves like a thin, elastic membrane, because the water molecules are more strongly attracted to each other than to molecules of air, a force known as surface tension. The strength of the surface film is well described by Louis Miall:

> Take a clean needle, poise it horizontally on the prongs of a fork, and lower the fork and needle steadily upon the surface of the water in a basin. If the fork is taken away from beneath, the needle will be left floating on the surface. Steel is many times heavier than water, but the resistance of the surface-film prevents the needle from sinking. Once beneath the surface, the needle sinks rapidly to the bottom . . . The extreme tenuity of the film, which is thinner than our imagination can realise, helps us to understand how it is that only small objects are affected by it. Ships, boats, swimming quadrupeds, and all objects whose weight is large in comparison with their contour,

are practically uninfluenced, but objects whose dimensions are given in fractions of an inch may be largely controlled by the peculiar properties of the surface film.

You can have a lot of fun with Miall's trick. Amaze your friends and win some pocket change by betting them that you can do the impossible, float a steel sewing needle on water. (It helps to rub the needle against your nose to make it a little oily.)

All insects that must penetrate the surface film, definitely not a trivial matter for these small creatures, have solved this problem in the same way. The parts of the body that penetrate the surface film are hydrophobic: they repel water because they are coated with wax, grease, or oil. When a hydrophobic body part touches the surface film, water is repelled, leaving the body part dry and with access to the air. The spiracles at the end of the rat-tailed maggot's air tube, for example, are surrounded by a fringe of hairs that repel water, because they are coated with oil from glands described in 1929 by zoologists at the University of Buffalo, William Dolley, Jr., and E. J. Farris. The hydrophobic hairs spread out at the surface, forming a pocket of air that surrounds the spiracles and is continuous with the atmosphere.

A few insects that have no gills can, nevertheless, stay beneath the surface indefinitely, because they inhale the air in hollow spaces in the roots of aquatic plants. "Aquatic insects," wrote Miall, "often find it a matter of some difficulty to procure a sufficient supply of air, and many ingenious contrivances appear as practiced solutions of the problem. None perhaps are quite so remarkable as . . . that the *Donacia* larvae should have found out the air-reservoirs of submerged roots, and possess special organs for tapping them." The slender, metallic green, bronze, or purple adult leaf beetles of the *Donacia* group walk on and feed on aquatic plants that protrude above the water, such as the floating leaves of water lilies, and only occasionally venture beneath the surface of the water. The larvae, however, remain permanently immersed in the water, feeding on the roots of aquatic plants and obtaining air through two spinelike tubes that pierce an air space in the roots.

Donacia larvae are not the only insects to have evolved this ingenious mechanism. The larvae of one group of mosquitoes (*Mansonia*), according to William Horsfall, pierce a root with a short, sharp air tube at the end of the abdomen, a modification of the snorkel with which other mosquitoes penetrate the surface film. They remain indefinitely attached to the root as they fan their hairy mouthparts to create a current from which they strain small particles of food. Similarly, larvae of the aquatic rice water weevil, probably the most common and destructive pest of rice in the United States, use sharp, spinelike spiracles to tap into air spaces in rice plants.

While watching the creatures in a pond through your glass-bottomed bucket, you may have seen a beetle, a predaceous diving beetle, swim to the surface, where it briefly hung, head down, before returning to its underwater pursuits. Like many aquatic insects, it had to come up for a breath of air—in this case for a bubble of air, silvery and glistening, that it took below the surface as a portable supply of oxygen. Of course the beetle must eventually return to the surface for another bubble—but, as we will soon see, not nearly as soon as would be expected from the limited oxygen content of the bubble.

Some insects come to the surface just to fill their tracheae with a fresh supply of air and do not take a bubble of air with them when they submerge. Among them are the larvae of most species of predaceous diving beetles, water scavenger beetles, and mosquitoes. They must return to the surface frequently, a mosquito larva at least once every 10 minutes.

Insects that use bubbles in respiration capture air in different ways and store the resulting bubble in different places on the body—but always where spiracles have access to the air in the bubble. For example, predaceous diving beetles break through the surface film with the tip of the abdomen, whose terminal segment bears hydrophobic hairs and a pair of spiracles. They simultaneously fill the tracheal system with air and draw even more air into the space beneath the wing covers. According to Reginald Chapman, surgically removing the hind wings creates more space for air under the wing covers, allowing the beetle to remain submerged for longer periods. When taking on air, another beetle, a water scavenger, lies horizontally at the surface and penetrates the surface film with the four terminal, clublike segments of its antennae, which are clothed with hydrophobic hairs. In this way it opens a water-free passage through which air flows to the spaces beneath the wing covers and is also trapped as a large but thin bubble in a thick pile of hairs on the underside of the body.

Although the giant water bug is not related to the beetles, it and its relatives acquire and store air much as does a predaceous diving beetle. On rising to the surface, the bug extends two hydrophobic, straplike appendages at the tip of the abdomen. They break through the surface film and let air enter two spiracles at the tip of the abdomen and simultaneously flow beneath the front wings, which are folded down upon the back.

Backswimmers rise to the surface bottom-side up, break the film with the tip of the abdomen, and store air beneath the front wings and in a thin film held by hairs on the wings' upper surfaces and in two troughs bounded by long rows of hydrophobic hairs on the underside of the body. They become so buoyant that they must hold on to something to keep from floating to the surface. Water boatmen also store air beneath the wings and as a film enveloping the underside of the body, but, unlike the giant water bugs and backswimmers, they break the surface film with the head and the forward part of the thorax.

All of these insects and the many others that use air bubbles can remain submerged without returning to the surface much longer than can those, such as mosquito larvae, that do not use bubbles. A backswimmer, noted George Edwards, can remain immersed for from 0.5 to 6 hours, a predaceous diving beetle for as long as 36 hours, and small, slow-moving bugs or beetles much longer: beetles of the family Dryopidae for days or weeks, some of the creeping water bugs and some riffle beetles indefinitely or even for a lifetime. In any case, all of these insects can remain submerged much longer than is to be expected from the rate at which they use up oxygen and the limited amount of oxygen in the bubble. The predaceous diving beetle's bubbles contain only enough oxygen for a 20-minute stay under the water, but we know that they can remain submerged for as long as 36 hours. How can this be? The answer is that the bubble itself absorbs dissolved oxygen from the water. In other words, the bubble acts as a gill, known to entomologists as a physical gill.

Larvae of the wasp *Agriotypus* are, as we have seen, external parasites that live on the bodies of case-building caddisfly larvae and pupae. The caddisfly larva or pupa forces a current of water to pass through its case, providing the parasite with oxygen that it absorbs through its skin, but when the parasite ultimately kills the pupa, the current no longer flows and there is not enough oxygen. But evolution has worked its wonders to enable the parasite to overcome this difficulty. H. Whitehead explained that it spins a ribbon of silk, two or three times as long as the caddisfly case, that trails in the water. Air trapped in the ribbon functions as a physical gill that enables the wasp, which will by then have transformed to the adult stage, to survive in the case under water until it emerges and flies away about 8 months later.

But how does a physical gill work? Because the insect is using up oxygen, its relative concentration in the bubble is constantly decreasing, thereby increasing the relative concentration of nitrogen in the bubble. Consequently, oxygen diffuses into the bubble from the water—where its concentration is greater—while nitrogen diffuses out of it into the water—where its concentration is lower. A bubble can function as a gill because oxygen diffuses into it at about three times the rate at which nitrogen diffuses out of it. Consequently, nitrogen tends to maintain the size of the bubble. Paradoxically, although nitrogen is not utilized by the insect, a physical gill could not function in its absence. The bubble would consist of virtually nothing but oxygen. Therefore, the relative concentration of oxygen in the bubble would always be higher than that in the surrounding water and, consequently, oxygen could not diffuse into the bubble. Indeed, the bubble of oxygen would shrink and soon disappear as its oxygen diffuses into the surrounding water. "For this reason," as Chapman explained, "an insect [in the laboratory] with a bubble of pure oxygen in water saturated with oxygen does not survive for very long unless it is able to come to the surface."

The ultimate physical gill is the plastron, a very thin film of air that permanently covers most of the body of riffle beetles and certain bugs. It is kept in place and its volume is kept constant by a protective pile of closely packed, almost microscopic, hydrophobic hairs. In a European creeping water bug, the hairs, densely packed at 2,500,000 per square millimeter (over 16 billion per square inch), are erect but bent over at the top to better contain the air film. The volume of a plastron is usually negligible because it functions solely as a gill rather than doing double duty as a store of air to be used up. Larval riffle beetles have gills and remain under the water, but when they become adults and lose their gills they must come to the surface, but only once, to form the plastron.

Most of the aquatic insects rely solely on atmospheric oxygen dissolved in the water, as do fish, tadpoles, crayfish, and clams, all of which have gills, as do many aquatic insects but by no means all of them. Some oxygen diffuses into the bodies of all aquatic insects through the "skin," the cuticle. Cuticular respiration, as it is technically but concisely known, provides all the oxygen required by some very small and sedentary insects, such as certain midge larvae. Although cuticular respiration does not supply enough oxygen for large or very small active insects, it is often a significant adjunct to other forms of respiration. As Wigglesworth pointed out, even if the gills of a mayfly nymph are snipped off, it can, by means of cuticular respiration, survive in winter, when it is at rest, or in highly oxygenated water, but in the summer, while the nymph is active, or is in water containing insufficient dissolved oxygen, the gills are indispensable.

The efficiency of cuticular respiration is often enhanced by a dense network of fine air tubes (tracheae) just beneath the skin, most often where it is thinnest. Oxygen diffuses into this network of tracheae and is dispersed throughout the body by way of the rest of the tracheal system. A short evolutionary step converts such an area into a gill—simply by everting the skin and the accompanying network of air tubes to form an evagination of the body. Gills, which can have many shapes—filamentous or tube-, feather-, or plate-like—are essentially a way of increasing the surface area of the skin to increase the absorption of oxygen. The gills of insects may be located on any part of the body, but are most often on the abdomen.

"If a gill breathing insect were to remain perfectly still, it would," observed Edward Popham, "sooner or later, exhaust the supply of dissolved oxygen in the water immediately surrounding it, but the situation could easily be remedied by the insects crawling to a new situation or by creating a current of water bringing them renewed supplies of oxygen." Many gill-breathing aquatic insects, among them certain mayfly nymphs, whirligig larvae, and the larvae of crawling water beetles move from place to place, leaving behind small pockets of temporarily oxygen-depleted water. Black fly larvae, mayfly and stonefly nymphs, and others that live in running water—especially turbulent mountain streams—have no such problem, because freshly oxygenated water constantly washes over them.

But many other insects, especially sedentary species, bring a fresh supply of water to themselves by moving their bodies or appendages so as to create a current. As we have seen, caddisfly larvae that live in cases, which are all open at both ends, can cause water to flow through the case by undulating their bodies. Mayfly nymphs that live in U-shaped, open-ended burrows in muddy bottoms use a similar tactic, creating a current that flows through the burrow by waving their gills. By undulating their abdomens, damselfly nymphs cause water to flow past the three leaflike gills at the tip of the abdomen.

In the nymphal stage, their close relatives, the dragonflies, "breathe" in a most unusual way. Their gills are in, of all places, the large, muscular rectum, lining its inner wall like shingles. The nymph constantly bathes its platelike gills with fresh, oxygenated water by alternately "inhaling" and "exhaling" through the anus, sucking in fresh water by dilating the rectum and expelling it by contracting the rectum. Some damselflies have a rudimentary and presumably more primitive version of this mechanism (and some turtles obtain oxygen from water they "inhale" through the anus). With those exceptions, the dragonfly's way of bathing its gills with fresh water is, as far as I know, unique in the animal kingdom. When I learned about this in an entomology course not long after being discharged from the army in 1947, I chuckled when I remembered that, after strenuous training, the GIs, ever colorful of speech, would gripe: "I'm so pooped my 'anus' is sucking wind." This is, of course, a slightly censored version.

The blood of humans and other vertebrates is red because it contains red blood cells, which are red because they contain the pigment hemoglobin, which has an affinity for oxygen. The blood, via arteries and capillaries, transports oxygen bound to hemoglobin from the lungs to the various organs and tissues where it is needed. If you swat a fly or step on a cockroach or some other insect, you will see that its blood (technically called hemolymph) may be pale yellow or pale green, but, with the exception of a very few insects, it will not be red. This is so because in almost all insects hemoglobin is not needed because oxygen is not transported by the blood but rather by the tracheal system, that branching and profusely rebranching system of tubes through which air flows directly to the cells of the body.

There are, however, just a few insects that do have hemoglobin, but it is not confined in cells in the blood. Most of them are midge larvae that live in the bottom mud of deep lakes, where the concentration of dissolved oxygen is very low. Because they are bright red, they are known as bloodworms. Although entomologists hold conflicting views on the role of insect hemoglobin in respiration, there is not much doubt that hemoglobin makes it possible for midge larvae to survive where there is little oxygen by storing it and by transporting it throughout the body. In an experiment, midge larvae raised on a diet with an adequate content of iron, an essential component of hemoglobin, had a large content of hemoglobin in the blood, were bright red, and did well even if there was little oxygen. But if the diet was deficient in iron, the hemoglobin content of the blood fell to a low level, the larvae became pale, and they were less tolerant of low concentrations of oxygen.

Oxygen is required to metabolize foods in order to release the energy that runs the body and fuels swimming, flying, running, and all other activities. Although most animals can survive longer without eating than they can without breathing, in the long run—which, depending on the animal, may be hours, days, or weeks—eating is as necessary as breathing. As we see in the next chapter, the energy derived from metabolizing food keeps the body functioning and makes possible essential activities such as searching for favorable dwelling sites, building shelters, escaping from predators, finding mates, and achieving evolutionary fitness by producing offspring.

Finding Food and Eating

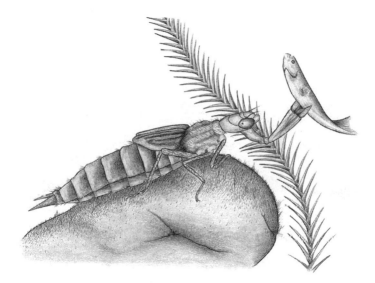

With its prehensile lower lip, a voracious
dragonfly nymph grabs a small fish

Once, when I was in the sixth grade, I put a large dragonfly nymph in my aquarium. It was a big mistake! The tank was already occupied by 15 or 20 fish, each little more than an inch long, that I had netted in Bunnell's Pond in Beardsley Park in Bridgeport, Connecticut. A budding naturalist enthralled by the wild creatures around me, I wanted only native fish in my aquarium—no alien tropical fish and certainly no bizarre goldfish. When I caught the dragonfly nymph, I had no idea what it was. But it looked interesting, and I put it in the tank. Soon my fish were disappearing one by one. What had happened to the missing fish was a mystery until I caught the dragonfly nymph in the act of catching and eating one. The nymph was clinging to a pondweed rooted in the sand at the bottom of the tank. When a little fish came close, a long "arm" lunged out from the nymph's *head* and in a split second grasped the fish and brought it back to its mouthparts. Then the nymph proceeded to devour my little fish. It had never entered my mind that an insect could eat a fish.

But what was the "arm" the dragonfly nymph used to grab my fish? I was familiar with a fair sampling of insects—grasshoppers, crickets, cockroaches, beetles, and a few others—but never before had I seen an insect with a long "arm" that shot out from its head to snatch something. A few months later I learned what the creature was and found the answer to this question in Frank Lutz's *Field Book of Insects,* which I found in the public library. The "arm" is actually the nymph's greatly lengthened lower lip. At the time, that was enough to satisfy my curiosity. It was not until I took my first entomology course at the University of Massachusetts, taught by the great entomologist Charles Alexander, that I learned the fascinating story of the evolutionary origin of the lower lip of insects, including dragonflies, and of the other mouthparts with which they ingest their meals.

While our "mouthparts," the teeth and tongue, are inside our mouths, an insect's mouthparts are outside the mouth opening. This seems strange to us, but it is the inevitable result of the way in which insects evolved the ability to chew, a tremendous step forward that opened a whole new world of opportunity to them. Their distant ancestors, segmented worms much like earthworms, had no mouthparts for chewing and could ingest only what they could suck in through their mouths. But the insects, with their newfound ability to chew, were able to feed on solids such as leaves, stems, fruits, or small animals.

An insect's paired mouthparts are derived from some of the legs of its ancestors, which clustered around the mouth opening when several segments of the body, three of which bore a pair of legs, came together around the mouth and joined to form the head. One pair of legs became the stout mandibles that snip and chew; the next pair the maxillae, the second jaws; and the third pair fused together to form the labium, or lower lip. The upper lip, the labrum, is not derived from legs; it is an outgrowth of the hard outer covering of the head. The two lips and the maxillae form a closed space in front of the mouth, the preoral cavity, in which food is chewed. Within this chamber is the tongue (hypopharynx), usually a mobile fleshy lobe, which is a forward extension of the lower wall of the throat.

After it has hatched from the egg, an insect's head shows no sign of being composed of separate segments and the mouthparts are not recognizable as legs. But in an early stage of embryonic development, these segments are still clearly separate and bear rudimentary appendages that look like the developing legs on the other segments of the body, unmistakable evidence of the evolutionary origin of the head and the mouthparts.

When I took my first biology courses back in the Dark Ages, I was taught that this lesson learned by examining the insect embryo is an example of the concept that ontogeny recapitulates phylogeny—that the developmental stages of an embryo reflect the stages in its evolution. This idea was overstated and it ultimately faded far into the backwaters of biology. But it has been revived—or reinvented—by the most recent generation of biologists. It is now called evo-devo, short for evolutionary-developmental biology.

The lower lip of nymphal dragonflies and damselflies—but of no other insects—has become an organ for snatching prey. It is always surprisingly long, at least one third the length of the body when fully extended. A hinge near its midpoint divides it into two segments. The first, the "upper part of the arm," connects with the head and is straight and narrow, while the second, the "lower arm," is triangular in shape, and at its broad tip, the "hand," there is a pair of opposable, fanglike hooks for firmly grasping prey. When the lower lip is not in use it is folded at the hinge and stowed out of the way under the body between the legs, and the hand covers the lower part of the face like a mask. Dragonfly nymphs eat a variety of creatures, mostly insects, but occasionally a tadpole or, as I learned to my cost, a small fish. Usually, wrote the entomologist Ernest Bay, they sprawl on the bottom or climb on an aquatic plant as they lie in ambush or stalk their prey.

Dragonfly and damselfly nymphs mature into consummate aerial predators. Some hover just above leaves as they glean prey such as aphids or spiders; some, like phoebes, kingbirds, or other avian flycatchers, sit on a perch and dart out at passing insects; but the most conspicuous ones, such as the large green darner, common in southern Canada and throughout the adjacent United States, fly with great agility and speed as they pursue small insects such as mosquitoes and gnats through the air, trapping them in a basket formed by their six bristly legs. Since this pursuit requires better vision than that of most other insects, adult dragonflies have huge, visually acute "wraparound" eyes that give them a visual field of almost 360 degrees; they see all but a small part of what is directly behind them. Describing those eyes, Philip Corbet quoted a Japanese haiku:

> The face of the dragonfly
> Is practically nothing
> But eyes!

When I first collected insects, I found it virtually impossible to net flying dragonflies, but I eventually realized that they have a blind spot and can be caught—but by no means always—if you swing the net at them from their rear.

You may see floating on the surface of a pond huge green mats that at first glance look like algae. On closer inspection, they will probably prove to be tiny, floating duckweeds, smallest of all the flowering plants. They and other green plants are the foundation of the food chains in most terrestrial and aquatic ecosystems. (A few ecosystems are founded on bacteria that derive carbon from carbon dioxide and otherwise subsist on inorganic substances such as hydrogen, hydrogen sulfide, or other forms of sulfur.) Only these plants—ranging from tiny, single-celled green algae to gigantic trees—can directly capture the energy of the sun and make it available to living things. By means of photosynthesis, they use the energy of sunlight to combine carbon, hydrogen, and oxygen into the energy-rich sugars that fuel most food chains on earth.

In aquatic ecosystems, the products of photosynthesis come from two sources, plants that grow in the water and plants that grow on land. Aquatic single-celled green algae, many of which are a part of the plankton (from the Greek word for drifting), the countless millions of mostly microscopic organisms that float below the surface of the water, are tiny but important photosynthesizers because they are very numerous. According to Elsie Klots, they may be responsible for 90 percent of the photosynthesis in an aquatic community. There are also multicellular plants such as water lilies, pondweeds, eel grass, watercress, and the tiny duckweeds. Some trees, such as bald cypress and sour gum, are rooted in the standing water of swamps.

Plants that grow on land contribute to freshwater ecosystems, less to some and more to others—notably to woodland pools and streams. Large trees fall into rivers and lakes when the current or waves undercut a bank. In autumn, fallen leaves are blown into ponds and streams—often in great abundance. Pollen, seeds, and the spores of ferns and mosses float on the breeze and fall into the water. Land-dwelling insects fall into the water, contributing nutrients from the terrestrial plants that nourished them. Those insects are certainly an important if not the major food of water striders, whirligig beetles, and other surface dwellers. I don't know how important they are in the diet of fish, but I do know that when I throw grasshoppers or caterpillars into a pond, bluegills and other fish dash to the surface to snap them up.

The filter-feeding insects, which I will consider next, consume the single-celled, planktonic green algae. Relatively few insects eat significant amounts of the larger multicellular aquatic plants. Among them—we have met them all—are a few midge larvae and larval moths (caterpillars) that chew on the leaves of plants such as water lilies, eel grass, and pondweeds. Adult beetles of the genus *Donacia* feed on the upper surface of the floating leaves of water lilies but seldom enter the water. Larval *Donacia* and both adult and larval riffle beetles feed on the submerged parts of aquatic plants.

Terrestrial plants or plant parts that fall into the water— some already partially decomposed by bacteria and fungi—are eaten by certain larval caddisflies, crane flies, and midges that gnaw on wood or eat autumn-shed leaves. What remains eventually disintegrates, to become a part of the detritus that is strained from the water by filter-feeding insects such as mosquito larvae. A caddisfly larva *(Desmona bethula)* makes a unique contribution to the food chains of aquatic ecosystems. On early summer nights, Nancy Erman found, large larvae leave the water to feed on land plants that grow at the edge of the stream. They return to the water when the air temperature nears freezing but continue to feed until dawn on warm nights.

Insects that feed on algae and other aquatic plants and insects that eat terrestrial plant matter that falls into the water are indispensable links in virtually all aquatic food chains. They are the intermediaries that make the nutrients that—with few exceptions—only plants can manufacture available to aquatic animals that do not eat plants. They convert plant tissues to the flesh of their own bodies, which is, in turn, eaten by predaceous insects such as dragonfly nymphs and by vertebrates such as fish and salamanders. Some of them, such as filter-feeding mayfly nymphs and black fly and mosquito larvae, also bridge the size gap between large predators and microorganisms, such as one-celled green algae, that are too small to be profitably eaten by the predators.

Like mosquito larvae, many other aquatic insects make a meal of the hordes of minute green algae and other planktonic organisms and the many tiny particles of organic detritus that float below the surface of the water, even in water that may look clear. The planktonic organisms are mostly exceedingly small. The smallest of them are the bacteria, all so infinitesimal—almost all less than 0.00004 inch long—that they are barely visible under a powerful light microscope. Considerably larger, but still microscopic in size, are diatoms and other single-celled algae, and the one-celled protozoans, relatives of the amoebas, such as *Paramecium*, which swims by beating minute hairs that ring its body, and tiny spherical colonies of the alga *Volvox*, which consist of dozens or hundreds of mostly identical, green, photosynthesizing cells. There are also some complex multicellular animals, among them the rotifers, commonly known as wheel animalcules, which are mostly very tiny although some are just big enough to be seen with the naked eye.

Insects harvest this abundance of mostly microscopic food by filtering it out of the water. According to J. Bruce Wallace and Richard Merritt, some aquatic insects, mainly mosquito and black fly larvae, are active filter feeders, whose mouthparts or other appendages are in some way modified for sieving out plankton and detritus particles as they fan through the water. Others, most of them caddisflies, are passive filter feeders, which live in flowing water and weave stationary nets of silk filaments that are fixed in place and trap food from the current that streams through them.

Most mosquito larvae are highly proficient active filter feeders. Because they live mainly in still waters, they must be equipped to create a current that brings food to them. A feeding larva is likely to be hanging from the surface film by its breathing tube. The rapid, rhythmic fanning, 180 to 240 beats per minute, of two large mouth brushes composed of long thin hairs produces a current of water that flows to the mouthparts. Food particles trapped between the hairs of the brushes are raked out by a comb of bristles on the mandibles, removed from this comb by other bristles near the mouth, and ultimately swept into the mouth by small brushes on the mandibles. The maxillae, which beat out of phase with the mandibles, trap particles on an array of short hairs. Serrated teeth (not bristles) on the mandibles comb out these particles, which are from time to time pushed into the mouth opening by deep inward thrusts of the maxillae. Large particles not caught by the mouth brushes or the maxillae are trapped by a few stout bristles on the mandibles and then ground up as the crushing parts of the mandibles press them against the hard surface of the "tongue."

Adult mosquitoes leave the water to find a mate and reproduce. The mouthparts of females are adapted for imbibing nectar and in some species also for piercing the skin of humans and other animals in order to suck blood, a protein source some require to produce eggs. Females of many other species do not require blood and, as do males of all species, drink only nectar, plant juices, and other liquids.

Anyone who has been in the north woods in the spring and early summer is all too familiar with the hordes of blood-sucking female black flies that plague both humans and beasts. A particularly bothersome African species was named *Simulium damnosum* in recognition of the misery it causes. The broad, serrated mandibles of a female black fly, overlapping like the blades of a scissor, are so sharp that they cause no pain when they snip through the skin. Thus the biting fly, not noticed by its victim, avoids the swat of a tail or the slap of a hand. Although its bite is painless, some time after the fly leaves, the site of the bite becomes a large, itchy welt.

Larval black flies live only in running water, many in fast-flowing mountain torrents, but others live in more sedate, broader rivers. In a 1932 publication on the black flies of the Adirondack Mountains in New York, Clell Metcalf wrote:

> To find the young of blackflies one should go to the swiftest part of a stream, where the water churns or boils over stones, sticks, logs or other obstructions, or where vegetation such as the leaves of trees or of grasses or sedges breaks the surface of the current into ripples. Remove the stone or other object from the water and examine it in bright light . . . On the down-stream side of the stones the dark gray to black appearing "worms" or

"maggots" . . . will be found squirming or writhing slowly over the moist surface.

Living in swiftly flowing water favors black fly larvae in two very important ways. First, the larvae are blessed with an abundance of oxygen, because turbulent waters are well aerated. Second, the current brings them a constant supply of food. Anchored to a rock or some other object by a sucker at its hind end and leaning downstream with the flow, the larva uses its fanlike mouth brushes to sift even tiny bits of detritus and infinitesimal microorganisms from the current. Although mainly sedentary, the larva can move about to a limited degree. "The larva," noted Harold Oldroyd, "can, like an inchworm, or measuring worm, move with a looping motion, using its fore and hind suckers alternately. This serves for limited local excursions, but for a controlled transit downstream, without being swept helplessly away by the current, the larva spins a silken thread, and pays it out as it goes, like a spider in a breeze. When it alights on a suitable object, the posterior [sucker] again takes a grip."

Because adult mayflies do not feed, it is up to the nymphs to obtain and store the nutrients they will require when they become adults. A few nymphs prey on insects, some munch on water plants, some scrape algae and other edibles from underwater objects, and a few, reported Vincent Resh, burrow in and feed on the bodies of freshwater sponges, as do the spongillaflies you met in an earlier chapter. A few other nymphs are filter feeders that strain plankton and fragments of detritus from the water. These filter feeders use their hairy front legs as sieves, not their mouthparts. Some nymphs *(Isonychia)*, according to the entomologist George Edmunds, Jr., and his coauthors, sit on the bottom, oriented so that they face into the current with their hairy front legs extended before them. The long, overlapping hairs on the legs strain food, much of it plankton, from the water. At intervals the nymphs eat the food trapped on the hairs. Other nymphs *(Ephoron)* use their tusklike mandibles to excavate U-shaped burrows in the bottom sediments that are open at both ends and lined with a silklike material. The nymph forces a current through its burrow by almost constantly waving the feather-shaped gills on its abdomen as its densely hairy forelegs sift food from the current.

Some aquatic insects are browsers that glean algae, other organisms, and detritus from the bottom ooze or from litter lying on stones, leaves, or other surfaces. Among them are the water boatmen. They are the only one of the 15 North American families (16 worldwide) of aquatic or semiaquatic bugs that are not strictly predaceous. Melvin Griffith summarized his investigation of a water boatman's diet this way: "the presence of algal, protozoan, and rotiferan remains in adult stomachs indicates . . . a diet neither wholly animal or vegetable. The scooping movements of the forelegs seem designed to winnow out of the ooze a nutritious salad from both kingdoms, mixed in one digestible mass." Robert Usinger added, "In addition to this 'salad' and the habit of evacuating the cell contents of filamentous algae, [some water boatmen] capture and feed upon whole [midge] and mosquito larvae."

The "scoop" on the stubby foreleg of a water boatman is a highly specialized segment of the leg, the foot (tarsus). The broad, paddle-shaped tarsus is larger than or almost as large as any one of the other segments of the leg. It is clothed with rows of closely spaced hairs that "winnow" food from the bottom ooze or from underwater surfaces. The water boatman's beak is very different from those of all other bugs, terrestrial or aquatic. The stylets of the broad, stubby, bluntly cone-shaped beak are adapted for rasping and sucking rather than for piercing and sucking. They do not join together to form the salivary and food channels characteristic of other bugs. The mouth opening on the face of the beak is unusually wide, wide enough to take in whole small organisms and also the cell contents of algal filaments.

Adult flies of the genus *Mallota*, which we have already met, visit blossoms to partake of nectar and pollen, just as do their relatives the drone fly and most of the other hover flies (family Syrphidae). Larval *Mallota*, like the larvae of drone flies, are rat-tailed maggots but live in tree holes rather than in sewage. Leaves and other organic debris drift into these tree holes and are decomposed by bacteria. The water in the tree hole is not only teeming with bacteria but has suspended in it an abundance of minute particles of detritus. Thus it comes as no surprise that natural selection has adapted *Mallota* and other rat-tailed maggots to take advantage of this bounty by straining the water. Lobes of their mandibles bear large combs, sieves, consisting of tightly packed bristles spaced less than 0.0002 inch apart. Only bacteria and very small particles of detritus can pass through. Large particles are blocked and cling to the outside of the sieve. The small particles are concentrated by another sieve behind the mandibles and are then swallowed. Rat-tailed maggots neither depend on a natural current nor produce one themselves. They suck a large gulp of water through the sieves and into the preoral cavity. As soon as the small particles that pass through have been swallowed, the water is forcefully expelled, sweeping away any large particles that obstruct the mandibular combs on the outside.

The small family Helodidae is worth mentioning because it is unique. Among the 300,000 species of beetles, only they—in the larval stage—have filtering mouthparts. Most adult helodids are small (most not much more than a tenth of an inch long) landlubbers that seldom enter the water. The aquatic larvae, which must come to the surface for bubbles of air, are filter feeders that consume detritus and plankton that they sweep from the surface of a stone or leaf with dense tufts of hair on the maxillae.

Insect larvae that are passive filter feeders weave silken nets that trap food suspended in the water—not unlike commercial fishers deploying gill nets to entangle mackerel, other food fish, and all too often innocent sea turtles, porpoises, and other "bycatch" that will be discarded. Some species of two distinct and only distantly related orders, caddisflies (order Trichoptera) and midges, flies of the order Diptera, weave miniature nets to strain plankton and detritus from a current of water—caddisflies from naturally flowing currents and midges from a current they themselves produce.

Midges, suggested Wallace and Merritt, are probably the most diverse family of all the insects in their choice of habitat and diet. As larvae, some species are terrestrial but most are aquatic, occupying virtually all aquatic habitats, even the seas and the profound depths of the Great Lakes. Their ways of obtaining food are varied, ranging from preying on insects to, of course, filter feeding.

Many midge larvae burrow in the bottom sediments of streams, rivers, or ponds. Some excavate and inhabit a U-shaped tunnel open at both ends. Rhythmic undulations of the larva's body cause a current to flow through the tunnel from rear to front. Food that comes in with the current is trapped on a net that blocks the front opening of the tunnel. At intervals, the larva eats both the net and the food adhering to it and then spins a new net to cover the opening. Wallace and Merritt reported that "the time interval required for spinning a food net, producing currents through it, and eating the net is about three to four minutes." Most adult midges rest by day and fly in the evening, night, and early morning. Although they are as small as mosquitoes and resemble them in other ways, they are not bloodsuckers and do not bite.

The mothlike adult caddisflies, usually less than an inch long, have rather broad wings usually densely clothed with hairs. Nocturnal and generally drab brown, they are seldom noticed except when they come to lights at night, sometimes large crowds of them. They seldom feed except for an occasional sip of nectar. Some of the larvae are the most wonderful spinners and weavers among the aquatic insects. A few weave shelters only when they are about to molt to the pupal stage. Many others construct and live in portable, usually tubelike cases made of sand, gravel, or bits of vegetation firmly bound together with silk. But the champion weavers are the filter-feeding species, which weave a variety of different trap nets. The nets of some species, with their adjunct structures, are architectural master-pieces, intricate and complex in design.

Broadly speaking, nets may be finger-shaped, cup-shaped, or funnel-shaped. The shape and form is typical of a species or a group of species, but may be modified as dictated by circumstances, such as the particular configuration of a location or the velocity of the current. In its simplest form, a net is finger-shaped with its opening facing upstream and is moored to a rock or some other support over which water flows. This type of net and some others often do double duty, serving both as a larva's shelter and the trap that provides its food. Other larvae attach a separate shelter to the net or construct one nearby. In either case, the larva frequently collects and eats the food caught in the net and removes any debris that clogs it.

Caddisfly larvae collected by J. Bruce Wallace and F. F. Sher-berger in the Altamaha River in Georgia build a small castle of sand with turrets that these entomologists believe is probably the most "elaborate feeding and dwelling structure" built by a caddisfly and "possibly one of the most complicated feeding structures constructed by non-social insects." They described the architectural marvel built by one of these caddisfly larvae *(Macronema transversum):* The larvae build of sand and silk a domed feeding chamber and larval retreat upon stones in large streams. The structure has two openings to the exterior. A vertical opening on an elevated tubelike turret serves as the entrance for inflowing water and a horizontal opening on a shorter turret serves as the exit. Both tubes connect with a large chamber divided by an extremely fine-meshed capture net. An adjoining smaller chamber, which serves as the larva's retreat, has two openings into the larger chamber, one on either side of the capture net. The larger opening connects with the upstream side of the larger chamber. The larva protrudes from it when feeding on particles trapped by the net. The smaller opening connects with the downstream side and allows for a flow of water over the larva's gills and is the exit through which the larva's feces pass into the outgoing current.

The flat landscape of central Illinois is not known for its rocky, fast-flowing streams, but there is such a stream, Stony Creek, near the little town of Oakwood. It is one of the few places in that area where hellgrammites, dobsonfly larvae, can be collected. I used to take students there to collect these wonderful insects. We would turn over stones, and if there was a hellgrammite beneath one, it would float downstream, to be caught in a strategically placed net. If you are careless handling one of these large creatures—they can be 3 inches long—it will give you a painful nip with its powerful mandibles. They are of the chewing type and are used to crush and masticate prey, usually animals smaller than themselves, among them caddisfly larvae, mayfly and stonefly nymphs, and even smaller members of their own species.

Just as mosquito larvae are intermediaries in food chains between tiny organisms such as bacteria and one-celled algae and small predators such as insects and little fish, hellgrammites and other large predaceous aquatic insects higher on the food chain are intermediaries between small aquatic insects and large predators, such as smallmouth bass. The hellgrammites, wrote Elsie Klots, "are of great importance in the ecology of the stream. They are secondary consumers feeding upon small animals and serving as food for still larger ones. They are thus 'middlemen' in the food chain, changing small units into larger ones."

The way in which larvae and adult predaceous diving beetles capture their prey is not particularly unusual, but the way in which the larvae consume their prey is, at least from the point of view of humans and other vertebrates, very unusual indeed. In his encyclopedic book about insects that eat other insects, Walter Balduf described how adults grasp their victims with the first two pairs of legs, which are armed with long, sharply pointed claws, and then chew them up with their short, stout mandibles. They, like the larvae, will eat almost anything that moves, mostly insects but sometimes snails or even some vertebrates, among them small frogs.

The larvae, often called water tigers because they are so ravenous and insatiable, lie in wait to ambush prey. When a potential victim comes close enough, the larva darts out, propelling itself by lashing its long abdomen, and grasps the surprised creature with its long, sickle-shaped, sharply pointed mandibles. "Not until then," wrote Balduf, "does the larva pass upon the edibility of its captive, but grabs at any moving thing not too large."

In his classic entomology text, John Henry Comstock wrote: "The mandibles are admirably suited for holding prey and at the same time sucking the juice from its body." The juice is sucked up through internal channels that pass through the mandible from its tip to its base, where the juice enters the mouth opening. This juice is not only the prey's blood but also includes its liquefied inner organs and tissues. They are dissolved by digestive juices and enzymes that the water tiger injects into its victim, along with a paralyzing poison, through the channels in its mandibles. This process, which insect physiologists call extra-oral digestion, was graphically described by Sir Vincent Wigglesworth: "The contents of the gut are regurgitated . . . through the perforated mandibles. As [a water tiger] feeds on some transparent insect, a black fluid can be seen to come from the tips of the jaws and spread among the organs. At once the [prey] is paralyzed and dies; the secretion seems to contain a nerve poison, making the prey quiescent. Very quickly the tissues melt away into a liquid with floating granules, which can be seen flowing back into the [mandibles]."

We will see that a few other insects, both aquatic and terrestrial, also practice extra-oral digestion. Spiders do too, but vertebrates—fish, birds, mammals, and other animals with backbones—do not, with the possible exception of some snakes, whose venom may begin the process of digestion even before the snake swallows its victim. The starfish of the seas, which are not vertebrates, practice an almost incredible form of extraoral digestion. When attacking an oyster or a clam, the starfish grasps the two hinged halves of the shell with suckers on its arms and exerts a relentless pressure until the shell gapes open. Then it everts its stomach through its mouth and into the shell. The stomach surrounds the soft-bodied clam or oyster, digests it, and is then withdrawn back into the starfish's body.

It is obviously advantageous for predators such as water tigers to secrete poisons that quickly subdue their prey. Justin Schmidt, an expert on insect venoms, postulated that many predators do just that, especially those that pierce and suck. There is reason to believe that beetles, including water tigers, produce their poisons in the gut, but generally speaking, other insects secrete them in their salivary glands. In 1924, R. Poisson, quoted by Schmidt, did a clever experiment which suggests that the salivary glands of backswimmers contain such a poison. When a backswimmer ate insects that Poisson had injected with a harmless blue dye, the backswimmer's saliva turned blue. When it subsequently attacked almost transparent insects that had not been dyed, its blue saliva was visible in the prey, which was soon immobilized.

Groups of shiny, black whirligig beetles gyrate on the surface of ponds in what looks like a crazed tarantella. A group may consist of anywhere from a few to hundreds of individuals, sometimes of several different species. These beetles are, like other surface dwellers such as marsh treaders and water striders, scavengers that feed on the many insects, mostly land dwellers, that rain down onto the water surface. Occasionally they prey on aquatic insects. Whirligigs swim with their short, stout antennae touching the surface of the water. The sensitive antennae perceive the ripples generated by a struggling insect that falls onto the water or one that rises to the surface for air. Although backswimmers are bugs rather than beetles, they have—through natural selection—evolved the same ability to perceive ripples. A simple but ingenious experiment done by G. A. Walton proves the point:

If a small object is spun in the surface film it will be attacked by the bugs, and I used a pin with the point doubled back and suspended from its head by a length of cotton, which could be twirled between the thumb and forefinger so as to spin the pin in the surface film. The [backswimmers] quickly detect the pin by the ripples created and swim up and attack it. So strongly do they grip the pin that they can be lifted out of the water without letting go.

When ripples alert the whirligigs to the presence of prey, they, often several of them, dash out to claim it. Balduf quoted C. B. Wilson's description of the feeding frenzy that occurs when more than one whirligig responds:

As many would seize the insect as could crowd around it, grasping it with their mandibles. Then they swim off, sometimes going fairly straight away, sometimes whirling around in wild curves and sometimes diving beneath the surface, but always holding on to their prey and tearing out mouthfuls of the insect tissues. When one bit off more than he could swallow at once, he would hurry away with it, pursued by a hungry crowd, each intent on snatching it from him, and he was lucky if he could keep it long enough to finish devouring it.

Although adult whirligigs are basically scavengers, the larvae are ravenous predators that live under the water, hiding on the bottom waiting for a prey animal—usually an aquatic insect—to come close. Festooned with two rows of large, feather-like gills on the abdomen, they need never leave their hunting grounds to go to the surface for air. As do diving beetle larvae, whirligig larvae digest their prey extra-orally. They too have long, sickle-shaped mandibles traversed from tip to base by an internal channel through which a lethal poison and digestive fluids are injected into the prey. Then, just as in water tigers, the liquefied organs of the prey are ingested through the same channels in the mandibles.

🦟 Whirligig beetle and predaceous diving beetle larvae have similar mandibles—possibly inherited from a common ancestor—that facilitate the capture of prey and the efficient and economical process of extra-oral digestion. This ability might well be envied by other insects, but not by the largely land-dwelling members of the order Neuroptera, antlions, aphid-lions, and many others, and the aquatic spongillaflies. Beetles and neuropterans are no more closely related than are mice and tigers. Nevertheless, they have evolved functionally similar although structurally different ways of accomplishing the same end, piercing their prey and injecting digestive fluids. For example, antlion larvae, famous for digging conical pitfalls in the soil to trap ants and other prey, have long mandibles that are sharply pointed and sickle-shaped, but rather than an internal channel, there is a long, narrow groove that traverses the length of the inner side of each mandible. The open grooves, useless in themselves, are made useful by the long, narrow maxillae that press against the mandibles and close the grooves. This is a striking example of what evolutionary biologists call convergent evolution. In this case, as in many others, natural selection has found more than one way to skin a cat.

🦟 The highly specialized mouthparts of both nymphal and adult giant water bugs form, as do those of all bugs—whether predators or herbivores—a piercing-sucking beak that is yet a third way of skinning a cat. The beak is marvelously designed for consuming insects or other animals by extra-oral digestion.

The two long, slender, stylet-like, and doubly grooved maxillae—outwardly braced by the long, thin, ungrooved mandibles—fit together snugly so that the grooves meet to form two closed channels, a "salivary" canal through which a paralytic poison and digestive fluids are injected into the prey, an insect or even a fish or tadpole, and a food canal that sucks up the predigested flesh of the prey animal.

The giant water bug's long, thin mandibles, adapted for piercing and sucking, cannot possibly grip anything, as do those of whirligigs and predaceous diving beetle larvae, but its front legs, specially adapted for seizing prey, take their place. Legs that can snatch and grab are said to be raptorial, as are the talons of a raptor, a bird of prey such as a hawk or an owl.

The way in which a raptorial insect leg works is most easily understood if we take a brief look at the structure of the typical insect leg. The jointed leg consists of five segments. The coxa articulates (is movably jointed) with the body; the trochanter, immovably joined to the long, stout femur, articulates with the coxa; the femur articulates with the long but slimmer tibia; and finally, the tarsus, or "foot," divided into as many as five articulating subsegments, articulates with the end of the tibia.

The exceptionally stout femur of the raptorial front legs of a giant water bug opposes the slimmer tibia, just as the two arms of a nutcracker oppose each other. The enlarged femur contains massive muscles that force the tibia against the femur in a powerful grip, and the end of the tibia is armed with a sharp claw, actually a modification of the tarsus, which helps to hold the prey.

Raptorial legs of this type have evolved independently in several unrelated groups of insects, another fascinating example of convergent evolution. Five of the 44 North American families (subdivisions of an order) of bugs have raptorial front legs: in aquatic environments, giant water bugs, water scorpions, and creeping water bugs; and on land, ambush bugs and assassin bugs. There are also terrestrial insects other than bugs with raptorial legs: praying mantises, distant relatives of the grasshoppers; mantispids, relatives of the antlions; and in New Zealand, according to Harold Oldroyd's *Natural History of Flies*, a very unusual wingless fly related to the house fly.

Other variations on the basic theme of raptorial appendages have evolved. For example, the adult scorpionflies known as hangingflies hang from a twig or a leaf in the understory of a forest by their exceptionally long and threadlike front legs and with the equally long hind legs dangling down. The tarsi of other insects play little or no role in grasping prey, but two of the four subsegments of the foot of a hangingfly's hind leg oppose each other and can snatch and grip an insect that comes within reach. But the most unusual grasping appendages of them all are surely those of the aquatic larvae of phantom midges. Their antennae, unlike those of all other insects, are raptorial. They hang straight down in front of the mouthparts and are used to capture mosquito larvae and other small aquatic insects or crustaceans.

The predators that I have discussed thus far are all opportunists that will eat almost any kind of prey that comes along. But aquatic marsh fly larvae—some live on land—are specialists that eat only snails. Lloyd Knutson and Clifford Berg described attacks that hungry marsh fly larvae made on snails: "The swift, forthright attack was followed by the snail's rapid withdrawal into its shell. Larvae that had penetrated the snail tissue were pulled into the shells as the snails forcibly withdrew.

If they had not penetrated the tissue, the larvae crawled rapidly after the retreating snails." When fully grown, usually after feeding on several snails, the larvae pupate within a puparium, the hardened skin of the fully grown larva, as do house flies and other "higher" flies, as opposed to the "lower" flies such as mosquitoes and midges. A larva ready to pupate changes its shape to the ovoid form of the puparium and darkens and hardens its skin. The molt to the pupal stage occurs within the puparium, but the puparium is not shed. The pupa remains within it and is protected by it as a moth is protected by its silken cocoon, a marvelous example of evolution's parsimonious aspect. Some marsh fly larvae pupariate inside a snail shell, but must first twist themselves into a shape that conforms to the spiral convolutions of the shell.

Although the great majority of species in several groups of aquatic insects are not carnivores, there are in all of these groups a few exceptional species that do feed on insects or other aquatic creatures. Among them are the nymphs of certain mayflies and stoneflies, a few water boatmen, and the larvae of a very few midges and mosquitoes. A tendency to become carnivorous is to be expected, because there is, nutritionally speaking, no more easily assimilated food for an animal than another animal. Data cited in Peter Price's comprehensive and authoritative book on insect ecology show this to be so. Carnivorous insects convert into body mass and use for growth more than twice as much of what they eat as do plant feeders.

Although most mosquito larvae are filter feeders, a few, perhaps 80 of the 2,500 known species, have become carnivores. In them the long, delicate hairs of the mouth brushes have coalesced to form stout spines for grabbing prey, usually mosquito larvae. All of the approximately 60 members of one genus (*Toxorhynchites*), a subdivision of the mosquito family, are predators. Ernestine Basham and her coworkers found that, during its entire larval life of 16 days, a North American member of this largely tropical genus devoured 118 mosquito larvae, more than seven per day. In his encyclopedic book, *Mosquitoes*, William Horsfall described the behavior of a hunting larva: "A larva ambushes prey, usually at the water surface. It hangs motionless or turns very slightly as prey approaches, and when the intervening space is less than the length of the predator, the body is flicked instantly toward the prey."

Some insects, among them at least one aquatic predator, are thieves that steal food from other insects. This piratical behavior, kleptoparasitism (from the Greek word for thief), is not unique to the insects. Bald eagles, for example, sometimes highjack ospreys to steal a fish. The oceanic jaegers and skuas steal food from other birds. At a pond in the county of Somerset in England, Walton watched a *Hydrometra* (marsh treader) slyly suck nutriment from an insect caught by a *Gerris* (water strider): "It will also take advantage of the kills of its more powerful relatives, *Gerris*, its fine sense of smell guiding it to the scene. With measured, silent tread the *Hydrometra* sidles up unnoticed by the feeding *Gerris*; hesitant and pausing it finally reaches out, stretching slowly forward and very, very gently inserts its [beak] into the victim. Should the *Gerris* make the smallest move, the *Hydrometra* quickly and slyly slips aside, waiting for another opportunity."

Food supplies the energy insects or other animals require to grow, to keep their bodies running, and to fuel their activities, which are many and varied. But, among other activities, males must find females and females must locate appropriate places to lay eggs; a predator is likely to burn a great deal of energy in hot pursuit of its prey; a prey animal runs or flies away so as not to be eaten. These behaviors and most others involve energy-consuming locomotion of one sort or another. I next consider how aquatic insects, using food energy, move about and go from one place to another—often in ways unique to them.

Going Places

*A water boatman, its oarlike legs briefly
at rest, clings to a pondweed*

A large dragonfly nymph lies sprawled on the silt at the bottom of a pond. Too slow to catch prey by pursuing it, he (or just as likely she) is an ambusher and does not move a muscle lest he alert possible victims or attract the attention of predators. He is, nevertheless, keenly aware of the creatures around him. If one is smaller than he is, it may make a meal if he can grab it with his raptorial lower lip. But if it is larger than he is, it may be a predator that will eat him, and it will be best to flee if it comes too close. Small insects and a tiny fish swim nearby but do not come close enough. But then a large fish approaches, and the frightened nymph escapes by abruptly and swiftly darting away.

How in the world did this usually slow-moving insect ever manage to move away so speedily? The basic mechanism is already in place: A dragonfly's gills are in its rectum, and it constantly bathes them with fresh water by alternately dilating and contracting the rectum so as to suck in and expel water through the anus. In an emergency, the rectum does double duty as a rocket engine by expelling a sudden rush of water far more forcefully than usual. According to Werner Nachtigall, large dragonfly nymphs have propelled themselves over 6 feet by making several consecutive thrusts, each of which rockets them forward about 20 inches. It is a fascinating fact that squids, which live in the seas, also use rocket propulsion, forcibly ejecting water, not through the anus but through a tubular siphon that connects with the body cavity, in which lie the digestive system and other organs. More versatile than dragonfly nymphs, squids can rocket either forward or backward by appropriately aiming the flexible siphon.

The dragonfly nymph's unusual means of rapid locomotion is often erroneously called jet propulsion, but it is really a form of rocket propulsion. Jet airplanes and rockets are both propelled by a powerful rearward blast of exhaust gases produced by burning fuel. But a jet engine cannot function unless it constantly scoops in air, while a rocket, completely self-contained, does not require the intake of air. If we could get a nymph with its rectum loaded with water to survive in airless outer space, its "rocket engine" would still work, because it is a law of physics that every action (ejecting water) has an opposite and equal reaction (forward movement). But it could "blast off" only once, because it could not refill its rectum with water—just as a rocket cannot fly after it runs out of fuel.

Mobility, the ability to move from place to place, serves an aquatic insect—or any other animal, for that matter—in several essential ways. By flying, it can find food or, as we will see later, find a mate, move to a different body of water, or even migrate to a more favorable climate. And, by moving through the water, sometimes by crawling and sometimes by swimming, it meets the demands of everyday life: finding food and shelter; finding places where physical conditions, such as the water temperature or the velocity of the current, are favorable; and, like our dragonfly nymph, escaping from predators.

If they are not frightened, dragonfly nymphs climb on water

plants or walk sedately on the bottom as do other aquatic insects, among them water scorpions, riffle beetles, and caddisfly larvae. Some insects walk on the surface of the water. We will come to them later. As is to be expected, many aquatic insects, but actually a minority of them, swim. Some propel themselves by variously undulating their bodies, mayfly nymphs by beating the abdomen, with its hair-covered tail fan, up and down with a porpoiselike motion, and damselfly nymphs by undulating the abdomen from side to side, as do fish. A few even swim with their gills. Walter Balduf, in his book on predaceous beetles, well described the swimming of a larval whirligig beetle: "The legs have no swimming fringes, but the eight posterior pairs of lateral gills are heavily fringed and serve for locomotion as well as for breathing. By lashing them up and down the larva can move either forward or backward with great rapidity. It can also jump quite a distance by snapping its body by a sudden contraction of the longitudinal muscles of the abdominal segments."

But most swimming insects paddle through the water. Fairyflies, those minute wasps that parasitize the eggs of aquatic insects, propel themselves with their paddle-shaped wings. But most insects that swim, such as beetles and bugs, row or paddle with their legs. One or more of their three pairs of legs have been adapted for swimming by being flattened and often further broadened by fringes of long, stiff hairs—all three pairs in water scavenger beetles, the middle and hind pairs in large predaceous diving beetles, and only the long hind pair in giant water bugs, backswimmers, and water boatmen. Making a stroke with these paddles is not as simple as it may seem, and has been made possible only by significant changes in the musculature and other anatomical characteristics of the usual walking leg. One of the difficulties of swimming under water was nicely explained by the entomologist and naturalist Peter Farb: "A canoe paddle can be lifted out of the water for the recovery stroke, but an underwater insect's paddle cannot be. Therefore, backswimmers have had to develop a leg action which gets a purchase on the water when it is pushing the insect along, but offers a minimum of friction when the leg is brought forward for the next stroke. This feat is accomplished by the hairs on the legs. One way, they spread stiffly and permit a powerful stroke; the other way, the hairs [fold backward and] hang limp."

Then there is the matter of steering, horizontally from one side to the other or up and down vertically. Predaceous diving beetles steer horizontally just as would a person rowing a boat. One leg (oar) is stretched out to the side with its "blade" motionless in the water, while the other leg continues to row. The beetle or the rowboat pivots to the right when the left leg or oar is rowing, and to the left when the right one is rowing. When the beetle is moving vertically, making a power dive or swimming to the surface, some of the legs act as motionless diving planes, analogous to the diving planes a submarine uses to dive or rise to the surface under power. If its forward diving planes are slanted downward, the submarine or insect dives, if they are slanted upward, it moves toward the surface.

Water is much denser than air and cannot be compressed. Consequently, it offers more resistance to a swimming insect than does air to a flying insect. To ease their progress through the water, insects are generally smoothly streamlined. Compare the sleek, hairless body of a diving beetle with that of some "rough-skinned" land-dwelling beetle covered with hairs that are short but that would, nevertheless, impede movement through the water. Diving beetles are so "smooth-skinned" and slippery that males would have difficulty holding on to females while mating if their front feet did not have large suction disks.

🜚 As my daughter Gwen and I walked along the shore of a small pond on an island near Buenaventura, Colombia, we flushed several lizards from the grass. They dashed to the water for safety and, much to our amazement, ran over the surface of the water on their hind legs for as much as 50 feet. They called to mind a flat stone thrown with such force that it skips over the surface of a pond. Commonly known as Jesus Christ lizards, these little creatures, I think they were about 6 or 7 inches long, did not immediately sink, because they have such fantastically long toes and run with such amazing speed. I know of no other animal that can walk or run on water except for certain kinds of insects.

Among such insects are water striders that skate over the surface of a pond on their middle and hind legs, the raptorial front pair reserved for taking prey. Their feet dimple the surface film, and the sun projects enlarged shadows of the dimples onto the bottom, shadows that skim along below as the insect glides above. Marsh treaders, long, thin, sticklike, and usually moving slowly, use all six legs to walk on floating vegetation— or occasionally on the surface film, but not nearly as adeptly as do water striders. Crowds of whirligig beetles gyrate madly as they swim on the surface, their upper sides above the surface film and their lower sides, with legs paddling, below it. A few kinds of rove beetles propel themselves across the surface in an amazing and, as far as I know, a unique way, by excreting a chemical substance that disperses the surface film.

Although the surface film is an impediment to insects that

must come to the surface for air, it and nothing else supports insects walking on the water. G. A. Walton's ingenious demonstration of the effect of a surfactant—a substance such as soap that reduces surface tension—on the ability of a water strider to stride makes the point:

> In the laboratory specimens of a [water strider] were placed on water from a spring . . . and the surface tension reduced by slowly adding a dilute solution of [a surfactant]. After the skaters had become incapable of standing on the water without getting their legs wet and falling spreadeagle upon the surface, and had recovered repeatedly by applying saliva to their legs, a point was reached when they were unable to do this any longer. That is to say, the aquaphobe force of the saliva on the tiny hairs on their legs was no longer great enough to overcome the reduced surface tension.

Water striders are very suitably adapted for living on the surface film, but I doubt that the "aquaphobe force of the saliva," if it exists, has anything to do with it. They are light in weight and have thin walking legs, two or three times as long as the body, that they spread wide to distribute their weight evenly. Their feet and much of the body are clothed with a velvety pile of oily, hydrophobic hairs that do not easily break through the surface film. The sharp claws, which might otherwise pierce the film, are not at the tip of the foot, as they are in other insects, but are set well back and out of the way. A water strider moves rapidly and can leap and then land on the water without getting wet, because the hairy pile on its body sheds water. Even if it accidentally submerges, it is buoyed up and kept dry by a film of air caught in the pile.

The lethargic marsh treaders or water measurers are, as Elsie

Klots put it, "the walking sticks of the aquatic world." (The scientific name of their family, Hydrometridae, is derived from Greek roots meaning water and measure.) Their brownish or greenish bodies, exceedingly slender and elongated—the narrow head alone may be about as long as the abdomen—and their very long, almost threadlike legs make them nearly invisible as they sit motionless or tread slowly and deliberately on floating vegetation. Their sharp claws are at the very end of the foot, not recessed as in the water striders. "This no doubt," observed Robert Usinger, "renders them less efficient in open water than such masters of the surface film as the [water striders]." While observing marsh treaders in Costa Rica, Chris Maier found that they usually walk slowly on mats of floating algae or on calm water. "When adults were walking, they slowly moved one limb forward at a time, alternating contralateral [diagonally opposite] limbs. At the same time they swung their heads from side to side and waved their antennae slowly but constantly." Although usually lethargic, they will sprint briefly, even across open water, if they are disturbed.

The shiny black whirligig beetles that gyrate on the surface (their family name is Gyrinidae) float on the water, supported both by their buoyancy and, since they are small and light, also by the surface tension. Like a boat, the lower part of the body, the "hull," is immersed in the water, while the upper part is above the water line. As a beetle paddles the legs on its hull, the water flows smoothly along the streamlined hull, minimizing the drag that would otherwise impede its progress. The middle and hind legs are powerful paddles that are short, flattened, broad, and have fringes of stiff hairs that further increase their surface area, thereby increasing the paddles' "bite" in the water.

Although they don't wear glasses, whirligigs do have four

eyes. (Virtually all insects have only two eyes, one on either side of the head, except for two or three small light-sensitive organs that cannot resolve images on the "forehead" between the eyes.) Each of the whirligig's eyes is divided into two well-separated parts. As the swimming beetle straddles the surface film, the upper part of the eye looks up into the air, and the lower part down into the water, each watching out for a meal or an enemy. The four-eyed fish of the West Indies has, according to Carl Bond, a similar adaptation, an eye with the iris divided into two parts, the upper exposed to the air and the lower in the water.

The sensitive antennae of whirligig beetles perceive ripples in the surface film caused by struggling insects that have fallen onto the water. In 1926, Friedrich Eggers reported that they use the same sense to avoid obstacles in the water, including their fellow whirligigs in a gyrating group. He noted that when they were confined in a glass container, they did not bump into the walls if they were swimming on the surface, but when they swam underwater they often hit the walls with an audible impact. There was, obviously, something about the surface film that guided the beetles. This observation and a series of experiments led Eggers to the conclusion that on the surface whirligigs become aware of obstacles by using a sense roughly analogous to the echolocation used by bats to locate insects in the air or to the sonar, another form of echolocation, used by navy ships to locate submarines. They perceive the "echoes" that bounce back when the arc-shaped waves that fan out in front of them strike an obstacle. (A recent publication by Vance Tucker includes a splendid photograph of a swimming whirligig and the waves it generates.) In a revealing experiment, Eggers showed that when a beetle's antennae were removed, it blundered and could no longer avoid obstacles.

🪰 An uncommon but extraordinary means of locomotion—certainly as unusual as the dragonfly nymph's rocket propulsion—is the way in which a few species of rove beetles glide on the surface of the water without moving a muscle and with no tail wind to push them. In *The Insects*, Reginald Chapman wrote that these beetles *(Stenus)* live "on grass stems bordering mountain streams in situations such that the beetles fall into the water quite frequently. They can walk on the surface of the water, but only slowly." If disturbed, however, they move very swiftly by releasing from glands at the end of the abdomen a surfactant that lowers the surface tension behind them, thereby dissipating the surface film. The beetle, standing on the retreating surface film, is carried away rapidly. By using a clever trick, K. E. Linsenmaier and R. Jander made visible the otherwise invisible, the retreat of the surface film. They spread a marker on the surface film, a thin layer of the minute, dustlike spores of a club moss *(Lycopodium)*. As the surfactant acted, the blanket of floating spores was driven away with the retreating surface film, revealing the spore-free track of its retreat.

🪰 Because food is not easy to come by, energy is precious and must be conserved. After all, a calorie saved can be devoted to producing offspring. Among the aquatic insects, the supreme conservers of energy are stream-dwelling insects that travel by just drifting with the current, expending a minimum of energy, as does a flying insect floating on the wind. In the early 1960s, when "drift," a technical term in aquatic ecology, was a hot

topic, I took my insect behavior students to see this phenome-
non in the Vermilion River where it flows through Kickapoo
State Park in east central Illinois. A little while before sunset, we
put our nets in the river but caught very few drifting insects.
When we put the nets out shortly after sunset, however, we
caught many, mainly mayfly nymphs.

The distance traveled by drifting insects varies from a few
inches to several yards and may occasionally be several hundred yards. Although the distance drifted in a single day may be
short, investigations cited by John Brittain and Tor Eikelund
showed that some insects could move cumulatively over 6 miles
downstream during the course of a single generation. Insects
may drift with the current accidentally, simply because they
lose their foothold, but more often they do so intentionally.
They may choose to drift away to escape unfavorable physical,
chemical, or biological conditions or to escape from fish or
other predators. Another and very important benefit of drifting
is that it enables them to move to new areas downstream that
may be less crowded or offer a greater abundance of food.

"Innumerable studies," wrote Brittain and Eikelund, "have
shown that drift increases during the night, especially during
the period just after sunset and to a lesser extent before sunrise." This daily pattern varies with the species and the circumstances. Mayfly and stonefly nymphs and black fly larvae drift
mainly at night, certain caddisflies in the daytime, and many
beetles throughout the day. Among the most important of the
circumstances that affects the daily pattern of drift is the presence of insect-eating fish. In western Colorado, Angus McIntosh
and his coworkers found that mayflies drift throughout the
day in streams not inhabited by trout but mostly at night in

streams with trout, which feed mainly during the day. Chemical cues that emanated from the fish alerted the mayfly nymphs to their presence.

Any animal must at some time in its life move from one place to another. Even the sedentary barnacle—a jointed-legged relative of the insects—with its hard, calcareous shell immovably and irrevocably cemented to a rock in the sea, began life as a larva that swam and drifted with the current until it ultimately settled down. The same can be said of sponges, oysters, sea anemones, and other sedentary animals.

In almost any species, at least a few females, sometimes accompanied by males, will at some time fly or otherwise leave the habitat in which they were born and find other places to live. By so doing, aquatic insects can colonize bodies of water not yet occupied by the competition, members of their own species. Even if they do not turn out to be pioneering colonists, they could still serve their offspring by not staying put to lay their eggs in a pond or stream that may be drying up or otherwise deteriorating, or they may favor them by moving to another body of water that may have fewer predators or fewer competitors for a limited food supply.

There is no shortage of newly created habitats that aquatic insects could profitably colonize, as Andrew Sheldon vividly noted:

For aquatic insects, the world is an everchanging mosaic of environments in which elements arise, vanish, and reappear . . . receding glaciers lay bare landscapes rich in aquatic habitats. Reservoirs are constructed. Ephemeral pools fill after rare desert rains or, more predictably, with the melting of winter snow. Dry streambeds bake in the sun, then fill and flow for days or years, and then dry again. Spates may destroy most of a stream's fauna or merely overturn a few stones to expose new surfaces for occupancy . . . If this kaleidoscopic view of the world is realistic, then colonization, broadly defined, must occur so frequently that it is an integral part of the life histories of all but a few extraordinarily specialized aquatic insects.

Aquatic insects have taken advantage of these opportunities to the fullest extent. The majority of them are on the move— exploring the environment—for most of their adult lives, often flying amazingly long distances. The rapidity with which they colonize newly available bodies of water is remarkable and is evidence that explorers are plentiful and that they search far and wide. An interesting example of this is the amazingly prompt arrival of aquatic colonists at James Sternburg's backyard fish pond in Urbana, Illinois. Every spring, Jim, fellow entomologist and longtime friend, thoroughly cleans and fills his plastic-lined pond with fresh water. Year after year, adult water striders arrive within a day or even minutes after the pond is filled. He has told me, with what I think is only a little exaggeration, that "the air must be crowded with cruising water striders looking for a pond."

But how do the water striders recognize Jim's little fish pond, or any other pond, as a body of water? Numerous observations suggest that some, perhaps many or most, different kinds of aquatic insects simply respond to any reflecting surface. A British ecologist, T. T. Macan, noted that mayflies that lay their eggs on the surface of the water seem to react to little more than a shiny surface. Some dragonflies are attracted to a white cloth or a piece of white paper placed on the ground. Female dragonflies, presumably looking for a place to lay their eggs, orient to the shiny roofs of cars or to panes of glass lying on the grass. Water bugs try to dive into paved parking lots wetted by rain.

Insects of quite a few species, notably monarch butterflies, dragonflies, and even leafhoppers only one eighth of an inch long, make a long-distance, migration, defined as a trip from an animal's birthplace to the birthplace of its offspring.

The migrations of insects, like those of birds, are often wind assisted. There are many known cases of insects carried by the wind for long distances. C. G. Johnson in *Migration and Dispersal of Insects by Flight,* published in 1969 but still a useful reference, told how certain mosquitoes, when leaving their resting place in the early evening, spiraled 12 to 15 feet up and then leveled off to fly downwind for as much as 16 miles. He also summarized other records of far more impressive distances that flying aquatic insects have been carried by the wind. In 1934, huge swarms of an infamous black fly, the Golubatz fly, named for a place on the Danube River in Serbia, were transported 50 miles from breeding sites on the Danube to Yugoslavia, where these blood suckers killed thousands of cattle. In Saskatchewan, another black fly traveled for nearly 100 miles on the wind. On September 11, 1927, salt marsh mosquitoes landed on a ship, the S.S. *Cristobal Colon,* 110 miles off the coast of North Carolina. Traps placed on offshore oil drilling platforms in the Gulf of Mexico by W. W. Wolf and several colleagues caught a predaceous diving beetle and dragonflies 100 miles from the closest land, black flies and damselflies at 66 miles, mayflies, mosquitoes, and caddisflies at 46 miles.

In 1954, William Horsfall, one of my mentors in graduate

school, reported a sudden influx into central Illinois of huge hordes of one of our most vexing mosquitoes, aptly named *Aedes vexans,* coincident with the arrival of a weather front from the north. They must have come from out of state, because in Illinois the only larval habitats that could have produced so many of them, the flooded bottomlands of rivers, were dry and the rivers were still falling owing to a severe statewide drought. The closest source of such a massive invasion of these mosquitoes was an area 230 miles to the north in south central Wisconsin, where heavy rains had flooded bottomlands.

The high altitudes at which aquatic insects have been caught in traps on airplanes or balloons leaves no doubt that they can be carried by the wind. Johnson reported that black flies, mosquitoes, caddisflies, and water boatmen have been trapped at 5,000 feet, mayflies at 3,000 feet, and predaceous diving beetles and water striders at 1,000 feet. In most if not all cases, these insects must have been carried aloft on thermals, the rising columns of warm air in which we sometimes see hawks and vultures spiraling to great heights. Glider pilots watch for these ascending hawks and move into the thermal to gain altitude.

Donald Borror of Ohio State University related an extraordinary experience with migrating insects:

On September 20, 1952, Mr. and Mrs. Allan D. Cruickshank observed an unusual flight of dragonflies at Todd's Point, on Long Island Sound near Old Greenwich, Connecticut. The flight was in progress when they arrived at the point at noon, and continued for the next two hours. Thousands of dragonflies passed the point during this period, all moving in a southwesterly direction; they passed in groups, and over a hundred were in sight at a time. Several species were present, but about 90 percent of the flight consisted of two species. Specimens of these two were collected and sent to [me] for [identification].

They were green darners *(Anax junius)* and a skimmer, the black saddlebags *(Tramea lacerata)*. Allan and Helen Cruickshank, well-known ornithologists, were probably at the point to observe the fall migration of plovers and sandpipers when they witnessed an awesome entomological spectacle, the southward migration of hordes of dragonflies. All-around naturalists that they were, they recorded the event and reported it to Borror, one of the outstanding entomologists of the time.

Worldwide, there are many migratory dragonflies, but in North America, according to Sidney Dunkle's field guide to dragonflies, the only migrating ones are some species of darners (family Aeschnidae) and some skimmers (family Libellulidae), the latter a large group of colorful species including the black saddlebags. In autumn, these insects move south to warmer climates just as do birds. But the birds make a round trip; the same individuals that went south in autumn return to their nesting grounds in the north the following spring. Migratory dragonflies, however, do not make a round trip. They breed in the south and die; it is their offspring that make the return trip.

We do know that migratory dragonflies make very long flights, but we know far less about their routes and distances traveled than we know about monarch butterflies, the most famous and by far the most studied of the insect migrants. The monarch's 2,000-mile route from southern Ontario to Mexico was traced by catching thousands of these butterflies in Ontario and elsewhere and releasing them with a tag with a return address glued to a wing. Tags returned by butterfly collectors and others to the University of Toronto traced the monarchs' southwesterly route. As Philip Corbet observed in *Dragonflies,* a similar approach is not likely to work with dragonflies, which fly faster, are less noticeable, and are more difficult to catch.

Observations made at various places in North America show that green darners migrate southward in autumn and northward in spring, but the entire route has not been traced in either direction. According to Corbet, adults destined to migrate south begin to emerge in southern Ontario in late June and in Indiana in mid-May. They forage nearby, growing fat, until they fly off days or weeks later. Their flight is surely wind assisted as witnessed by the fact that individuals in flapping flight on windless days are quickly exhausted and descend to the ground. Nevertheless, green darners have been caught almost 1.5 miles above the ground and are known to have traveled for a distance of almost 200 miles with the assistance of a tail wind.

On several occasions, large flocks of migrating dragonflies have been seen hunting for insect prey, the fuel that will sustain them on their southward journey. R. G. Emery, Jr., described a huge flock that he saw foraging on a peninsula called Presque Isle (French for peninsula) that juts into Lake Erie:

On August 28, 1932, I returned to Presque Isle, Pennsylvania . . . This day was very cloudy, cool and rainy, but I noticed as I walked [that] many large dragonflies darted up ahead of me out of the bushes. They were all *Anax junius* [green darners]. After a short flight they would alight and hide. On Tuesday the sun came out bright, so I was afield early . . . the air was swarming with dragonflies. They were there in the thousands, flying about 15 to 25 feet above the ground . . . They seemed to be flying in a circle, over quite a large area, as if feeding, for soon they would move to another place.

The rest of Emery's report suggests that these dragonflies were migrants from elsewhere rather than a local population: "I left this wonderful sight to see if there was any activity on the local ponds, but found there was not an *Anax* to be seen. I had found numerous *Anax* nymphs in [nearby] Niagara Pond while collecting during the summer, so I thought I would see if these had emerged, but on examination I found them to be as plentiful as ever and not an *Anax* to be seen over this pond."

Near the coasts of Maine and Massachusetts, green darners have been observed moving southward in the company of birds on northerly winds. During 6 consecutive years, an observer on the coast of New York watched green darners migrate southward in September with the assistance of northerly winds associated with the passage of cold fronts. Corbet wrote, "Such air movements convert the barrier beaches of southern Long Island into great highways for migrating insects, which pursue a steady, unfaltering, southward flight, occasionally interrupted by bouts of foraging." Migrating green darners first appear at Cape May, New Jersey, about 150 miles to the south, in September. At that time, many dragonflies, presumably migrants from the north, arrive in association with cold fronts. They increase in number until October and in most years leave not long thereafter to fly across Delaware Bay.

About 400 miles inland, flocks of migrating green darners fly westward along the north side of Lakes Ontario and Erie and congregate at the end of a long peninsula, Point Pelee, on the north shore of Lake Erie, thereby shortening the over-water portion of their southward flight across the wide lake. (Point Pelee, like Cape May, is a famous Mecca for birders, including me, because migrant birds crossing the lake take advantage of the point as do dragonflies.) F. M. Root of Oberlin, Ohio, noted that "on Point Pelee in 1911, about the middle of August . . . great numbers of dragonflies appeared . . . The great bulk of these were [green darners] and towards evening they clustered so thickly on the cedars near the end of the Point that eight or ten could be captured any time by a single sweep of the net."

"Migrating [green darners]," wrote Corbet, "roost overnight, choosing warm, west-facing surfaces on trees, and bushes where they settle during the hour before sunset. The next morning [before proceeding across the lake] they make a brief presunrise adjustment flight to east-facing perches where they warm [their bodies] as the sun rises. The adjustment flight, which occurs at about . . . 35 minutes before sunrise, follows several minutes of [body] warming accomplished by wing whirring." The metabolic work, done by the wing muscles, work required to whir or vibrate the wings, produces sufficient heat to increase the body temperature of these "cold-blooded" creatures—as are all insects—enough to permit flight.

Birds and mammals are commonly said to be "warm-blooded" and all other animals "cold-blooded." But in this instance the technical terms are more interesting and enlightening. Birds and mammals, whose metabolism generates heat inside the body, are endotherms (from Greek roots for inside and heat). The body temperature of "cold-blooded" animals is maintained by heat, usually sunshine, from outside their bodies. They are ectotherms (ecto is Greek for outside).

In early spring, usually during the first warm spell in March or April, adult green darners, presumably migrants from the south, appear in the northern United States and southern Canada, well before green darner nymphs that stayed behind the previous fall have completed their development and emerged as adults. Many of the returning individuals are mature females that have mated, as revealed by small scars on their eyes caused by the genital claspers of a male. (More about this seemingly inexplicable situation later.) The returnees are scattered and "sneak in" as individuals or small groups, but never in the large conspicuous flocks seen in autumn.

On April 4, before any local nymphs had become adults, Terese Butler saw two green darners flying near Kitchener, Ontario. These returning migrants had been blown north by strong southerly winds from a low-pressure system that spawned tornadoes from Georgia to Ohio. Canceled checks, other papers—and probably dragonflies—were blown 200 miles northeast from Xenia, Ohio, hard hit by a tornado, to Cleveland. The day the green darners arrived, the low-pressure system from the south had reached Kitchener, which is about 160 miles northeast of Cleveland, and afternoon temperatures had risen to an unusual 68°F.

Finding a mate—as well as distributing eggs—is the ultimate reason for insects to go from place to place. Every organism strives to produce offspring that will bear its genes. Some animals of the seas—jellyfish, starfish, oysters—reproduce by simply releasing eggs and sperm into the water, where they may, with luck, find each other. But insects, like mammals, have evolved a far more efficient system, internal fertilization. The males of 99.8 percent of the insects—all but the most primitive species—have a penis with which they inject their sperm into the female's genitalia.

The Next Generation

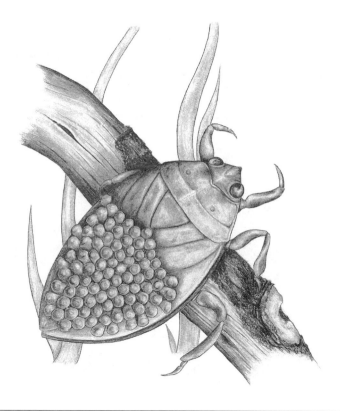

A male giant water bug, his mate's eggs glued to his back, rests near the water surface, where there is plenty of oxygen for his progeny

Female giant water bugs glue their eggs to their mate's back and then abandon both him and the eggs. At first, naturalists assumed that the egg-bearing bugs were females and that they had placed their eggs on their own backs. In 1886, the American entomologist George Dimmock, echoing an imaginative 1863 speculation by a French entomologist, wrote that "these eggs are set nicely upon one end, and placed in transverse rows, by means of a long protrusile tube, or ovipositor, which the insect can extend far over her own back." It was not until 1899 that Florence Slater reported that she had dissected many egg-bearing bugs and found them all to be males. José de la Torre-Bueno, a Peruvian-born American entomologist, found, as did Slater, that females do not have a long protrusile tube and assumed that the males are the *unwilling* victims of their mates. The egg-bearing male, he wrote, "like others of the same sex, dislikes exceedingly this forced servitude, and does all he can to rid himself of his burden. From time to time he passes his third pair of legs over [his back], apparently in an endeavor to accomplish his purpose."

Seventy years later, by which time natural selection and evolution had become the undisputed central theme of biology, Robert Smith pointed out that the "humiliated male hypothesis" is absurd because "natural selection could not have favored females programmed to dispose of their own ova on the back of a male only to have them discarded in places or conditions that might impede their development. On the contrary, females are always under intense selection pressure to choose oviposition sites that will maximize egg viability."

In reality, a male giant water bug is an attentive caretaker of the 100 or more eggs that cover his back. After all, these are his very own offspring, which will pass his genes on to future generations. From 95 to 100 percent of the eggs that remained attached to their father's back, Smith found, survived to hatch, but eggs removed from a male and placed in a dish of water were infested with a fungus within a week and all died.

Females and males not encumbered with eggs, Smith found, mostly stayed on their pond's muddy bottom, surfacing only occasionally for air. But males with eggs on their backs spent a great deal of time perched near the surface on a plant, positioned so as to expose the tips of the eggs to the air. When they were in deeper water, the fathers frequently patted and stroked their eggs with the hind legs while they supported themselves with the front and middle legs, a behavior intended not to dislodge the eggs, but to rid them of fungal spores and debris.

Most female insects live for only a few days or weeks, but in that short time lay several hundred or even several thousand eggs. But, according to Smith, female giant water bugs live for a year or more, and during that period, long for an insect, lay comparatively few eggs, a total of less than 350. It is a general rule that animals, including insects, produce relatively few young if they give parental care, as do the giant water bugs, but if they do not, they lay a great many eggs, gambling that a few will survive even though they are left to shift for themselves.

Brooding his mate's eggs can enhance a male's evolutionary

fitness—increase the number of his offspring—only if it is his sperm that fertilizes those eggs. Consequently, the male is genetically programmed to be jealous, to minimize the risk of being "cuckolded" by another male. He never allows a female to place eggs on his back until after he has copulated with her. "Even then," as Randy Thornhill and John Alcock put it, "he allows her to glue no more than three eggs in place before insisting on another copulation, repeating this cycle [several] times before the pair separates." In an extreme case, Smith found, a pair coupled over 100 times in 36 hours as 144 eggs were transferred.

A female may already have mated with some other male before she takes up with her current consort. When Smith paired a female giant water bug with a vasectomized male, the eggs that she placed on his back hatched despite the fact that, although he copulated with her, he could not have contributed sperm. Obviously, the eggs had been fertilized by the sperm of a previous mate. Indeed, he found that a female can retain living sperm in her spermatheca (sperm-storage organ) for as long as 5 months after her last mating. But he also showed that the male's libidinous behavior assures that he is the father of the eggs he broods. This is the result of what evolutionary biologists call sperm precedence. As Thornhill and Alcock pointed out, "multiply-mating females of many, if not all, insects tend to use sperm of their most recent mate when they fertilize their eggs." In other words, the last sperm to enter the spermatheca are the first to be used. Thus by copulating with a female just before she lays her eggs, the male thwarts her previous mates. Smith demonstrated the pervasiveness of sperm precedence by mating female giant water bugs that had already been inseminated by another male with a second male that had a distinctive genetic trait. The results showed the highest level of sperm precedence ever reported for an insect; 99.7 percent of the eggs laid by 24 different females produced nymphs with the distinctive trait, which proved that they were the progeny of the second male—not of any previous male.

In the vast majority of animals, as Anthony Wilson and his coauthors pointed out, the male's sperm are his sole contribution to his offspring. There are, of course, even among insects, cases where mother and father cooperate to give parental care. But the giant water bugs are among the few animals in which parental care is provided only by the father. Among the few others is the male stickleback fish, which builds a nest and broods the eggs; the male seahorse, another fish, which has a pouch, a marsupium, on the abdomen in which he broods the eggs and young; and several birds, in North America, the phalaropes, species in which the females are the colorful sex and do the courting—they mate with several of the plainer males, which have already built a nest and will incubate the eggs and care for the chicks.

A tiny aquatic bug of the Australian tropics, a cousin of the water striders and a member of a recently discovered genus, has turned the tables. In this case, the male burdens the female. Only a bit more than half as long (0.05 inch) as his mate, he rides on her back for days, sipping nutrient solutions from two glands on her back. Göran Arnquist and his colleagues proved that the females do indeed nourish the males by showing that males become radioactive if their mates are fed radioactively labeled fruit flies. The male obviously benefits by being fed, and it is my guess that he benefits most by preventing his mate from being inseminated by other males. The female benefits because the male protects her from the harassment of importuning suitors that could interfere with the all-important business of finding food and developing and laying eggs.

Giant water bugs of both sexes are capable fliers. They are strongly attracted to lights, and in the early days of electricity were called electric light bugs, because they swarmed around street lights at night. In her book on the American language, Mary Dohan wrote that late in the nineteenth century "*electric arc lights* brightened the streets, although they were somewhat obscured by clusters of *electric light bugs,* which, it was [falsely] believed, were spontaneously generated in the arc carbons and had a bite as deadly as a tarantula's." Like the giant water bugs, all other aquatic bugs and some aquatic beetles—although strictly aquatic only as nymphs and larvae—are amphibious in the adult stage, and are as adept in the air or on land as they are in or on the water. They mate and lay eggs in the water. Among them, in addition to the giant water bugs, are water boatmen, backswimmers, marsh treaders, water striders, whirligig beetles, predaceous diving beetles, and water scavenger beetles. But to the contrary, the great majority of other aquatic insects, although aquatic as larvae, are strictly terrestrial as adults and most can fly. Among them are the mayflies, dragonflies, stoneflies, dobsonflies, caddisflies, moths, and true flies. These insects fly or walk in search of mates and suitable places to lay their eggs.

In the same area and at almost the same time on the same day, usually in the evening, millions of mayfly nymphs molt to the adult stage, their synchronized emergence triggered by some environmental factor and fine-tuned by their internal clocks. This close synchronization of the members of a species maximizes an individual's chance of finding a mate. Nymphs rise from burrows in the muddy bottom and molt to the adult stage as they float on the surface. Within moments, they are ready to leave and fly to shore, but, even so, many are gobbled up by fish. Once perched in shoreside vegetation, they—unlike all other insects—molt again, to a second adult stage. They live for only a day, and get on with the business of reproduction as soon as possible.

At dusk, second-stage adult males congregate above trees or other plants and form large, airborne mating swarms. Each male, wrote George Edmunds, Jr., and his coauthors, bobs up and down, flying rapidly upward for several feet and then drifting down to rise again. Females fly into the swarm and are soon seized by males. As the pair slowly drifts downward, they copulate, a behavior complicated by the fact that mayflies are unusual in that males have two penises and females two vaginas. Within 30 seconds, the two separate while still in the air. The males usually reenter the swarm, which persists until just after dark.

The females immediately fly out over the water to lay their eggs, on average about 4,000 of them per individual. Females of some species, Edmunds and his colleagues wrote,

> plunge to the water, and others fly back and forth ten to twenty feet above the water surface for several minutes before dropping to the water. As the females lie on the water with the wings outspread, the last two abdominal segments are raised sharply upward and the eggs are extruded. More rarely, the females barely

touch the water surface, release some of their eggs, and then rise again to repeat the performance. Usually within thirty minutes after the first females appear over the lake, all those taking part in the mating flight have oviposited. After ovipositing, the females are generally taken by fish; those not eaten have been observed flying for more than an hour after releasing their eggs.

Other aquatic insects also congregate in mating swarms: some caddisflies, and a few or many species of several families of true flies: crane flies, midges, mosquitoes, phantom midges, black flies, horse flies. Swarms form in daylight, at various sites of different types, and vary in size from a few dozen or few hundred individuals up to millions of individuals in swarms so large and dense they may be mistaken for plumes of smoke. (Frederick Knab cited a German entomologist's report that in 1807 the fire department was summoned because a huge swarm of gnats that had formed over the steeple of St. Mary's church in Neubrandenburg had been mistaken for a cloud of smoke.)

On a late afternoon one summer, I came upon a dense, cohesive but wavering swarm of insects hovering at the edge of a country road over a post to which was nailed a sign that warned against trespassing. A sweep of my net through the swarm caught many of the insects, all mosquitoes, apparently of the same species, and to judge by their big, bushy antennae, all were males. I knew about mating swarms of mosquitoes, but then being a beginning entomology student, had never before seen one. My net had dispersed most of the swarm, but the males did not go far, and in less than a minute the swarm was back together again right over the same post. Several more sweeps of the net through the swarm caught only males, and again, after each disturbance, the swarm quickly reformed over the post. Many entomologists, such as John Downes, have demonstrated that such congregations of males are mating swarms.

Mating swarms of mosquitoes or other insects often form along the edge of a stream, pond, or road, and always above some distinctive landmark, or swarm marker, such as a bush, a clump of grass, a rock, or a post. "Swarm markers," wrote Downes, "though of many different forms, are usually objects of a kind that human beings also would regard as useful landmarks; the relatively infrequent objects of large size or notable contrast against the ground . . . or sharp boundaries or conspicuous angles." Males aggregate over a swarm marker, not because they are attracted to each other, but because each one is attracted to the marker and then hovers above it, facing into the breeze and keeping the marker continually in sight. Downes did a simple experiment which showed that midges, and presumably other swarming flies, orient to markers by sight. He found swarms of midges hovering above wet spots or piles of cow dung darker than the sandy road on which they were located. Wondering if the swarms formed in response to odors or moisture rather than visually, he placed three dark cloths on the road: one dry and odorless, one moistened with water, and another smeared with cow dung. Swarms assembled over all three cloths, which leaves little doubt that the midges perceived the marker by sight.

Females are attracted to the marker but do not join swarms to participate in the aerial dance of the males. When Frederick Knab swept his net through a swarm of mosquitoes, he caught almost 900 males but only 4 females. His observations tell us why mating swarms include almost no females:

Repeatedly females were seen to issue from the foliage, dash into the swarm, and emerge united with a male. When in copula the male and female face in opposite directions, their bodies in a horizontal plane; the female dragging the male after her. The pair (or rather the female) would fly upward for a while and then slowly drift towards the ground. Once a pair in copula was seen to issue from one swarm and plunge into another swarm close by. The pair made great haste to extricate itself while the swarm was immediately thrown into frantic excitement and the mosquitoes danced up and down at a furious pace for some time, until at last the ordinary measure of speed was regained. With the growing darkness . . . the swarms rapidly diminished, the males flying off into the air.

How does a male mosquito distinguish a female from the hundreds of males crowded around him? The answer is that he recognizes her by the sound produced by the rapid beating of her wings, a sound somewhat lower pitched than his own flight tone. You have probably heard this sound when kept awake in the dark by the droning of a female mosquito flying around in search of a victim from whom she can take a blood meal. In 1948, Louis Roth published experimental results that show conclusively that male mosquitoes can recognize females by their flight tone. He struck a tuning fork behind a cloth in a cage full of virgin male mosquitoes. If the pitch was right, like that of a flying female, the sex-starved males clustered on the cloth as close as possible to the tuning fork and tried to copulate with the cloth and even with each other.

As do the giant water bugs and virtually all other insects, male mosquitoes take measures to guarantee that it will be their sperm that fertilize their mates' eggs. Nothing as crude for them as the chastity belts that the knights of old put on their ladies before leaving on a trip. The male mosquito drugs the female with a pheromone—a chemical signal that affects behavior or physiology—that he injects into her along with his semen. Experiments done by George Craig, formerly one of William Horsfall's graduate students at the University of Illinois, show that glands associated with the male's genitalia produce the pheromone, and that when these glands are dissected from a male and implanted in the body of a female (a microscopic surgical tour de force not uncommon in entomology), her behavior becomes "matronly," and she rejects the advances of other males. Accordingly, Craig named this newly discovered pheromone matrone. He also showed that injecting matrone-containing extracts of these glands had the same effect as implanting whole glands.

How do mosquitoes, midges, and other hovering insects manage to beat their wings rapidly enough to sustain themselves in hovering flight? The wings of a hummingbird hovering at a flower beat so rapidly, 50 to 70 times per second, that they are only a blur to the human eye. Some insects beat their wings much faster, mosquitoes about 300 times per second and certain very small midges an amazing 1,000 times per second, but butterflies only about 10 times per second and dragonflies only 28 times. For decades there had been two hypotheses to explain how insects manage to beat their wings so astonishingly rapidly, neither testable until a few years ago, because of technological difficulties. One hypothesis held that the wing muscles, which are in the thorax, are fantastically (and implausibly) efficient. The other, shown to be correct by the technological prowess of Michael Dickinson and John Lighton, is that the power of the wing muscles is augmented by power, which would otherwise be lost, stored in elastic elements, "springs," in the thorax. Before the wings make their downstroke, their upstroke is braked as they stretch these springs, thereby transferring some of their kinetic energy to the springs. When the springs recoil, this energy is released and helps to power the down-stroke. Dickinson and Lighton suggest that the protein resilin, which is in the wing hinge, may constitute the springs. Resilin is one of the most efficiently elastic materials known.

In two groups of the stoneflies, as Kenneth Stewart and his coauthors explained, adult males and females communicate with each other by tapping or rubbing the surface on which they sit with the end of the abdomen, a behavior known as drumming. They perceive drumming not as sound waves in the air, but as vibrations conducted by the leaf mats, wood debris, live plant parts, or other substance beneath their feet. As a male roams in search of a female, he often pauses to tap, and females that perceive his signal respond by tapping. These signals carry well for short distances, sometimes up to several yards. Males zero in on the females, and the two mate immediately. Only virgin females answer males, and they probably mate only once, although a male will mate with several females.

The ancestors of these stoneflies did not drum, hypothesized Monchan Maketon and Stewart; instead "incidental tapping of the abdomen in some ancestral . . . species probably enhanced mate-finding, and this success reinforced a continuation and refinement of the behavior." As more and more species of drumming stoneflies evolved, their signals had to become recognizably typical of their own species so as to prevent a fruitless inappropriate response to—or even coupling with—a member of some other species. Consequently, mating calls became ever more complex and males evolved a variety of structures used in drumming on the underside of the end of the abdomen: lobes, knobs, hammers, or liquid-filled sacs described and illustrated by Stewart and Maketon. We see a similar evolutionary pattern in birds. Their songs, used in proclaiming territorial boundaries and attracting mates, are all different. But their alarm calls, which warn of the approach of a hawk or some other predator, tend to be very similar, probably because all species benefit by understanding their meaning.

The drum calls of male stoneflies range from a simple series of taps, probably the ancestral call, to complex patterns of bursts and rubbing. In some species, each burst of tapping is like a drum roll on a snare drum, with taps coming faster and faster as the burst goes on. But the responsive drumming of females is far simpler, usually nothing more than a few taps. Because females will respond only to the drumming calls of males of their own species, a male "knows" that a responding female must be a member of his own species. Consequently, there is no need for her to reply with a complex call that proclaims her specific identity.

Female stoneflies *(Pteronarcella badia)* responded to artificial male calls that Rodney Hassage, Stewart, and David Zeigler generated with a computer. The typical call of a male from a Colorado population—there are slight differences in regional "dialects"—consists of 7 beats, and in different males the call ranges from 5 to 9 beats. Females seldom responded to artificial calls of only 3 or 4 beats but frequently responded to calls consisting of from 5 to 11 beats and having a duration of from 57 to 154 percent of the typical call. Hassage and his coworkers pointed out that a 5-beat call "conveys the minimal information necessary for substantial female response, and longer calls . . . have the minimal calls embedded in them." It seems that more than the usual signal will do as long as it is not too much.

A few days after mating, according to H. B. N. Hynes, female stoneflies extrude a mass of eggs that adhere to the abdomen. "In most species, she then flies down to the water surface where the mass becomes detached." Sometimes it is dropped onto the water, but usually the female dips into the current and then flies up from the surface without her eggs. Wingless species run across the water surface as they drop their eggs. Most species produce several egg masses within a few days.

Stoneflies are not the only insects that communicate by drumming. Termites produce a presumed alarm call by vibrating their heads or abdomens against the ground. Termites are deaf but are very sensitive to vibrations carried in solid substances. Leafcutter ants communicate by means of vibrations transmitted through leaves. Beetles that burrow in the wood of old houses make a sound audible to people by striking their heads against the walls of their burrows, possibly as a signal between the sexes. Superstitious people believe that these sounds, made by "death-watch beetles" portend a death in the house.

While stoneflies send vibrating messages through solid objects, water striders communicate by generating waves on the surface film. When they repeatedly depress the surface film by pumping their legs up and down, a succession of concentric, circular waves radiates outward—just as waves radiate from pebbles dropped into the water. Different messages can be sent by changing the amplitude (size) of the waves, their frequency (delay between them), and the pattern in which waves or bursts of waves are generated. As you have surely guessed, wave messages are used in a sexual context, to court females, to excite or encourage them to lay eggs, and to warn other males away from a defended territory.

Even when blinded by a mask, adult males could distinguish between the sexes, treating individuals that broadcasted signals as males and those that remained silent as females, R. Stimson Wilcox discovered. He made tiny masks by applying liquid black silicone rubber to the head of a dead male and peeling it off after it had hardened. The resulting mask could then be slipped over a live male of the same size.

With a series of more technical experiments, Wilcox demonstrated that males depend upon the presence or absence of a wave signal to discriminate between the sexes. He noted the response of masked males to females that were electronically forced to emit a male signal. Females with a tiny magnet glued to a foreleg were allowed to swim freely within an 11-inch coil of wire in an aquarium. When a computer-generated male signal was transmitted into the coil, the magnet oscillated, forcing the female's leg to move up and down so that, like a marionette, she did a rough imitation of a male's signal. Males copulated with "silent" females, but shortly thereafter rejected the same female when she was forced to emit the signal of a male.

A male water strider, according to Wilcox, guards his mate by staying coupled with her for as long as 24 hours, thereby preventing her from being inseminated by other males, making certain that it will be his sperm that fertilize his mate's eggs.

A coupled female, not greatly encumbered by the small male perched on her back, moves about freely and continues to hunt for food. Although his presence limits her sex life, the female benefits because he wards off the sex-starved males whose harassment, Wilcox found, would otherwise interfere with her hunting and reduce her catch of prey by more than 50 percent. This would be a significant loss for her because it takes many meals to supply the nutrients necessary for developing her eggs and fueling the energy consumed by carrying around her male passenger. As Wilcox pointed out, the male generally succeeds in protecting his parentage, because the female usually lays her eggs shortly after separating from her mate and because she lays them under the water, precluding copulations with other males until after she has laid the eggs fertilized by her current mate.

Dragonflies are harmless, beautiful, and beneficial, but to some they look fearsome with their long, needle-like abdomen, spiny legs, bulging eyes, and wings that rustle when they fly. Bizarre myths have grown around them. They are called devil's darning needles and are said to sting horses and even to sew up the ears of boys. But their real peculiarities, and those of the more petite damselflies, are even more bizarre than the myths. Not only do nymphal dragonflies have a long lip that they use like an arm and a rectum that serves both as a "lung" and a rocket engine, but both adult dragonflies and adult damselflies have a bizarre sexual anatomy and mating behavior that is unique among the animals.

The females' reproductive organs are, as in almost all insects, at or near the tip of the abdomen. But the males' sexual anatomy is very unusual, to say the least. Hundreds of millions of years ago, males of the ancestors of the modern dragonflies and damselflies had a penis and genital claspers located at the end of their abdomen, and, like any other insect, it was with these organs that they coupled with females. But, as Ray Snodgrass has pointed out, in modern dragonflies and damselflies, the penis is rudimentary and useless for copulation, although the genital claspers remain strong and eminently useful for gripping. The functional intromittent organ of a male dragonfly or damselfly is a secondarily evolved penis, complemented by other secondary copulatory organs, on the underside of the base of the abdomen, almost as far removed as possible from the original penis at the tip of the abdomen. (It is as if a man had accessory genitalia on his belly just below the breastbone.) A bizarre arrangement by all insectan standards, but one that serves the male well.

Odonates recognize members of the opposite sex visually—according to Philip Corbet, damselflies mainly by color and pattern and dragonflies by the same cues plus body shape and style of flight. In 1992 Ola Fincke described the behavior of a male giant damselfly defending against other males a territory around a tree hole, to which he sought to attract egg-laying females. "Using a low number of synchronized wing beats/second, a territorial male appears as a pulsating, blue and white beacon, signaling his presence (perhaps both to competing males and potential mates as well as to human observers). Males also make themselves conspicuous by perching . . . and holding their broad wings horizontally, or by flying high into the clearing and then gliding down into it."

She demonstrated experimentally that the differences in wing coloration between males and females facilitate sexual recognition. Males normally court females peacefully, but Fincke found that they tried to fight with them if their wings had been artificially colored to look like those of a male. Conversely, males tried to clasp other males in a sexual embrace if the gender-denoting white patches on their wings had been covered.

Before mating, the male odonate "loads" his secondary copulatory apparatus by looping his long, thin abdomen downward and forward to transfer sperm from his rudimentary primary penis into a receptacle associated with his secondary penis. Only then is he ready to inseminate a female. After a period of courtship, or sometimes without warning, the male grips a flying or perched female just behind her head or by the head itself with the claspers at the end of his abdomen. (The claspers often leave telltale scars, visible with magnification, on the eyes.) Edward Butler, an early observer of these insects, wrote: "With his claspers the lover seizes his betrothed by the neck, and the two then fly about in line, one behind the other, tandem fashion." But Butler, possibly because he was writing in 1886 during the absurdly prudish Victorian era, made no mention at all of what follows, the amazing way in which odonates copulate.

The next step, the prelude to copulation and insemination, is that the tandem pair, either perched or in flight, assumes the "wheel" position. The female, first lifted up by her consort if they are perched, loops her abdomen forward and up to link the genital opening at the tip of her abdomen with the secondary genitalia at the base of his abdomen. Because the male continues to grasp the female's head, the two are then doubly joined, forming an unbroken loop, a circle, or as odonatologists put it, a wheel. After this comes copulation and the insemination of the female. Corbet noted that the formation of the wheel is a sine qua non for copulation, but that the pair are not necessarily copulating all the time that they are in the wheel formation.

The females of most species, wrote Elsie Klots, scatter their eggs as they skim over the surface periodically dipping the abdomen into the water. They may be alone or, in some species, in tandem with a male. Some drop their eggs in midair several feet above the water. Females of some species alight on a plant or some object protruding above the surface and dip the abdomen into the water when laying eggs. Some stick the eggs to leaves of aquatic plants and others use a sharp ovipositor to insert eggs into the tissues of plants above or below the water, even crawling down beneath the surface. The members of one family, wrote Corbet, lay eggs by thrusting the abdomen into sediment beneath the surface as they hover over shallow water in streams; he saw one female make 200 consecutive thrusts. Some lay their eggs in mud or litter just above the water line. Fincke watched giant damselflies first dip the abdomen into the water and then lay their eggs just above the water line on the wall of a tree hole.

In sexually reproducing animals, a female knows that her offspring contain her genes, but a male can never be absolutely certain that he is actually the father of his mate's progeny, that they contain his genes. A dragonfly or any other organism attains evolutionary fitness, its closest approach to "immortality," by leaving behind offspring that carry its genes. Consequently, males of many species have evolved ways of ensuring their paternity.

Female damselflies and dragonflies may lay their eggs while alone, but the female is often closely guarded by a watchful male who wants to prevent her from mating with rival males. He may just hover and fly nearby or actually hold his mate in the tandem position. The male's secondary copulatory organs have freed his genital claspers so that they can be used for this purpose. A male may hold onto a female for as long as the rest of the day, but always releases her as nightfall approaches. By holding her in the tandem position he benefits his mate—and thereby indirectly his offspring—by leading and doing most of the energy-demanding flying and by picking out favorable places in which to lay eggs. Furthermore, if a female goes under the water to lay eggs, the male may maintain his hold on her and help to pull her out of the water. Alternatively, he may just wait nearby, hovering or perched, and attempt to resume guarding when she emerges from the water. Male giant damselflies and males of some dragonfly species defend mating territories from which they exclude males of their species but welcome females.

A male odonate's efforts to ensure his paternity may consist only of guarding his mate, but in some species the male can interfere with the sperm of the female's previous mate. For example, male dragonflies of certain species have large, membranous, inflatable lobes at the tip of the secondary penis. Jonathan Waage, an evolutionary biologist, suggested that these lobes become inflated with blood during copulation and are forcefully pushed into his mate's sperm pouch, packing the sperm of a previous male deep into its rear. He then covers them with his own sperm, which, being on top, will take precedence and be used by the female to fertilize her eggs. Waage discovered that a male damselfly *(Calopteryx maculata)* is even more ruthless. The male uses his secondary penis not only to transfer sperm to the female but also to first remove sperm deposited in the female's spermatheca by previous mates. The secondary penis is anatomically modified for this function with an extensible head, horns, and backward-pointing hairs which entangle sperm so that they can be pulled out of the female's body and discarded with a flick. According to Waage, "no such sperm removal function has previously been attributed to any other animal." But four years after Waage's amazing discovery, Nick Davies, a zoologist at the University of Cambridge in England, observed that, just before mating, male dunnocks, also known as hedge sparrows although they are not true sparrows, stimulate the female to eject the sperm of a previous male by repeatedly pecking her cloaca, which includes both the excretory and genital openings.

Some animals have many offspring, give them no care, and "hope" that a few "lucky" ones will survive. Others, like giant water bugs, have relatively few offspring but improve their odds for survival by caring for them. Codfish spew out about 6 million eggs and abandon them. Robins have a clutch of only five eggs but care for the young until they can make it on their own. These are, of course, the extreme ends of a spectrum of various degrees of parental care. Among the aquatic insects, the giant water bugs are the most caring parents. The male protects the eggs until they are ready to hatch, but after that the newly hatched nymphs must fend for themselves. Other aquatic insects give their offspring much less care, at best depositing their eggs in places that give them some protection from egg-eating predators and the physical environment.

Dragonflies and damselflies that hide their eggs by thrusting them down into the bottom sediment or, more commonly, by inserting them into the tissues of an aquatic plant lay far fewer eggs than do those that simply release their eggs into the water, where they are easy prey for any passing fish or other predator. Corbet summarized the available data on the number of eggs in each clutch laid by dragonflies and damselflies. On average, those that insert their eggs into a plant produce clutches of about 500 eggs, but those that do not hide their eggs in this way produce clutches of more than 1,500 eggs and some of as many as 3,500 or even 5,000.

I was doing research at the University of Michigan Biological Station, a few miles south of the Straits of Mackinac, when Ola Fincke did an exhaustive field study of the reproductive behavior and lifetime egg production of damselflies (*Enallagma hageni*) that laid their eggs in a small, shallow pool less than 100 yards in circumference. (It was hard work. In the morning, Ola, with waders and an insect net, walked past my cabin to her pool. It wasn't until late afternoon that she trudged past wearily on her way back to her cabin.) She observed that females, usually flying in tandem with a male, separated from their escort and crawled down beneath the surface onto an aquatic plant, usually a stonewort (*Chara*) and inserted their eggs into its stem. Meanwhile, the male waited on the surface, and when the female came up he tried to reengage her, but often failed. The many females that Fincke observed laid during their lifetime an average of slightly less than two clutches that, on average, contained 361 eggs each.

All aquatic bugs and some aquatic beetles are amphibious in the adult stage, and, like giant water bugs, mate and lay their eggs in the water. Most bugs attach their eggs to some surface in, above, or very close to the water. Some backswimmers cement their eggs to the surface of aquatic plants, but others insert them into the plants with a sharp ovipositor. Like their marine cousins, water striders in ponds and streams often glue their eggs to some floating object. Most water boatmen attach their stalked eggs to an aquatic plant, but one species has the unusual habit of preferably, but not necessarily, gluing its eggs to the body of a crayfish. There are, according to Melvin Griffith, at least three ways in which this could benefit the water boatman *(Rhamphocorixa acuminata)* in question. The crayfish's habit of migrating overland from one body of water to another could save the eggs from dying in a pond that is drying up; the pugnacious crayfish may in protecting itself chase away predators that might eat the eggs; and the current caused by its gills probably aerates the eggs.

As do the bugs, many aquatic beetles attach their eggs to the outer surface of aquatic plants, and some, such as certain predaceous diving beetles, insert them into the tissues of plants. Unlike most other beetles with aquatic larvae, the leaf beetles of the genus *Donacia* usually stay out of the water, although females of some species go beneath the water surface briefly to lay eggs on plants. Females of other species sit high and dry on the upper surface of a floating lily pad, chew holes through it, and then insert the long ovipositor through the hole into the water and attach their eggs, arranged in concentric rings, to the underside of the pad. Water scavenger beetles enclose 50 to 100 eggs in an air-filled silken boat that floats just below the surface and is completely sealed except for the tip of a long "snorkel" that pokes up into the air and provides the eggs with oxygen.

Dobsonflies, spongillaflies, and some other aquatic insects glue their eggs to a plant or some other object that hangs over the water. Dobsonflies lay several thousand eggs arranged in long, straight, parallel, and contiguous rows. The newly hatched larvae drop down into the water. Spongillaflies lay only a few eggs in each of many masses and cover them with a layer of silk. The larvae fall to the water, and Elsie Klots said that they "often have trouble breaking through the surface film and, when finally they do, seem quite ill at ease, swimming jerkily and apparently aimlessly until . . . they come in contact with a sponge."

As we have seen, aquatic insects—like almost all other insects—produce far more offspring than are required to replace them and their mate. No wonder. Their offspring, as did they, must run a gauntlet of physical and biological hazards. They are subject to the vagaries of the weather. And, as we will see next, they may be infected by bacteria, fungi, and other disease-carrying organisms, and are likely to be eaten by a host of predators ranging from other insects to mammals such as bats.

On Being Eaten

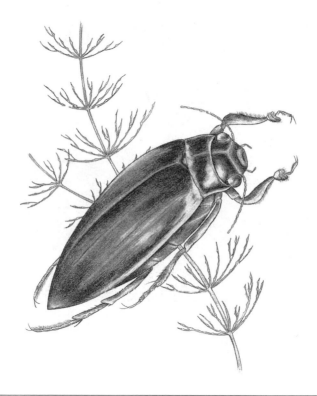

*This predaceous diving beetle injects digestive
fluids into its prey and then sucks out
its liquefied tissues*

If 2 of a giant water bug's 350 eggs survive to become reproducing adults, they will have replaced their parents and the water bug population will remain stable from year to year. But if 4—only 2 more—survive to adulthood, the population will double with each generation, and after only 10 generations (a relatively brief span of 10 years or less) it will have multiplied by an ecologically disastrous 1,000 times, throwing the bug's ecosystem into turmoil. (House flies have 10 generations in a *single year*.) In 1798, Thomas Malthus recognized that all plants and animals, including humans, are programmed to bear more offspring than are likely to survive, a form of insurance that improves the odds that, despite the many physical and biological hazards their progeny will face, at least a few will live. Malthus's book was to influence Charles Darwin, guiding him to the insight that the few survivors are likely to be those that are best suited to their environment—which is, of course, natural selection.

Population explosions seldom happen, because physical and biological threats take a heavy toll on the progeny of all organisms, plants and animals. Physical factors such as storms and droughts can be devastating to aquatic insects. A rushing flood may wash stream-dwelling insects downstream, perhaps to a hostile environment where they are not likely to survive. During a drought, aquatic insects may die because their stream or pond goes dry. Even if a stream or pond does not dry up completely, it will shrink in size and thereby limit the growth of populations. Floods and droughts are often sporadic, but biological factors—notably creatures that eat or parasitize aquatic insects—tend to be less sporadic inhibitors of population growth.

Aquatic insects, both in their adult and immature stages, are fodder for many predators—ranging from spiders to bats. In their classical *Biology of Mayflies*, James Needham and his co-authors graphically describe the havoc that a variety of predators inflict on mayflies during the brief span of their winged, adult life:

> The perils of this brief period are manifold. Robins and other birds search the shore—a reception committee for them at their arrival upon land! We have seen robins at the waterside with bulging crops and half a dozen mayfly tails hanging out of the angles of their beaks. Other birds search the foliage for them; others harvest them when they swarm. Spiders lay snares that capture them by the thousands . . . Dragonflies of many kinds hover about the swarm, capturing them at will, as hawks follow coveys of pigeons and quail. Bullfrogs sit by the waterside, alert to catch them whenever they fly past, and the return of the females to the water for egg-laying marks the renewal of attack by carnivorous fishes. Trout, bass, pickerel, and many other fishes snap them up at the surface, or even spring into the air to seize them while in flight.

Parasites and predators, the main biological threats to almost all insects, have a unique role in population control, because, unlike physical factors, they can and usually do respond on a "sliding scale" to changes in the abundance of their prey. (Insects that parasitize other insects are often called parasitoids, because, although they live as nonlethal parasites at first, they generally kill their hosts in the end.) As their food, the prey, becomes more abundant, parasites and predators progressively become more numerous and destroy an ever increasing proportion of the prey population. Parasite and predator populations inevitably decrease as they destroy more and more of their prey and a meal becomes harder to find. Largely released from predation pressure, the decimated prey population then proceeds to increase and bounces back. In turn, parasite and predator populations, favored by this growing supply of prey, increase until they catch up with the prey population. In this way, the population pendulum swings back and forth, but usually rather moderately, thereby maintaining the ecological balance, which is really a dynamic equilibrium of alternating increases and decreases of predator and prey populations.

A great many different viruses, bacteria, fungi, protozoa, and roundworms (nematodes) parasitize aquatic insects in one or more of their life stages. Some roundworms are free-living, some infest plants; one that may be as much as 16 inches long lives in the intestines of humans and pigs; and many are parasites of insects. In Louisiana, for example, O. R. Willis found anywhere from one to seven or more roundworms as much as 2 inches long coiled up within the bodies of damselfly nymphs that were only about three quarters of an inch long. Up to 81 percent of the nymphs in some populations were parasitized. The mature roundworms escape from the nymph's body by breaking out through the skin in the vicinity of the anus. The nymphs die within a few hours.

Some parasitic worms have complex life cycles in which they

survive only if they pass through the body of more than one host animal. For example, an adult parasitic worm in a water bird such as a heron, its definitive host, lays eggs that are released into the water with the bird's droppings. If an egg is lucky enough to be swallowed by a copepod (a tiny relative of crabs and shrimps), the first intermediate host, it hatches, enters the copepod's blood-filled body cavity, and molts. If the copepod is then eaten by the second intermediate host, a dragonfly nymph, the worm penetrates the nymph's gut to enter the body cavity and molts once again. If the dragonfly nymph is eaten by a fish, the third intermediate host, the worm migrates to its body cavity and forms a dormant cyst covered with a protective layer. If the fish is then eaten by a water bird, the definitive host, the cyst is activated and the worm's life cycle is finally completed as it lays eggs in the bird's intestines.

Many entomologists have said that insects are their own worst enemies. In 1909, H. A. Gossard argued, quite rightly, that "the greatest and most fertile lands in the world would shortly become lifeless deserts—except for the check put upon insect multiplication through warfare within the insect household, by which one species of insect destroys [other species]." Gossard had land-dwelling insects in mind, particularly those that damage crops, and their parasites and predators. But there is no doubt that what he said is equally true of aquatic ecosystems.

Although there are many predaceous insects in the water, there are only a few insects that parasitize the aquatic stages of insects, although, according to R. R. Askew's book on parasitic insects, about 112,000 known insects parasitize land-dwelling insects. About 100,000 of them are wasps, about 10,000 are flies of the family Tachinidae, and the rest are scattered among other groups of insects. Most of the parasitic aquatic insects are the wasps that we met earlier, but there are not many of them. For example, fewer than 100 of the thousands of North American parasitic wasps are aquatic. These few pioneers may some day, in evolutionary time, be followed by others that will also evolve means to survive in the aquatic realm and thereby take advantage of the many as yet unexploited opportunities it offers to parasites.

Only a few insects other than wasps parasitize insects that live in the water. Included among them, according to Harold Oldroyd's *Natural History of Flies*, is the very aberrant larva of a midge. Almost none of the larval midges are parasites, but this species *(Symbiocladius)* sucks the blood of its host, a mayfly nymph, as it lies hidden in a silken sac that it spins under the developing wings of the nymph. The maggot stage of a tachinid fly, J. T. Lloyd found, is a parasite within the body of an aquatic caterpillar. The caterpillar has gills and, enclosed in a silken web attached to a rock, lives in the water of fast-flowing streams. When the caterpillar is about to pupate, it replaces its web with "an impenetrable, oval-shaped, roof-like silk covering, . . . which has a number of semicircular openings at the ends facing up and down stream." The upper part of the cocoon is filled by a bubble of air that accumulates from the fast-flowing, well-aerated water that continually passes through the cocoon. The host pupa, which has no gills, gets its oxygen from the bubble. When both host and parasite are still in the larval stage, the maggot pokes a Y-shaped breathing tube out through the caterpillar's skin and up into the bubble. After the maggot kills its host and itself pupates, it remains within the bubble until it emerges as an adult.

The terrestrial stages of aquatic insects, whether eggs, pupae, or adults, are more likely to be attacked by parasites than are the aquatic stages. The larvae of spongillaflies, as we have seen, leave the water and pupate within a silken cocoon enclosed in a loose, meshlike net attached to a branch, the hull of a boat, or some other object. They are parasitized by the larvae of a small, black wasp. Harley Brown wrote of them:

> During their normal activities, [the adults] seldom take flight; instead, they hurry about . . . investigating every object encountered . . . Neither a migrating larva nor an exposed pupa nor an adult of the host species appears to arouse any interest on the part of a wasp, but a cocoon of the host excites immediate enthusiasm, at least in the female. Upon discovering a [spongillafly] cocoon, or the net covering such a cocoon, the female wasp explores the entire surface of the net and as much of the inner cocoon [as] she can reach with her vibrating antennae.
>
> If the host is satisfactory . . . the female wasp inserts her ovipositor in the wriggling host . . . and proceeds to pump venom into it for a minute or longer. After it has become quiescent, she withdraws her ovipositor, then shifts position slightly before reinserting the ovipositor through net and cocoon to deposit an egg upon the host.

The larval parasite clings to the body of the host and sucks up the contents of its body until nothing remains. It pupates within the spongillafly's cocoon, and after about 6 days, the adult wasp emerges through a neatly cut hole that it chews through the cocoon and the net.

Some aquatic insects, among them spongillaflies and alder-flies, lay their eggs in masses on leaves or other objects over-hanging the water. As soon as they hatch, the larvae drop into the water. Spongillafly eggs, Harley Brown reported, are at-tacked by egg-sucking mites. According to George Salt, a very tiny parasitic wasp parasitizes the eggs of an alderfly that lays its eggs in masses of hundreds on the leaves of a semiaquatic grass. The female parasite lays one egg per host egg, and each of her offspring spends its entire larval and pupal life in that egg until it becomes an adult and gnaws its way out of the egg shell.

Nymphal water striders, Bruce Smith found, were signifi-cantly injured by parasitic mites. They were more likely to die and grew more slowly than did uninfested individuals. About half of the adult damselflies of one of the species from a pond in Poland were infested with "blood-sucking" water mites that clung to the underside of the thorax, usually between the mid-dle and hind pair of legs. Klaus Reinhardt found that infested damselflies flew shorter distances than uninfested ones, not be-cause of the weight of the parasite or because they were distrib-uted so as to throw the host off balance, but rather because they damaged the flight muscles.

Years ago, when I temporarily "wore the hat" of medical en-tomologist and examined hundreds of adult mosquitoes under a microscope, I noticed that many of them were parasitized by mites. Some of these mites were clinging to the side of the tho-rax under the wing. Almost always, if there were mites on one side of the thorax, there was an equal number on the opposite side. I supposed that the mites had a way of distributing them-selves on a mosquito so as not to throw their host off balance and thereby interfere with its ability to fly. After all, the mites have everything to gain. A handicap will probably decrease a mosquito's chance to survive, and the mites will, of course, die with the mosquito.

A few years later, my conjecture was confirmed by systematic observations Asher Treat recorded in *The Mites of Moths and Butterflies*. For one thing, he remarked that "most mites that travel in numbers on insects distribute themselves quite symmetrically upon their hosts. In some such instances, where the mites become attached and only a small odd number are present, the odd mite will occupy a median position." In other words, the odd mite will be on the center line so as not to weight one side of the host more than the other.

Treat also discovered that some of the mites that infest the ears of moths—land-dwelling species—are *not* symmetrically arranged. They generally infest only one of the moth's two ears so as not to totally deafen the insect. Why this should be so becomes apparent once we realize that moths take evasive action to escape from bats when they hear the ultrasound that bats, flying in the dark, emit so as to sense obstacles and prey by the echoes that bounce back from them. Treat wrote:

The mites normally invade and occupy only one of their host's two ears, leaving the other ear intact and fully functional as a detector of ultrasound. The adaptive value of this behavior is obvious, for if an infested moth is caught by a hungry bat, not only does the moth perish, but the mites as well. A one-eared moth may have its acoustic defenses somewhat impaired, but it is still a safer mite vehicle than a moth that is deafened altogether. The chosen ear may be either the left one or the right, but regardless of which it is, and regardless of how crowded it may become, the other ear is almost invariably left wholly un-disturbed.

There is an exception that proves the rule. Ear mites of a species that does not cause deafness usually occupy both of a moth's ears.

As you saw earlier in some detail, many aquatic insects are predators that feed on other water-dwelling insects; among them are the ferocious nymphal and adult water bugs, larval and adult diving and whirligig beetles, dragonfly and damselfly nymphs, some stonefly nymphs, and even a few mayfly nymphs and mosquito larvae. The aerial stages of aquatic insects are preyed upon by strictly terrestrial predators such as birds, bats, praying mantises, robber flies, and predaceous wasps. They may blunder into a spider's web or be snatched by a crab spider waiting in ambush on a blossom. They are also pursued by "mosquito hawks," the flying adults of the aquatic dragonfly and damselfly nymphs.

Many aquatic insects eat other aquatic insects. But do these parasitic and predaceous insects put an ecologically signifi-cant limit on prey populations? This question was answered by the masterly experiments of Barbara Peckarsky and Stanley Dodson in streams in southern Wisconsin. They placed in the stream stainless steel cages made of a mesh with openings small enough to exclude large predaceous stonefly nymphs but large enough to permit the entry of smaller colonizing insects. Some cages contained no predaceous stonefly nymphs; in others they placed unconfined nymphs free to roam; and in yet others they put nymphs enclosed in smaller cages so they could not move about or capture prey. The presence of predaceous stonefly nymphs significantly reduced the number of colonizing prey insects that became established in a cage. This was so even if the predators were confined in small cages, apparently because potential colonizers were somehow alerted to their presence, probably by some chemical cue. Amazingly, potential colonizers were able to distinguish between predaceous and nonpredaceous stonefly nymphs. Nonpredaceous, detritus-feeding nymphs, either free or caged, did not affect the number of colonizing insects that established themselves in a cage.

An extensive study done by Ola Fincke and her coworkers on Barro Colorado Island in Panama showed that damselfly and dragonfly nymphs have a significant depressing effect on the populations of several species of mosquito larvae in tree holes. (In the adult stage, some of these blood-sucking tree hole mosquitoes disseminate the viruses that cause such diseases as dengue, yellow fever, and encephalitis.) Fincke, in fact, thought that these odonate predators are keystone species in the community of organisms that inhabit tree holes. Keystone species are those that have, in one way or another—predation in this case—a significant effect on the structure—species composition—of their ecosystem.

One fine summer day, Harold Hayes and I approached the Esopus Creek, a famous trout stream in the Catskill Mountains of New York. We stopped when we noticed an osprey hovering over the water. Suddenly, it plunged in feet first and came up with a large trout caught in its talons. This "fish hawk" was the ultimate link, the top predator, in a complex food chain. The beautiful, shining trout grew to its impressive size by eating mainly aquatic insects as well as small fish that themselves eat insects. Some of the insects in the stream ate other insects, but many fed, at least in part, on plant matter, on living aquatic plants including algae or on the decaying fallen leaves and other detritus of land-dwelling plants. Green plants are the foundation of this and practically all other ecosystems. As we saw, only they can capture the energy of the sun and, via photosynthesis, produce the essential calorie-rich sugars and starches that are passed up the food chain as animals eat plants and each other.

Trout and other fish are the most important vertebrate predators of insects in most freshwater ecosystems. Worldwide there are about 30,000 known species of fish and, according to Carl Bond, about 12,000 of them live in fresh water, although a few, such as salmon, eels, and shad, spend a part of their lives in the sea. Insects are at least a part of the diet of most of them, including, among others, species well known to anglers: trout, bluegills, crappies, largemouth and smallmouth bass, bullheads, channel catfish. When they are still small, the majority of large carnivorous freshwater fish feed on insects—even the fish-eating pike and the mighty muskellunge, which, when it has grown large, eats not only fish but even ducklings and young muskrats.

Fish have the five senses familiar to us: taste, smell, touch, hearing, and vision, plus a sixth sense that we will revisit later. Different species of fish use different sensory modalities in seeking prey. Pike and muskellunge, for example, rely largely on vision. Fish that can be taken with artificial lures respond visually to a disturbance in the water or to some combination of these stimuli. Many fish rely largely on their chemical senses, as do catfish such as bullheads, eels, carp, and the burbot of European rivers.

Some fish are very sensitive to chemicals in the water that passes over the small odor receptors in the two nasal organs in their heads. The sense of smell is used not only in locating prey but also in navigation. After spending a year or more in the ocean, salmon return to spawn in the stream where they hatched from the egg. Orienting to the distinctive odor of their natal stream, they swim upstream in rivers that empty into the sea, ascending many branching tributaries as they follow the odor trail until they arrive at their spawning site, usually a shallow pool in the upper headwaters of a small stream many miles from the sea.

Taste receptors, useful only at close range, are the final arbiters of whether or not a fish will actually swallow something. A trout, for example, may mistakenly snatch a floating twig from the surface but will reject it "on the advice" of taste receptors in its mouth. The taste receptors of a fish, unlike ours, are not necessarily confined to the mouth. In a wide variety of fish taste buds are scattered over the body including the fins. Over 100,000, according to Karl Lagler and his coauthors, are on the skin of a bullhead, with the greatest concentration usually in the region of the mouth, on top of the head, and especially on the barbels (whiskers).

Fish also have sensory receptors that are stimulated by the pressure of moving water impacting their body. In most fish these "touch" receptors are arranged in a long, thin line, the lateral line, that extends along the flank from the tail to the head, where it may split into several branches. Norman Marshall, a British icthyologist, described the lateral line:

> The skin of fishes and certain amphibians houses lateral line sense organs, which respond to disturbances in the water and to changes in flow patterns near the swimming animal. This "distance-touch sense" . . . is a special attribute of the lower aquatic vertebrates. When the vertebrates became masters of the land, these sense organs must have been lost. Nothing like them is found in the reptiles and mammals that have returned to the water, not even in whales and dolphins, which rely largely on their sense of hearing.

The lateral-line sensillae enable fish to sense nearby obstacles, predators, or—more to the point of this chapter—moving insects or other animals that may become a welcome meal. "The lateral sense," Carl Bond wrote, "is of great importance in food detection in most fishes that feed on active prey. Even species that are strongly sight-oriented can continue to locate moving prey when forced to rely on the lateral line in experimental situations."

The sixth sense that fish possess is not mysterious, but perceives a natural aspect of the fish's environment just as do its other five senses. Many fish can detect weak electrical fields—not only the famous Amazonian eels that themselves emit high-voltage electrical discharges to stun their prey, but also many other fish that do not have this ability. Among them are the familiar bottom-feeding bullheads, which you may have fished for in a pond with a cane pole. The bullheads and all other catfish, according to Thomas Finger, have an "electroreceptive capability." Tiny, pitlike sense organs, the electroreceptors, are spread all over the surface of the fish, most numerous on the tail and the top of the head, but absent from the barbels.

All animals, including insects and all the other prey of fish, generate low-frequency electrical fields by the activity of their muscles. For example, R. C. Peters and F. Bretschneider found that electrical fields are emitted by midge larvae and mayfly and dragonfly nymphs that live in the mud in which bullheads search for their prey. Behavioral experiments summarized by A. J. Kalmijn show that bullheads use their electrical sense to locate other animals. In an experiment, bullheads located the position of live goldfish shielded by a layer of agar gel, which allowed electrical stimuli to pass but blocked all visual and chemical stimuli. But when a thin film of electrical insulation covered the agar, bullheads were no longer able to find the goldfish. Experimental results published several decades earlier had already shown that, in an aquarium, catfish oriented to a weak electrical field between two copper electrodes. The fish often nibbled at the empty region between the electrodes.

Fish are, with the possible exception of predaceous insects, probably the most effective of the predators that keep populations of insects within ecologically tolerable bounds in ponds, lakes, and streams.

One of the most unusual of them, the amazing little archerfish of the estuaries and lower reaches of rivers of the Indo-Pacific region, can knock down and capture insects sitting on overhanging foliage or flying over the water. Many of them are, of course, likely to be the aerial forms of aquatic species. In *The World Encyclopedia of Fishes,* Alwynne Wheeler described how the archerfish, or sharpshooter, knocks insects into the water.

"It can spit drops of water with great accuracy at 1 m (3¼ ft) distance, and after a few ranging shots can hit a small target at 3 m (10 ft)."

"Exclusion experiments"—like Peckarsky and Dodson's with stonefly nymphs—have revealed the importance of insectivorous fish in establishing and maintaining the the species composition and organization of aquatic communities of plants and animals. For example, Peter Morin's exclusion experiments in a North Carolina farm pond showed that bluegills and largemouth bass control the magnitude and species composition of the dragonfly population. In screen enclosures that kept out fish but not insects, the total population of dragonfly nymphs increased by a factor of 10, and the small species that were normally dominant were replaced by larger species, probably because when fish were present they weeded out the larger dragonfly species, usually eating them rather than the smaller ones.

In a California river, Mary Power used enclosures of screening through which insects and fish fry could pass but large fish, mainly California roach and steelhead trout, could not. By excluding large fish from some enclosures and including them in others, she showed that these insect-eating fish have an important ripple effect on the natural ecosystem, but only in stretches of the river that have a bottom of mainly boulders and bedrock rather than gravel. In these stretches, the large fish suppress the population of damselfly nymphs and other small predators, including roach and steelhead fry, thereby releasing the predation pressure on midge larvae that live in and feed on the "turf" of algae that covers the boulders and bedrock. Consequently, midge populations grow large and dramatically decrease the "standing crop" of algae.

Power found that this was the case in enclosures with fish. Small predators were scarce because they were eaten by the fish. Consequently, midge larvae were abundant and diminished and matted down the algal turf, maintaining it at its usual level, less than an inch thick. But in enclosures without large fish, the ecosystem was unnaturally altered. Predaceous insects were more than usually numerous and greatly decreased the midge population. Consequently, the algae flourished, were erect rather than prostrate, and were heavily covered with a growth of bacteria and other microorganisms.

How great an impact a fish can have on an ecosystem was demonstrated on a grand scale by a biological control, in this case the introduction of a small fish, the inland silverside, to alleviate an insect problem at Clear Lake, a 40,000-acre body of fresh water in central California. Mary Flint and Robert van den Bosch wrote, "Visitors to Clear Lake and residents of the area, [a] popular holiday resort, were bothered by the presence of occasionally dense populations of a nonbiting gnat." Although commonly known as the Clear Lake gnat, this insect is actually one of the phantom midges that we met in an earlier chapter. The nearly transparent larvae stay in the bottom sediments during the day, but at night come out into open water to feed on water "fleas" *(Daphnia)* and other tiny crustaceans barely visible to the naked eye.

According to Sherburne Cook, other lakes nearby have similarly dense populations of these gnats. But in Midwestern lakes phantom midges never become annoyingly numerous. Cook attributed the difference to the absence in the California lakes of fish that feed away from shore in the open water, where the larvae of the Clear Lake gnat feed. Fish with this feeding behavior do live in Midwestern lakes, but no fish in Clear Lake "utilized any developmental stage of the gnat as a primary food source." With this in mind, the silverside, a fish of Midwestern and southern lakes, was stocked in Clear Lake in 1967. It ultimately became the most abundant fish in the lake and reduced the population of the gnats to little more than 5 percent of its original size. But Norman Anderson and his coworkers found that the silverside did not actually eat enough gnat larvae to account for all of this decrease. Since both the gnat larvae and the silversides feed extensively on tiny planktonic crustaceans, the fish probably reduce the population of gnats both by eating them and by competing with them for food.

From 1949 to 1958, before the introduction of the silverside, the Clear Lake gnat was controlled by the application of DDD, an insecticide closely related to DDT, at the maximum rate of just 1 part of DDD in 50 million parts of water. This concentration killed the gnat larvae, but was far too low to directly harm fish, birds, or other vertebrates. Nevertheless, many bass died and dead western grebes were found along the shore. Originally about 1,000 pairs of these fish-eating birds built floating nests among the reeds at the lake's margin, but by 1958 only about 30 pairs survived. They nested, but their hatchlings died. The grebes were found to be free of disease and their deaths remained a mystery until someone finally thought to examine their bodies for DDD.

The results were absolutely astonishing. The grebes' body fat contained well over 2,000 parts per million of DDD, over 100,000 times its concentration in the lake water. How could this be? The answer is that DDD, almost nonbiodegradable and very persistent, was concentrated in the food chain that supports the grebes, a process that is most accurately described as bioaccumulation or bioconcentration but is usually and less logically called biomagnification. The floating, single-celled, green algae, which are the foundation of the food chain, absorbed the insecticide from the water and concentrated it to about 10 parts per million. Algae-eating fish accumulated about 900 parts per million of DDD in their body fat, and bass and other carnivorous fish about 2,700 parts per million. The grebes, which eat both algae-eating and carnivorous fish, accumulated about 2,130 parts per million, more than enough to cause death. DDD was last applied to Clear Lake in 1958, but the poison lingered in the lake for years, not in the water, but held in the bodies of the plants and animals in the lake. Three years after the last application of DDD, the grebe population was down to only 16 pairs, and none of their young survived. Since the introduction of the silverside, the grebe population has continually increased.

Although adult frogs and toads are insect-eating predators, in the aquatic larval, or tadpole, stage most are vegetarians that feed mainly on algae—in North America, all species except for the spadefoot toads. Tadpoles of the dart poison frogs of the New World tropics are predators that, as Ola Fincke observed, live in water-filled tree holes and prey on mosquito larvae and other aquatic insects.

Most frogs and toads, including all of the American and Canadian species, must return to the water to mate and lay eggs, but the marvelous, brightly colored, little dart poison frogs are, as explained in *Grzimek's Animal Life Encyclopedia*, among the few that have freed themselves from the water in this respect. The male inseminates and guards a small clump of eggs laid on the ground by his mate. The newly hatched tadpoles climb onto their father's back and cling there until he brings them to a water-filled tree hole, where they must then fend for themselves by preying on aquatic insects.

A skin secretion of these adult frogs is very poisonous, and their bright colors warn away animals that might try to eat them. Long before the conquistadores came to Central and South America to steal gold from the Indians, some Indians used these frogs to poison the tips of their blowgun darts and arrows. They hold frogs impaled on a stick over a fire and catch the poison that drips from their skin glands in a small vessel. After the poison has fermented, they dip their blowgun darts in it and let them dry. A monkey or bird hit by a poisoned dart is paralyzed almost immediately.

The salamanders, the amphibians other than frogs and toads, are all basically predators and most include insects in their diet. Most salamanders are terrestrial as adults, and in the larval stage are aquatic and feed, at least to some extent, on aquatic insects. A few, mudpuppies, hellbenders, and the eel-like sirens, are aquatic throughout their lives and some of them feed heavily on insects. According to James Oliver, aquatic insects constitute 17 percent of a mudpuppy's diet and 34 percent of a siren's.

Almost all reptiles are predaceous, but only a few are aquatic. In fresh water, the omnivorous turtles known as sliders and cooters feed on aquatic plants, fish, and insects. Alligators of all ages eat spiders and insects—large individuals sparingly—but young ones, only 8 inches long when hatched, subsist almost exclusively on aquatic insects.

A strange little insect-eating bird lives along fast-flowing, rocky streams in the mountains of western North America. I saw my first one while I sat on the bank of a small stream in Rocky Mountain National Park in Colorado. Slaty gray, plump, short-tailed, and about 2 inches shorter than a robin, it came flying in and perched on a rounded, spray-drenched stone in the middle of the stream. It bobbed up and down and occasionally its eyes flashed a startling white as it wiped them with bright white "eyelids" (actually the nictitating membranes). After a while it dropped from the stone and disappeared under the water but soon reappeared on another nearby stone. Arthur Cleveland Bent, an eminent early-twentieth-century ornithologist, pointed out that this bird, the dipper, known as the water ouzel in Europe, uses its stubby, rounded wings to literally "fly" under water and its clawed feet, which are not webbed for swimming, to clamber over submerged rocks as it searches for prey. According to Steven Ormerod, it is looking for caddisfly larvae and other aquatic insects, the major part of its diet except for the occasional snail and small fish.

Wading birds with long, sharp beaks, such as ibises, snowy and great egrets, green and little blue herons, and yellow- and black-crowned night herons, stalk the margins of ponds, marshes, and slow-moving streams hunting for their aquatic prey, including but not limited to dragonfly and damselfly nymphs, bugs, beetles, and other aquatic insects. In marshes, king, Virginia, and sora rails wade in the shallows, and purple gallinules walk on floating lily pads as they hunt for aquatic creatures, including a variety of insects. Graceful black terns swoop down from the air to snatch aquatic insects such as adult mayflies from the surface of a pond. Ruddy ducks, buffleheads, goldeneyes, scaup, and other diving ducks plumb the depths of ponds and lakes to catch insects and other aquatic creatures. Dabbling ducks such as mallards, shovelers, and green- and blue-winged teal, also known as puddle ducks, tip hind end up in shallow water to scoop up their food, including aquatic insects and other prey from the water and the bottom sediments.

Bent wrote that the upper and lower mandibles of the shoveler, like those of all surface-feeding ducks, are serrated to form rows of comblike "teeth" that strain out water and mud but retain food that no doubt includes insects. He notes that it is in the huge, shovel-shaped bill of this duck that these teeth "reach their highest development," because, more than any other ducks, shovelers dabble not only on the bottom but also along the surface to obtain their food. Bent quotes the British ornithologist John Guille Millais, who said of the shoveler, which occurs both in the New and the Old Worlds:

I have watched with pleasure the wonderful sight, calculation, and quickness of a male shoveler . . . on a small marshy pond . . . About the last week in April a certain water insect . . . would "rise" from the mud below to the surface of the pool only to be captured by the shoveler, who, rushing at full speed along the water, snapped up the beetle the moment it came to the surface. How it could see the insect in the act of rising I could never make out, for it was invisible to me standing on the bank above . . . After each capture the duck retired to the side of the pool again and there awaited the next rise—commonly about 25 feet away. While thus occupied he seemed to be in a high state of tension: the feathers are closely drawn up and he kept his neck working backwards and forwards, in preparation, as it were, for the next spring, exactly like a cat "getting up steam" for the final rush on a victim.

On the memorable evening in 1960 when Bill Downes and I were plagued by that immense swarm of salt marsh mosquitoes as we camped on a Gulf Coast beach in Texas, the mosquitoes were being gobbled up by hordes of aerial predators—probably every kind of flying insectivore in the area. The predaceous insects were represented by dragonflies, the mammals by bats, and the birds by cliff swallows, purple martins, chimney swifts, and nighthawks. The dragonflies and the diurnal birds continued their feast in the glow of our camp fire for a while after they would normally have stopped because of the failing light. Long after they had left, we could still see the shape of hunting bats in the light of our fire.

Bats are voracious feeders, because flying is energetically expensive and requires a large intake of calories. Not surprisingly, the daily food intake of some bats is equivalent to half of their own body weight. Whether they are gleaners that pluck prey from leaves or other surfaces or aerial hunters that fly in pursuit of prey, insect-eating bats are generally opportunists that will take whatever insects are available, including adult aquatic insects. The big brown bat of the eastern United States includes mayflies, caddisflies, and stoneflies in its bag of prey, reported Wilfried Schober. According to Philip Corbet, flying dragonflies are seldom taken by bats that are aerial hunters, but are "a regular though small component of the food of foliage-gleaning insectivorous bats." Ola Fincke found that the tropical giant damselflies are, even when roosting at night, susceptible to predation by insect-gleaning bats, as indicated by their severed wings lying under the roosts of these bats.

Many know that some land-dwelling plants that live on nutrient-poor soils—among them sundews, the famous Venus flytrap, and pitcher plants—trap insects, digest them, and assimilate their mineral nutrients. But not many people know that there are aquatic insect-eating plants. In nutrient-poor ponds and lakes of Europe, Asia, Africa, and Australia grows the waterwheel *(Aldrovanda vesiculosa)*. According to Kenneth Cameron and his colleagues, this aquatic plant is a close cousin of the terrestrial Venus flytrap, which grows only on a small area of the sandy coastal plain of North and South Carolina. The Venus flytrap is a small rosette of long, winged, green stalks that bear the trap leaves, which consist of two opposing lobes with long, stiff spines at their margins. If an unwary insect touches one of the long, thin trigger hairs on a leaf, the two lobes snap shut and their spines intermesh. The trapped insect is then digested. The waterwheel's leaves are basically similar and work on the same principle. The rootless plant is submerged and bears its green trap leaves arranged in whorls of seven or eight that are closely spaced along the length of a long, thin stem. A leaf's two lobes snap shut when some of its 20 trigger hairs are touched by a small aquatic insect or some other animal. Although the lobes of a waterwheel's leaf must push through water to close the trap, Thomas Givnish reported that they snap together in an amazingly fast 0.2 second. They manage this despite the fact that water is 800 times as dense as air and is not compressible, as is air.

The aquatic plants known as bladderworts have received little popular attention, although they occur virtually all over the world, including North America, and their suction trap is the most sophisticated of the plant traps—even more amazing than the snap traps of the Venus flytrap and the waterwheel. But most bladderworts are very small and likely to be noticed only when they grow long stalks that poke high above the water and bear small white, purple, or yellow blossoms. The bladders are the traps. Those of many species are too small to trap insects, some only a hundredth of an inch long, and capable of catching only microorganisms such as protozoa. But the bladders of some species are large enough to catch small insects.

The traps vary in the details of their structure, but all work in essentially the same way. The greater bladderwort, one of the larger species, illustrates the basic principle. The bladder's wide mouth, usually closed by a valve, is surrounded by long, thin, branched hairs that shield the shorter trigger hairs that extend out from the flap of the valve. When the trap is set, the walls of the bladder are concave and compressed, greatly decreasing its inner volume. The long, branched hairs form a loose funnel that may lead unwary prey, perhaps a young mosquito larva, to the trigger hairs. If the larva brushes against a trigger hair, the compressed walls of the bladder suddenly spring outward, greatly increasing the bladder's volume and thereby producing a vacuum that sucks water and prey into the bladder through the now open valve in as little as 27 milliseconds, 27 thousandths of a second. The valve then snaps shut, the bladder secretes digestive enzymes, and the trap is reset after the prey has been digested and absorbed.

As is to be expected, natural selection has equipped many insects, including aquatic species, with various ways—not always successful—of protecting themselves from the many species of animals that prey on or parasitize them. As we will see next, these ways are various and some are amazingly ingenious.

How Not to Be Eaten

*A caddisfly larva protrudes from the portable case it
made of tiny sticks to protect it from predators*

One of my professors at the University of Massachusetts, Charles Alexander, told his students that an entomologist—even if he does laboratory research—should have a taxonomic hobby: he should collect, learn to identify, and study the lives of a family or some other not-too-large group of insects. Some years later I heeded his advice, but only after I had been fooled by a "bumble bee" that, on closer inspection, turned out to be the *Mallota* we met earlier—a harmless hover fly, a member of the family Syrphidae. Mimics such as *Mallota* are likely not to be attacked by insect-eating birds because of their resemblance to stinging or otherwise noxious insects, the models, whose conspicuous colors, yellow and black in bumble bees, warn the birds. Mimicry is not uncommon. In the Philippines edible cockroaches—none of them household pests—are generally passed up by birds and other insect eaters, because they mimic noxious and colorful ladybird and leaf beetles. The orange and black toxic monarch butterfly of North America is mimicked by the more palatable viceroy.

The hover flies became my taxonomic hobby—a hobby that evolved into serious research on the fascinating topic of mimicry, of fundamental interest in both the fields of evolutionary biology and animal behavior. Early on, field work that I did with Joe Sheldon showed that mimetic syrphids, including *Mallota*, are present as flying adults in the spring when their wasp and bee models are very scarce, but in the summer, when their models are most numerous, they are in the larval stage safely hidden away in water-filled tree holes.

Our finding is contrary to what had then been the "conventional wisdom" of mimicry researchers: that mimics should be active only when their models are the most numerous and they, the mimics, can get lost in the crowd. On the face of it, this seems to make sense. Consequently, I wondered if *Mallota* and the other mimics might somehow benefit by not coinciding with the peak abundance of their models. Being active early in the season would, of course, give them access to the nectar of spring flowers. But there must be more to it than that. Plenty of plants blossom in the summer.

The most likely alternative explanation is that by emerging as adults in the spring they somehow elude predators. But their major predators, birds—even migrants from the south— are present both in the spring and the summer. My graduate students and I ultimately showed that by emerging early *Mallota* and its mimetic cousins avoid the dangerous period in the summer when young insectivorous birds that have not yet learned to avoid bees and wasps leave the nest and begin to feed themselves.

In controlled experiements with captive birds, David Evans and I found that young birds that we raised in the laboratory and that had never so much as seen a bumble bee greedily ate *Mallota*—but not after they had been stung by a bumble bee. But do migrants remember this lesson when they return in spring? They do. Adult migrants that we trapped in the early spring, when they were not likely to encounter bumble bees, did not even try to eat the bumble bee–mimicking *Mallota*s we offered them. *Mallota*'s seasonal timing is clearly important to its survival.

🪰 Natural selection, as is to be expected, has favored aquatic insects or any other animals that manage to avoid encountering predators or to protect themselves against them in one way or another. The most reliable defensive tactic, but by no means the most common of them, is not to be where the predators are— not to coincide with them in space or, like *Mallota*, in time. Among the other aquatic insects that make their escape in the fourth dimension, time, are some phantom midge larvae that, Carl von Ende found, forage in the open water only at night and during the day bury themselves in the bottom sediments to avoid predators, particularly fish, that hunt in the open water during the day and spot their prey visually. The winter stone-flies leave the water as adults only when most insectivorous birds have gone south and ectothermic, land-dwelling predators such as spiders, insects, frogs, and toads are hibernating.

Some aquatic insects that do coincide in time with predators minimize the risk of being eaten by not coinciding with them in space. Andrew Sih discovered that small juvenile backswimmers in small pools in California are preyed upon mainly by the cannibalistic adults of their own species, which spend most of their time hunting in the open water near the center of the pool. Juveniles avoid the cannibals by lurking at the edge of the pool, where they are relatively safe. After Sih removed all adults from a pool, small juveniles were much more likely to be seen at or near the center of the pool.

Pools that dry up from time to time are relatively safe havens for some aquatic insects, because fish and other vertebrate predators are likely to be absent. Insects that live in such temporary pools generally have special anatomical, physiological, and behavioral characteristics that adapt them to life in these changeable habitats. For example, if their pool dries up, some dragonfly nymphs can survive for months by burrowing into the moist bottom sediments and becoming dormant. Others, as we have already seen, leave the drying pool in the adult stage to fly off in search of temporary pools that still hold water. Insects in temporary pools need not be as vigilant as their relatives that coexist with fish. Damselfly nymphs in temporary pools escape by swimming away if approached by a predatory dragonfly nymph, but their close relatives in permanent ponds stay put and "hope" not to be seen by the nymph, presumably so as not to expose themselves to fish, which are even more dangerous predators than dragonfly nymphs.

Just by being one of a group, an individual decreases the probability that it will be taken by a predator. A lone individual that encounters a hungry predator is sure to be eaten, but if it is 1 of a group of 10, there is only 1 chance in 10 that it will be eaten—if we assume that only one individual satiates the predator. Many animals, herds of sheep, schools of fish, swarms of locusts, tend to cluster together for safety. The synchronous emergence of huge swarms of mayflies facilitates mating but also decreases an individual's risk of being eaten, because predators are soon satiated, long before they make a significant dent in the swarm.

Even small swarms of only a few hundred mayflies can satiate a local population of predators, as Bernard Sweeney and Robin Vannote found. In a small river in South Carolina, fully grown nymphs of *Dolania* swim to the surface just before sunrise and molt to the adult stage as they float downstream. Males patrol the river searching for mates. Females, usually mated within seconds of rising from the surface, immediately lay their eggs and die within a half hour. Males may live for as long as an hour. Sweeney and Vannote caught the floating nymphal skins and dead bodies of adults, virtually all of which fall to the water surface, in a net stretched across the river downstream of the swarming site. The difference between the number of dead adults and the number of molted nymphal skins is an estimate of how many adult mayflies have not been accounted for, presumably because they had been eaten by aerial predators such as bats, swallows, and dragonflies. On mornings when swarms were small, 30 or fewer, from 80 to 90 percent of the adult *Dolania* of both sexes, were missing, but when swarms included from 100 to 250 of them, only from 20 to 30 percent of the females were missing, but up to 50 percent of the males, which are more exposed to aerial predators because they spend so much time in the air as they search for a mate.

In a classic article, William Hamilton theorized that gregariousness can evolve even if it has no selective advantage other than "diluting" the threat from predators. He argued that, even in nongregarious species, natural selection is likely to favor individuals who stay close to others even when no predator is in sight. He made his point with a beguiling fantasy:

Imagine a circular lily pond. Imagine that the pond shelters a colony of frogs and a water-snake. The snake preys on the frogs but only does so at a certain time of day—up to this time it sleeps on the bottom of the pond. Shortly before the snake is due to wake up all the frogs climb out onto the rim of the pond. This is because the snake prefers to catch frogs in the water. If it can't find any, however, it rears its head out of the water and surveys the disconsolate line sitting on the rim—it is supposed that fear of terrestrial predators prevents the frogs from going back from the rim—the snake surveys this line and snatches *the nearest one.*

It is obviously not a good thing to be the nearest frog when the snake approaches. But how can an individual not be the nearest frog when the snake appears? The closest he can come is to be one of a shoulder-to-shoulder cluster of frogs, all of which are about equally close to the snake and are constantly pushing and shoving as they try to get into the middle of the cluster, the safest position. Clearly, a behavioral mutation for snuggling would be beneficial. It would pass the muster of natural selection and foster the formation of groups.

It has not been easy, wrote W. A. Foster and J. E. Treherne, to obtain evidence that the "dilution effect" can in and of itself reduce the risk of predation, because "it is likely to be masked by other advantages of group living, such as improved efficiency of feeding and reproduction or, more importantly, improved detection and confusion of the predator." But Foster and Treherne avoided these complications by the judicious choice of subjects for their observations, single individuals or "flotillas" of up to a hundred or more juvenile marine water striders in the shallows near the shoreline of one of the Galápagos Islands in the Pacific. Their subjects were not feeding and were, of course, too young to be concerned with reproduction. Furthermore, unlike Hamilton's frogs, they were not forewarned of an attack by one of their major predators, a small fish that, unseen, swiftly darted up from below the surface. Their data support Hamilton's theory. A lone water strider was about 100 times more likely to be eaten by one of these fish than was a member of a flotilla of 100 or more individuals.

In a similar study of these insects, Treherne and Foster observed that, although the water striders gave no overt response to the unseen predators, they did respond very energetically to predators that they saw before they were actually attacked, surface-feeding fish and yellow warblers (the same species that nests in North America) that swooped down from mangroves growing in the shallows. With early warning, the members of *large* groups remained aggregated but "initiated behavior changes which are likely to confuse predators by transforming a group of slow-moving, oriented individuals into a collection of rapid and randomly moving ones." But, under similar circumstances, *small* groups of water striders suddenly fled when a predator came close—a confusing "last-minute explosive dispersal."

Just as the deer runs from the cougar or as shiners leap from the water to escape a school of bluefish, many, but not all, insects flee to escape from diving beetles, fish, or other predators. In an earlier chapter we saw a dragonfly nymph use rocket propulsion to dash away from a fish that came too close. Several studies, as Barbara Peckarsky noted, have shown that some stream-dwelling insects escape from predators by "letting go of their hold" and drifting away with the current. Gary Scrimgeour and Joseph Culp showed that in artificial laboratory streams mayfly nymphs reacted to predaceous fish or stonefly nymphs by drifting away—although if food was unusually abundant the nymphs were reluctant to leave and the predators had to come closer to provoke them to escape. If threatened, some insects flee by retreating to a safe haven. Larval midges in ponds pull back into their burrows. Stream-dwelling cadisfly larvae stop monitoring their trap nets and retreat to their shelters. But not all animals flee when they sense an approaching predator. As you come near, a cottontail rabbit "freezes," not moving a muscle but relying on its camouflage to keep it safe. But if you come too close, it abruptly dashes off with its white tail flashing. And so it is with most insects. In daylight, underwing moths cling motionless to a tree trunk with their superbly camouflaged front wings covering the hind wings. But if you poke the moth with a forceps to simulate the peck of a bird, it suddenly flies off, revealing colorful hind wings. When it lands on the trunk of another tree, the hind wings are immediately covered by the front wings, and the moth seemingly disappears, confusing the pursuing bird, which has a "search image" for something brightly colored.

Remaining motionless until a predator comes dangerously close is a simple behavior that serves camouflaged animals well. But some species have more complex behavioral attributes that protect them from predators. The hunting methods of some dragonfly nymphs have been molded by natural selection to adapt them to habitats with insect-eating fish and others to habitats where there are no fish. According to Dan Johnson and Philip Crowley, dragonfly species that live in waters with few or no fish can afford to make themselves conspicuous by moving about as they search for their prey. They tend to be well fed and grow rapidly. By contrast, other dragonfly species that live in habitats where fish are numerous and a significant threat are loath to make themselves conspicuous, and simply sit and wait for suitable prey to get close enough to ambush. In keeping with this less productive method of hunting, they grow slowly and, unlike the others, can tolerate long periods without food.

With some remarkable exceptions that we will come to later, all small animals, including insects, are camouflaged. A few resemble inedible objects of no interest to a predator, as do caterpillars that resemble bird droppings or treehoppers that resemble thorns, but most insects are colored and patterned so as to blend in with their background and thereby escape notice, as does the undisturbed underwing moth. I know of no aquatic insect that resembles an inedible object, but most are camouflaged so as to blend in with the background.

The classic example of camouflage is the nocturnal peppered moth of England, which, during the light of day, rests motionless on a tree trunk. Before the Industrial Revolution these moths were light in color and inconspicuous on the light colored bark of trees. But beginning in the early nineteenth century, coal-burning factories belched smoke that stained the tree trunks black, and the light-colored moths, now conspicuous, became easy prey for birds. A black mutant peppered moth was first noticed near Manchester in 1878. Better camouflaged and less likely to be noticed by birds, the black form increased rapidly and 50 years later had almost supplanted the light form. The same thing happened to this and other insects in woodlands near factory towns all over northern Europe and North America. This story has a sequel that illustrates the constant operation of natural selection. As Britain cleans up air pollution, the trunks of once soot-stained trees are reverting to their original light color, and the few light moths that persisted in smoke-polluted areas, now better camouflaged, are less likely to be eaten by birds and are supplanting the black moths.

Camouflage is, in essence, a way of trying to be invisible. Whereas most insects blend in with the background, the light sand of a beach, the dark bark of a tree, or the green of a leaf, some phantom midge larvae are virtually transparent and almost truly invisible. The only phantom midge that lives in certain Swedish pools occupied by fish is almost completely transparent. When Jan Stenson removed the fish from these pools, not only did this species become more abundant, but it was joined by another, less transparent, yellowish-brown species that Stenson thought would not survive in the presence of fish, because it is darker and more visible. He tested his idea by presenting fish in tanks with both species of phantom midge. The fish almost always ate the darker ones and virtually ignored the more transparent ones. But the darker species was also more conspicuous because of its activity. Did the fish attack the darker midges because of their color or their more conspicuous movements? Stenson found the answer by giving the fish a choice between naturally dark larvae and transparent larvae stained to resemble them. The fish attacked both species equally, although the naturally dark larvae were more active.

The English entomologist E. J. Popham noted that individuals of the same species of water boatman vary in color, but that in eight different ponds both nymphs and adults roughly matched the colors, different shades of brown, of the bottom. He calculated that "the chance of the pigmentation of the insects coinciding with the colour of the ponds, in the eight cases

. . . is 1 in 6561, a chance which is too large to be coincidence." There are two different explanations for this. The insects could select ponds that match their own color, or they could orient to colors randomly, and only those that happen to match their background are likely to survive. Popham's observations and experiments indicate that water boatmen actually oriented to backgrounds that matched their own color: "It is a matter of common experience that . . . in an aquarium the colour of which differs greatly from their own, the insects become very restless and attempt to fly away. This does not occur if there is no contrast in colour." He observed that in an aquarium with the bottom evenly divided into three different colors, most water boatmen settled down on the area of the bottom that most closely matched their own color.

The camouflage of these water boatmen, Popham showed, gives them considerable protection from insect-eating fish. He placed a lone water boatman in several different aquariums, each with a bottom of a different color. Of 200 that contrasted with the background in their aquarium, 151 were eaten by fish, but of 200 that matched it, only 49 were eaten. He also found that the threat to these insects varies with the fidelity of their camouflage. "In varying populations the most obvious insects are first eliminated and then those which are less so, and, finally, those which are best adapted to the background."

Neither an adult water boatman nor a nymph can change its color quickly at any time as can a chameleon or many fish, but the water boatman's color can change when it molts. "The colour acquired by a nymph or young adult," wrote Popham, "depends directly upon the environment in which it has lived during the process of moulting. A light-coloured background inhibits the formation of [dark] pigment, but a dark background allows pigment formation to proceed." Of 66 nymphs transferred to aquariums with background colors that did not match their own and confined there for more than 3 days, 45 closely matched their new background after molting to the adult stage and only 21 did not.

Almost 50 years after Popham's discoveries, Blair Feltmate and Dudley Williams of the University of Toronto did a similar but more detailed and meticulous study of a stonefly. Streams in southern Ontario have beds composed of stones that range in color from light to dark, and, according to casual observations, the dark-colored species of stonefly nymph that was the subject of their research tended to be found on dark stones. A careful survey of several sections of a stream confirmed the casual observation. The majority of stoneflies were on dark stones, almost none on light stones, and only a few on stones of intermediate color. Experiments done in aquariums or in a natural stream showed that swimming stoneflies were most likely to settle on dark objects. They clearly made the selection on the basis of color; if their eyes were covered with Liquid Paper correction fluid, they did not discriminate between dark and light objects. In experiments in aquariums containing two artificial stones, cubes constructed of dark-colored or light-colored tiles, Feltmate and Williams found that stonefly nymphs preferred to settle on dark cubes and that this tended to protect them against rainbow trout. After 24 hours, 19 of the lone trout in each of 24 aquariums with two light-colored cubes had found and eaten the one nymph in their aquarium, but in 24 aquariums with two dark-colored cubes, only 3 trout had found and eaten the nymph.

Certain mosquito larvae, the medical entomologists Mark Benedict and Jack Seawright showed, can, like water boatmen or stoneflies, change color during a molt in response to the color of the containers in which they develop. Larvae of one of the malaria mosquitoes, *Anopheles,* are white if reared in a light-colored container and very dark if reared in a black container. When reared in a black rather than a white container, larvae of a species of *Culex* also became darker but less so than did *Anopheles* larvae. Benedict and Seawright observed that these larvae respond similarly in nature, and postulated that the ability to match the color of their background is "a form of camouflage that should enhance their chances of not being discovered by a predator." Under the same circumstances, larvae of the yellow fever mosquito do not change color at all. But why don't these larvae have the ability to match their background? The answer is probably that camouflage would be of little or no help to them. Whereas *Culex* and the malaria mosquito larvae live in well-lighted pools, larvae of the yellow fever mosquito live in tree holes or artificial containers, where the light is dim at best and predators probably do not hunt by sight.

Effective camouflage involves more than just resembling the background in color and pattern. As you have probably noticed, almost all animals are dark on the dorsal (upper) surface and light on the ventral (lower) surface. This pattern, known as counter shading, is so nearly universal that Roger Tory Peterson, in *A Field Guide to the Western Birds,* wrote that the male bobolink in breeding plumage is unique, "our only songbird that is *solid black below and largely white on back,* like a dress suit reversed." Counter shading tends to obscure the three-dimensional form of the body. When light, which usually comes from above, falls on an object such as a ball, it lights the upper side but leaves the lower side more or less shaded. On a uniformly colored ball, this contrast between the light and shaded areas reveals its three-dimensional form, making it stand out from its background. If an animal were uniformly colored, not counter shaded, this contrast would counteract the camouflaging effect of color and pattern, thereby attracting the attention of predators. The lighter color on the underside of a counter-shaded animal obscures this contrast. Aquatic insects, generally speaking, are counter shaded. Those that swim in the open water or skate on the surface are benefited by counter shading not only as is a ground-dwelling insect but also by being obscured when seen from below against the bright sky or from above against the dark bottom.

Caterpillars that habitually hang upside down from a twig or a leaf are, according to Hugh Cott, reverse counter shaded, light on the back and dark on the belly. And so it is with other insects whose usual posture is upside down. Among the aquatic species, the backswimmer immediately comes to mind. It and the water boatmen are roughly similar in appearance and the way in which they swim, but the water boatmen, which are normally not upside down, are dark colored on their backs and light on their bellies. But the backswimmers, which, as their name tells us, lie on their backs as they swim, are reverse counter shaded, light on the back and dark on the belly.

In *Defence in Animals,* Malcolm Edmunds wrote, "some animals carry parts of their environment around with them and so become cryptic [camouflaged]." Bedecking themselves with camouflaging substances is not by any means unknown in freshwater insects, but is most spectacularly developed in crabs, seagoing relatives of the insects. Robert Shelford described a crab in Borneo that lives near the shore and holds a large leaf over its back, making it hard to spot among the waterlogged leaves that wash to and fro in the current. In 1889, William Bateson wrote:

> As is well known, certain crabs . . . have the habit of fastening pieces of weed, &, on their backs and appendages until they are almost indistinguishable from the surrounding weeds . . . The crab takes a piece of weed in his two chelae [pincers], and . . . deliberately tears it across as a man tears paper with his hands. He then puts one end of it into his mouth, and, after chewing it up, presumably to soften it, takes it out in the chelae and rubs it firmly on his head or legs until it is caught by the peculiar curved hairs which cover them.

Bateson went on to say that the crabs camouflage themselves with various kinds of plants and even small animals such as sponges and hydroids, the latter being relatives of the jellyfish that can sting like nettles. He also found that if a crab's camouflage was removed, then it would "*immediately* begin to cloth itself with the same care and precision as before."

A stonefly nymph that lives on the silty bottom of brooks in Chile and Argentina disguises itself much as do the crabs described by Bateson, by bedecking itself with particles of silt. Joachin Illies wrote of this stonefly: "The entire upper side of the nymph, except for the eyes and the last segment of the abdomen, is covered with a thick mantle of silt particles that adhere to hairs and are difficult to remove. Beneath its mantle the body of the nymph is soft-skinned and very pale. It is no wonder that these insects, which live on the bottom of still pools, camouflage themselves with silt. A new covering of silt is acquired after each molt. They move sluggishly and in their natural habitat are hard to find—easily mistaken for a lump of silt" (translated from the German). An Australian stonefly nymph, wrote H. B. N. Hynes and Mary Hynes, is covered on its upper side with long soft hairs that entangle "flocculent silt." "We also observed that through the spring and early summer . . . many were covered with green algae which, together with the silt in their hairs, made excellent camouflage."

A caddisfly larva's case hides its body, making it difficult for a predator to recognize it as a living thing that might make a meal. The case may itself be hard to find because it is camouflaged. Caddisfly cases blend in with their surroundings, because they are usually made of abundant materials such as sand or vegetation that are a major element of their habitat. Anker Nielsen observed that caddisfly cases made of short lengths of dead twigs blend in almost imperceptibly with the broken bits in the habitat. Larvae in cases made of leaves, Christian Otto and Björn Svensson found, were more often eaten by trout when they were on a contrasting sandy bottom than when they were on a bottom littered with dead leaves. In addition, however, caddisfly larvae, like those we will meet next, are physically protected from predators by the cases they construct.

Anita and Frank Johansson of the University of Ulmeå in Sweden noted that two species of caddisflies construct two distinctly different kinds of cases that give them physical protection in different ways. One species uses small pieces of leaf to make a thin, smooth-walled, cylindrical case. The other builds a shorter, wider case that bristles with lengths of stem and other plant debris arranged tangentially, crosswise rather than lengthwise, giving it, as the Johanssons put it, a hedgehog-like appearance. The Johanssons found that the hedgehog case is much stronger than the tube case; it takes well over three times as much force to crush it. Dragonfly nymphs attacked these two kinds of cases differently. They almost always removed the tube larvae through a hole they tore in the weak wall of the case, but the walls of hedgehog cases were apparently too strong for the dragonfly nymphs to penetrate. They managed to capture hedgehog larvae only when the head and thorax protruded from the opening at the front of the case.

The Johanssons used a mechanical device, the "caddis case crusher," to measure the force required to breach a caddisfly case. Designed by Dr. S. Thelandersson of the School of Civil Engineering of the University of Lund in Sweden, it is essentially a combination of a guillotine and a nutcracker with one movable arm and another attached to the surface of a table. A case is put on the "block" beneath the free end of the hinged moveable arm, which can be pulled down by a weight suspended from it on a string. The weight is a small bucket that is gradually filled with water until it is heavy enough to pull down the movable arm and crush the case. The weight of water required to crush the caddis case is a measure of its strength.

Many insects are armed with weapons, especially chemical weapons, that usually discourage attacking predators. Among land-dwelling insects, the bombardier beetle sprays a threatening predator in the face with irritating chemicals at the temperature of boiling water. Monarch butterflies are laced with toxins they sequestered from their food plants when they were caterpillars. Female wasps and bees have sharp stingers that inject potent venoms. These defenses are effective. Thomas Eisner showed that toads sprayed in the face by a bombardier beetle are obviously distressed, gaping wide and rubbing their tongue against the ground. After eating a monarch, inexperienced blue jays, Lincoln Brower found, vomit, may retch at just the sight of a monarch, and thereafter refuse to eat monarchs or a butterfly, the viceroy, that mimics them.

Noxious insects are generally colorful and conspicuous rather than camouflaged. Bombardier beetles are yellow and blue, monarchs orange and black, and bumble bees yellow and black. Today we know for a fact that conspicuousness is often, but not always, a warning to predators, but in Charles Darwin's time, the evidence that proves this point had yet to be uncovered. Darwin thought that some animals, such as butterflies, are "beautiful," colorful, to attract mates, but did not understand why some are colorful and conspicuous when they are in the caterpillar stage and not yet sexually mature. Darwin wrote, "I then applied to Mr. [Alfred Russel] Wallace, who has an innate genius for solving difficulties." Wallace's response was:

Distastefulness alone would be insufficient to protect a larva unless there were some outward sign to indicate to its would-be destroyer that his contemplated prey would prove a disgusting morsel, and so deter him from attack. A very slight wound [is] sufficient to kill a growing caterpillar, and if seized by a bird, even though afterwards rejected as nauseous, its death would nevertheless ensue; the distasteful larvae therefore required some distinctive mark, something by which they may be contrasted with and separated from the agreeable larvae, in order that they might be freed from the attacks of birds. Brilliant coloration.

The bombardier beetle's weapon is fired from a distance and the beetle usually escapes. But the monarch's toxin has no effect unless it is eaten, and a bumble bee is likely to be seriously injured even if it is not swallowed when it stings. What purpose, then, is served by a toxin or venom that is effective only after the death of the animal that it is supposed to protect?

Predators, sickened but rarely killed by these toxins or venoms, learn to recognize and not attack these noxious insects. Therefore, a victim's death is likely to protect other members of its own species, possibly relatives genetically similar to itself, which are likely to live nearby and in the "educated" predator's territory. In most animals, half of an individual's genes will survive in its offspring or siblings, one quarter in a niece or nephew, and one eighth in a first cousin. Consequently, although it dies, a victim may enhance its inclusive fitness by promoting the survival of its own genes in a relative. This seeming paradox is understandable if we view an organism as the genes' way of surviving by making copies of themselves—something like the not altogether improbable argument that a chicken is an egg's way of making another egg. In other words, an individual's fitness is ultimately the survival of its genes.

Some aquatic insects, particularly beetles and, to a much lesser extent, true bugs, are repugnant to predators because of noxious chemicals secreted by glands that open onto the surface of the body. According to Steve Scrimshaw and W. Charles Kerfoot and to Konrad Dettner, some, if not all, whirligig and riffle beetles and predaceous diving beetles and creeping water beetles are rejected as food by various species of fish because of their potent chemical defenses. Ernest Benfield found that bluegill sunfish and rainbow trout seldom swallowed adult whirligig beetles, although they would take them into their mouths and then spit them out, apparently without harming them. They often did not attack them at all if they had had a previous experience with a whirligig. Benfield established that whirligigs are made unpalatable by their external secretions: Bluegills eagerly ate freshly killed house flies but rejected those that he had smeared with the defensive secretion of a whirligig. Similarly, salamanders ate pieces of beef liver, but not if they had been coated with the whirligig secretion. According to Thomas Eisner, the foremost expert on the defensive chemicals of insects, a secretion of the predaceous diving beetles is toxic to frogs and fish. Frogs swallow them but then regurgitate the still living beetles.

A noted evolutionary biologist, G. Evelyn Hutchinson, once remarked on the "dinginess," lack of colors contrasting with the background, of the great majority of the insects and other invertebrates of fresh water. This is certainly true of many aquatic insects. Nymphal or larval mayflies, stoneflies, dragonflies, dobsonflies, and caddisflies are certainly "dingy," although they are delicious morsels for fish. Their only protection seems to be the camouflage that makes them dingy, thus inconspicuous.

But what of the many beetles that have potent chemical defenses? Are they dingy creatures who do not advertise their toxicity to predators as do so many land-dwelling insects? A few are quite colorful, and many others also advertise their toxicity, although not so obviously to the human eye. There is no doubt that predaceous diving beetles and whirligig beetles have potent chemical defenses, but I have found little mention of warning coloration or warning behavior on their part. Yet many of these beetles are indeed warningly colored.

Adult predaceous diving beetles often swim in open water where they are in clear view and exposed to insect-eating fish. Of the many species I looked at in the collection of the Illinois Natural History Survey, one of the largest and best insect collections on the continent, many of these diving beetles were not counter shaded. They were black or almost black both above and below. Black is a warning color, conspicuous against many aquatic and terrestrial backgrounds, and, seen from below by a fish, the beetle must be flagrantly conspicuous, starkly silhouetted against the bright sunlight from above. A few diving beetles are rather gaudily colored. Many of the common large species have contrasting yellow margins on the dark thorax and wing covers and may have yellow legs. A smaller species, about a half inch long, is brown with yellow markings and has a fringe of bright, golden hairs on its long, oarlike hind legs. Another small species is black above and marked with red spots, suggesting the warning colors of a noxious ladybird beetle.

To my mind, there is no doubt that whirligig beetles give predators unmistakable warnings of their noxiousness. When a group of adult whirligigs swimming on the surface of a pond—their usual occupation—is disturbed by a predator or a person who comes too close, they may escape by diving down into the water or, at least in my experience, more often stay on the surface, form a tight group, and call attention to themselves by whirling and spinning around each other in a frenzied tarantella. Most whirligigs are black above, and according to Ross Arnett and Michael Thomas, on the underside most are entirely red, brown, or black with various contrasting markings in some species. In 1866, the Reverend Hamlet Clark described an Australian species that is bright green above with narrow, bright coppery red streaks on the wing covers, metallic black on the underside, and with reddish hind legs. Whirligigs are surely warningly colored, both when seen from above and from below.

In 1922, C. S. Elton wrote that some aquatic mites, eight-legged relatives of the insects, are unpalatable to fish and scarlet red in color. Sixty years later, W. Charles Kerfoot noted that in New England ponds not inhabited by fish the various species of mites are of subdued and inconspicuous colors. But in ponds or small lakes with perch, shiners, and other fish, there are many other species of water mites that are bright scarlet, clearly a warning color. According to Elton, a three-spined stickleback that had been starved for 4 days enthusiastically ate dingily colored prey put into its tank, but when offered a brilliant scarlet mite, "went up to it and took the mite into its mouth, but immediately spat it out. It went up to the mite repeatedly after this without eating it, and followed it round for some time, clearly torn between its ravenous hunger and the unpleasantness of the mite." Other aquatic biologists have reported that fish will "mouth" and then spit out noxious prey unharmed. In this way, a toxic mite or insect could educate a predator to shun members of its species without itself being injured or killed.

Adult riffle beetles, small insects that do not swim but crawl slowly on the bottom eating microorganisms and debris scraped from rocks, would seem to be easy pickings for predators, but, as H. P. Brown pointed out, they are rarely eaten. He noted that many are conspicuous. "Some . . . are jet-black and shiny, with contrasting silvery-white areas . . . Others . . . are black with colorful spots or streaks of yellow, orange, or red on their [wing covers]." These colors, wrote David White, are reminiscent of warning coloring in terrestrial insects. In the laboratories of the University of Michigan Biological Station on Douglas Lake near Pellston, Michigan, White offered adult and larval riffle beetles to perch, pumpkinseeds, and other fish from the lake. The fish almost always rejected them. They took them in their mouths but within seconds spit them out. "All prey appeared to be unharmed and were moving after being expelled, but none of the fish attacked the prey a second time." A turtle also rejected these beetles, wiping at its mouth with its forelegs until the beetle was expelled and continuing the wiping action for some time. Larval riffle beetles are not warningly colored, but they live out of sight buried in gravel, beneath rocks or logs, or in crevices.

In order to survive, aquatic insects must not only avoid being eaten or parasitized by some other creature but also cope with an often hazardous and always unforgiving physical environment. They may be threatened by droughts, racing floods, the cold of winter. As we will see next, aquatic insects have evolved some truly remarkable ways of coping with these difficulties.

Coping with the Climate

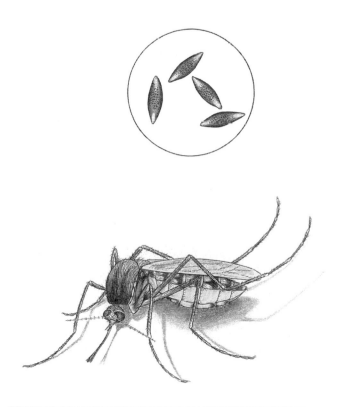

The eggs of this floodwater mosquito, a common pest but not a transmitter of disease, hibernate in the soil during the winter

Many years ago, I heard a sermon that was really a simple lesson in physics meant to underscore the perfection of the creation. Water, the Methodist minister pointed out, is an exception to the general rule that the density (weight per volume) of liquids is greatest at their freezing point. Although water freezes solid at 32°F, it is densest at 39°F. Consequently, the warmer but denser water sinks while water at the freezing point floats to the surface and turns into ice. If water were densest at its freezing point, water at 32°F would sink to the bottom, and streams, ponds, and lakes would freeze from the bottom up and eventually become solid blocks of ice. Life in the water, and probably on land, could not exist in the temperate zones and the Arctic.

As the minister implied, most aquatic habitats are fundamentally hospitable to life. But they are not totally benign and, in fact, do have physical aspects that may hinder the growth and development of insects or even threaten their survival. The heat of summer and the cold of winter can be inimical to land-dwelling as well as aquatic insects. High midsummer temperatures may cause a drought that dries up aquatic habitats; it may be too hot for an insect to keep its body temperature at a safe level by dissipating the heat generated by muscular activity; the laying of eggs may have to be delayed if it is too hot for the young that will hatch from them to survive. In winter, food will not be available or, at best, very scarce. Winter temperatures are usually too low to permit muscular activity by most insects and may even kill them. After all, insects are ectothermic and cannot internally regulate their body temperature as do the endothermic birds and mammals.

Generally speaking, the activities of life, wrote C. Ladd Prosser in *Comparative Animal Physiology,* occur only at temperatures between the freezing point of water, 32°F, and 104°F. Most animals live within much narrower limits, but a few aquatic insects survive and grow at temperatures well above 104°F. Dragonfly nymphs that live in shallow pools heated by the sun survive at temperatures approaching 113°F. A midge larva lives and survives to breed in the water of a hot spring at 124°F, and a brine fly larva is at home in thermal pools with a water temperature of 130°F. Fresh water at or below 32°F is not liquid, which excludes the aquatic stages of insects except for a very few that survive in a state of dormancy embedded in solid ice, such as larval pitcher plant mosquitoes. But a few aquatic insects can, in the adult stage, live and be active at *air* temperatures well below 32°F. For example, a tiny midge, Bernd Heinrich wrote in *The Thermal Warriors,* "walks on glacier ice even when its body temperature is chilled to −16°C [3.2°F]. It is so sensitive to heat that, when taken from its natural environment and held in one's hand, it is killed by the warmth of one's skin."

Some exceptional insects can grow and develop in water that is close to the freezing point. Among them are the fierce mosquitoes of the Arctic tundra. In *People of the Deer,* Farley Mowat described their immense swarms and how they plague and madden people and caribou. One of these mosquitoes *(Aedes communis),* reported William Horsfall, completes the larval stage in only 2 weeks at a very cool water temperature of 49°F. Even at 36°F, only 4 degrees above freezing, it feeds and grows, although at that temperature it takes 4 months spread over more than 1 warm season, the brief Arctic summer, for it to complete the larval stage. Andrew Spielman and Michael D'Antonio said of this mosquito, "The eggs survive subzero winter quite nicely. When the ice thaws and the water rises, they hatch almost instantaneously." They are in a big hurry. The Arctic summer is very short. To judge from Victor Shelford's account of the ecology of the tundra on the northeastern coast of Alaska near Camden Bay of the Arctic Ocean, late May and June are spring, July is summer, autumn begins in August, and winter at the beginning of September.

On a warm winter day with Herbert Ross, an authority on stoneflies, as my guide, I collected adult winter stoneflies that clung to the concrete abutments of a bridge on the Middle Fork River in central Illinois. The winter stoneflies are so named because they are active only during the cold months of the year. It is then that they grow to maturity, leave the water, mate, and lay eggs. This despite the fact that they live in streams in the temperate zone, where summer is long and warm, and they are not compelled to adapt to cold temperatures, as are the mosquitoes of the tundra. In *A Textbook of Entomology*, Ross wrote:

There is a peculiarity about certain groups of stoneflies that is only rarely encountered among insects. Winter signals the end of the active season and the beginning of the quiescent period for most insects. With many of the stoneflies the opposite is the case. Apparently the [recently hatched] nymphs do not develop further during the warmer months of the year. With the approach of winter, nymphal development becomes accelerated, and the adults emerge during the coldest months of the year, beginning in late November or early December, and continuing through March. The adults are active on the warmer winter days and may be found crawling over stones and tree trunks, mating, and feeding on green algae.

In southern Ontario, according to H. B. N. Hynes, nymphs often molt to the adult stage in the space under the ice that forms as the water level falls after freezing. Many adults may accumulate in these spaces, where the air temperature is relatively warm, to await the sunshine that will lure them out onto the snow. P. P. Harper and Hynes observed that no adults come out on days when the air temperature is much below freezing. On such days, nymphs ready to molt to the adult stage will leave the water only to turn around and return to its relative warmth.

Most aquatic insects live at more moderate temperatures than those in hot springs or Arctic pools. In southern Ontario, Robert Trottier determined that nymphs of the green darner dragonfly begin to feed and grow at a water temperature of about 48°F. At 54°F, they complete the final phase (instar) of the nymphal stage in 69 days, at 68°F in 24 days, and at 86°F in only 15 days. While the Arctic mosquitoes grow well at 49°F, a floodwater mosquito *(Aedes vexans)* and the yellow fever mosquito *(Aedes aegypti)* of temperate and tropical areas will, according to Horsfall, die at 49°F and grow optimally at 80°F or above. Rangathilakam Krishnara and Gordon Pritchard found that the optimum temperature for growth by the damselfly *Lestes disjunctus* is about 84°F, while that of another damselfly *(Coenagrion resolutum)* is somewhat lower than 73°F.

These temperatures were determined with insects confined in containers of water at constant, unchanging temperatures. They are useful comparisons of the relative effects of temperature on growth and survival, but do not reflect what actually happens when, as in nature, aquatic insects experience a kaleidoscope of temperatures. Water temperatures vary with the season and even the time of day. In any body of water, temperature varies from place to place. Generally speaking, the water at the bottom of a pond is cooler than water at the surface. Water shaded by vegetation is cooler than water exposed to the heat of the sun. The windward side of a lake is likely to be cooler than the leeward side, because as the wind blows warm surface water across the lake cold water wells up on the windward side and warm water accumulates on the leeward side. For these and various other reasons, the temperature of the water that surrounds an insect could be unfavorable or changeable. Sedentary insects must adapt to changing temperatures or die, but mobile insects can escape by moving between microhabitats.

The elegant experiments of Martin Kavaliers show that aquatic crane fly larvae are perfectly capable of aggregating in a place where the temperature is to their liking. In a long, narrow, water-filled trough with translucent Plexiglas sides and an aluminum bottom covered with stream gravel, he established a gradient of temperatures from 50°F to 68°F by cooling one end of the trough while heating the other end. The gradient was measured with ordinary thermometers inserted into the trough at intervals. The precise temperature at a larva's location was measured by a thermocouple, a tiny electronic thermometer, glued to its back. Kavaliers' laboratory had an artificial day with 12 hours of light and 12 hours of dark. During the "day" the larvae preferred a water temperature of about 55°F and during the "night," about 61°F.

🦟 Although the ectothermic insects have no internal metabolic mechanism to control their body temperature, they do have other ways of controlling it. Many can raise their body temperature well above that of the surrounding air to a level at which their muscles and other internal organs can function. Numerous insects—grasshoppers, butterflies, dragonflies, damselflies—bask in the sun with their bodies oriented so as to absorb as much heat as possible. Butterflies perch at the tip of a branch with their opaque wings spread wide and facing the sun. Dragonflies and damselflies, reported Philip Corbet, expose the thorax and long abdomen to the sun, but different species of damselflies hold their transparent wings in different positions. For example, some hold them so as to reflect sunlight onto the body, while others hold them over the body to form a sort of greenhouse that traps heat.

"Underwater basking" is an aptly descriptive term coined by J. R. Spence and his coworkers to describe a remarkable behavior of water striders. They determined that at air temperatures below 46°F both sexes of four related species crawl beneath the water surface if the water is warmer than the air. They cling to a support just below the surface, but leave the water when the air temperature rises above the threshold temperature at which the eggs in the ovaries begin to develop. This behavior increases the rate of egg development and also the number of eggs laid. Adult stoneflies other than winter stoneflies, William Tozer found, are killed by a 2 to 3 minute exposure to 38°F. They survive lethally cold nighttime air temperatures, which may fall below freezing, by returning to the water. The water temperature may be a relatively balmy 47°F even when the air temperature is only 20°F. These stoneflies, observed Tozer, crawled beneath the surface on protruding stems, remained there for 20 to 60 minutes, and then came to the surface for air and floated there for a few minutes before submerging again.

Some large flying insects, moths, katydids, bees, and dragonflies, warm up before taking flight by "shivering," rapidly vibrating the wings with the massive flight muscles in the thorax. All muscles produce heat as a byproduct of doing work, but in dragonflies only the wing muscles produce enough heat to significantly affect body temperature. The heat produced by the wing muscles continues to keep the body temperature elevated in flight.

A water temperature that is too warm has a bizarre and unexpected effect on larval mosquitoes. As is to be expected, temperatures that are too high can be lethal, or less drastically, decrease growth rates, body size, life span, and the ability to reproduce. But Horsfall and John Anderson made the surprising discovery that a rather small increase in the rearing temperature can, in some species, cause mosquito larvae that would have become males to become females instead. If larvae of Aedes stimulans are raised at 75°F, about half become males and half become females. But if they are raised at 84°F, only 9°F higher, they all become almost complete females. Larvae that would have become males lack the big bushy antennae of the normal male and have mouthparts and external genitalia that are indistinguishable from those of a "real" female. Furthermore, "feminized" males have no testicles or other internal male organs of reproduction, but they do have ovaries and the other internal female organs of reproduction. Some feminized males have even mated with normal males and been insemi-nated, but they laid no eggs. Similar sex reversals have been noted in only a few other insects, but according to Sir Vincent Wigglesworth, in no known case are feminized males capable of reproducing. The feminization of male insects seems to be, inexplicably, a dead end with no apparent adaptive value.

With few exceptions, the sex of most animals, particularly insects, birds, and mammals, is genetically fixed at the time of conception. But to paraphrase R. Shine and his coauthors, in some species, an individual's sex is determined not genetically but partway through its development by some environmental influence. In some ectothermic vertebrates—certain fish and reptiles such as turtles, some lizards, and all of the alligators, crocodiles, and their relatives—sex is determined by the tem-perature an individual experiences during its early develop-ment, in crocodiles, for example, by the temperatures the eggs experience during incubation. Contrary to what we saw with the mosquito, males and females of these species are anatomi-cally and physiologically normal and capable of reproducing. This method of sex determination can have benefits. For exam-ple, David Conover and Stephen Heins found that in nature, most offspring of the Atlantc silverside, a fish, become females early in the season when temperatures are low and become males later in the season when temperatures are higher. Conse-quently, females feed for a longer time and grow larger, which increases their fecundity. Males are smaller, but that does not significantly affect their ability to father offspring.

As the cold of winter or the heat of summer approaches, virtually all temperate zone insects must "decide" whether to mature and reproduce, or defer reproduction until a more favorable season. Most insects survive unfavorable conditions by going into the inactive hibernation-like or estivation-like state called diapause (estivation is the summer equivalent of hibernation). But some insects, as we will see later, escape the cold of winter or the heat of summer by migrating. A few others, among them certain mayfly, dragonfly, and stonefly nymphs, and dobsonfly, caddisfly, and black fly larvae stay put and do not go into diapause. They continue to feed and grow, albeit slowly, if the water is a few degrees above freezing but become quiescent, inactive although not in diapause, at lower temperatures. Some continue to grow at temperatures almost down to the freezing point.

Insects may diapause in any life stage, but—almost invariably—all members of a given species diapause in the same life stage. Most diapausing insects are inactive, and—without exception—development to the next stage stops. Eggs do not hatch; nymphs do not molt to the adult stage; larvae do not become pupae; pupae do not become adults; and adults do not lay eggs or, like aphids or tsetse flies, give live birth to offspring.

If an insect freezes, ice crystals form in the cells of its body, the cells burst, and the insect dies. Diapausing insects protect themselves against freezing by producing an antifreeze. Just as we put alcohol or some other antifreeze in our car radiators in winter, diapausing insects permeate their bodies with an internally secreted antifreeze, glycerol or some other alcohol such as mannitol or sorbitol, which lowers the freezing point of water, or proteins that prevent the formation of damaging ice crystals.

Food is scarce in the winter, and even if it were not, it would be too cold for most insects to be active enough to feed. Consequently, they must survive the long winter on the limited amount of energy, much of it in the form of fats, they can store in their bodies. To this end, diapausing insects not only remain inactive but also drastically reduce their basal metabolic rate to a tenth or even a twentieth of its usual level. If its winter metabolic rate falls to a tenth of the summer rate, an insect reduces its consumption of energy by 90 percent and can, therefore, survive on its stored energy 10 times as long as it could if it were not in diapause.

Temperate zone insects face the all-important question of whether or not another generation can be completed before winter. If not, the insect must either migrate or go into diapause. But if diapause is initiated too early, the opportunity to produce another generation will be lost; and if it is initiated too late, the next generation will die. Is there an unfailingly reliable cue that foretells the approach of winter? The onset of cold weather is definitely *not* a reliable cue. In some years it may come atypically late or there may be an abnormally early—and misleading—cold spell. Furthermore, slow-growing insects with a generation time of 10 or 12 weeks may be ready to enter diapause in August, well before there has been a significant fall in temperature. By contrast, fast-growing insects with a generation time of only a week or two may not have to enter diapause until late September.

The only reliable cue is the length of the day. In the North Temperate Zone, the days gradually shorten after June 22, the longest day of the year, and gradually lengthen after December 22, the shortest day of the year. Insects are "triggered" to enter diapause by the short days of late summer and fall. The trigger is usually pulled before the insect actually stops developing. A slow-growing caterpillar, for example, may be triggered, and thereby predestined to diapause, in the summer but continue to feed and grow for several weeks and not exhibit the attributes of diapause until after it has spun an elaborate cocoon and molted to the pupal stage.

But how does an insect "know" when to terminate diapause? Diapause may be terminated by the long days of spring, but at different day lengths in different species and even in different individuals of the same species. In some species it may be terminated by warm weather—but generally not by warm weather alone. If it were, the insect could be unseasonably reactivated by warm days in the autumn or by a warm spell in the winter. In either instance, it would perish in the cold weather that would inevitably follow. Insects avoid this danger by not responding to warmth until after they have experienced a sufficiently long period of cold. I demonstrated this to my children with the beautiful, land-dwelling cecropia moth, a favorite of amateur naturalists. Cecropia spends the winter as a diapausing pupa in a large silken cocoon. We collected cecropia cocoons in the fall, and kept one group at room temperature and another in a refrigerator. After 10 weeks, we took the cocoons out of the refrigerator and put them next to the cocoons that had been at room temperature all along. Over a period of several days, beginning about 3 weeks later, a moth emerged from every one of the chilled cocoons, but none had as yet emerged from the others.

Some insects "wake up" early in the spring and others "wake up" much later. The terminating mechanism not only reactivates an insect, but synchronizes it with the availability of the particular biological resources, food plants or prey, that it requires. The bumble bee–mimicking fly that we met earlier spends the larval stage in water-filled tree holes, terminates its pupal diapause in May, and emerges as an adult in June when the nectar plants, especially viburnums and dogwoods, that it favors are in full blossom. And, as we will soon see, a sequence of "triggers" assures that the eggs of floodwater mosquitoes hatch only when there is abundant food for the larvae.

Some mosquitoes diapause in the adult stage, a few in the larval stage, and most of the really abundant ones—the ones that ruin backyard barbecues—diapause in the egg stage. In Canada and the United States, mosquitoes of the genus *Anopheles* and the genus *Culex* survive the winter as adult females in diapause. In the fall, they mate with males that do not enter diapause and do not survive. In the winter, inseminated females of both genera rest in dark, damp places protected from the wind: barns, abandoned buildings, cellars, hollow trees, caves. According to Horsfall, *Culex pipiens*, the common house mosquito, survives temperatures well below freezing. Horsfall noted that when the females of one of our most common species of *Anopheles*, *Anopheles quadrimaculatus*, the malaria mosquito, are disappearing from barns, sheds, and other summer daytime resting places in October, they begin to appear in caves. The population of these diapausing adult females grows rapidly in November and peaks near the end of the month. In a field study in Delaware, Carl Huffaker found diapausing females of this species mainly in sites with temperatures between 30°F and 43°F, although some survived at a low of 3°F.

Larvae of the mosquito known to science as *Wyeomyia smithii* live, as we have seen, in a most unusual habitat, the liquid—mostly water—in the urnlike pitfall traps of the extraordinary insect-eating pitcher plant of the eastern United States and southern Canada. Although insects that tumble into the trap are digested, a few creatures, including larval *Wyeomyia*, the pitcher plant mosquito, live safely in the pitcher. Late in January, during a bitter cold spell (the temperature had fallen to −2°F), J. Turner Blakeley found the liquid in the pitchers frozen and saw mosquito larvae embedded throughout the solid core of ice. His friend John Smith wrote:

> A number of leaves were gathered, the cores of ice with all they contained were removed and the lumps were placed together in a jar in a moderately warm room. The ice melted slowly, and as the larvae were gradually freed they dropped to the bottom where for a time they rested, apparently lifeless. But as the amount of ice decreased, feeble motions here and there indicated a revival, and long before the lumps were completely melted, those first released were moving about actively. This be it noted was in water not much above the freezing point.

Over 90 years later, Mark Campbell and William Bradshaw mentioned the then well-known fact that the pitcher plant mosquito overwinters in a larval diapause that is induced and maintained by short days and averted or terminated by long days.

Many species of mosquitoes, among them *Anopheles* and *Culex*, lay their eggs on the surface of the water, but others—known as floodwater mosquitoes—lay them in crevices in the moist soil of places that are subject to periodic flooding: river bottoms, depressions in fields, ephemeral woodland pools. These species—among them *Aedes vexans*, the most annoying and abundant of the biting mosquitoes in most of the United States—spend the winter as diapausing eggs. They can survive in dry soil for 2 years, but few survive longer. The eggs hatch only after the following sequence of events: the completion of embryonic development, a period of drying and cold temperatures, being covered by water that is favorably warm, and, finally, a sharp drop in the concentration of dissolved oxygen in the water.

The last step of the sequence is unusual but is essential to the survival of the tiny larvae that hatch from the eggs. They feed on microorganisms that they filter from the water. The sharp drop in oxygen concentration signals that microorganisms, which use up oxygen, have become sufficiently abundant. Alfred Borg and Horsfall demonstrated experimentally that a decline in the oxygen concentration is without doubt the effective signal. In their laboratory experiments, eggs hatched immediately if placed in a beaker teeming with microorganisms feeding on decaying vegetation, but they never hatched in a beaker of pure distilled water, in which there were no microorganisms. However, when the level of dissolved oxygen in the distilled water was decreased by bubbling nitrogen through it, the eggs soon hatched, even though there were no microorganisms in the water for them to eat.

The eggs of many other aquatic insects, wrote H. B. N. Hynes, are "resting stages in the life cycle and allow them to evade unfavorable periods in a [dormant] condition." Among the many are the eggs of certain mayflies that have a winter diapause and, as F. J. H. Fredeen found, also the eggs of some black flies, which can survive in the laboratory for up to 2.5 years. According to Hynes, a stream-dwelling stonefly that occurs on both sides of the Atlantic lays eggs of two types, both of which will be in the same batch laid by a single female. The eggs of one type are not in diapause (or perhaps are in a brief diapause), and those of the other type remain in diapause for up to 11 months. This is probably a "bet-hedging" strategy, a case of not putting all the nymphs that will hatch from the eggs in just one "seasonal basket." One of the two groups is likely to prosper if the other is decimated or even wiped out by a disaster. As I explained in a review article on the subject, bet-hedging is not uncommon among insects.

Some of the diapausing offspring of a single cecropia female molt to the adult stage and escape from the cocoon in late May, but others do not become adults until late June. If, for example, one of these groups does not fare well in a cold spring or a drought-stricken summer, the other group may do much better. We see the same sort of bet-hedging in the aquatic larvae of a phantom midge. William Bradshaw discovered that some larvae terminate their winter diapause and resume development very early in the spring, while others do so a few weeks later. He found that in a pond in Michigan the early group did well in a year when spring came early and the water became progressively warmer. But in a year when an early thaw was followed by the refreezing of the pond, few of the early group survived, but the late group, emerging after the thaw, fared well.

Like the phantom midge, some aquatic insects diapause in some stage other than the egg. Among them are a common European stonefly that overwinters as a partly grown nymph, some caddisflies that diapause in their cases as full-grown larvae, and a variety of aquatic beetles and water bugs that overwinter in the adult stage. In 1920, H. B. Hungerford quoted from C. Wessenberg-Lund's English summary of a 1913 article in German in which it was noted that the air-breathing adults of some aquatic insects, especially predaceous diving beetles, water scavenger beetles, and some water bugs hibernate beneath the ice. Wessenberg-Lund wrote that "insects which in summer die, when only for a few minutes or hours excluded from air, in winter at a temperature near zero [32°F] are quite able for months to support a total exclusion from air. When every possibility of getting air for breathing is excluded, it seems that the animals settle down in a winter sleep—in which respiration is extremely lowered."

Some aquatic insects spend the winter diapausing on land. In fall, full-grown spongillafly larvae abandon the freshwater sponge on which they have been feeding and come ashore to spin a cocoon in a sheltered spot. There, according to Elsie Klots, they remain in diapause until they molt to the pupal stage in the spring. Adult marsh treaders come ashore in the fall to lie concealed in debris or damp moss near the water. Similarly, adult water striders diapause in the winter under logs, brush, or other shelter near the water.

Diapause, as T. R. E. Southwood put it, is a "sit-tight tactic" for surviving adverse conditions. Its alternative is migration to a more benevolent climate or place, "seeking pastures new," as Southwood expressed it. In deserts, certain nomadic dragonflies mature in temporary rain pools that will soon go dry, not leaving enough time for another generation to survive and grow to maturity. In the Sahara and other drought-prone areas, pools form in depressions when it rains, but soon dry up and may stay dry for years. Such pools, wrote Corbet, are colonized by dragonflies whose progeny are genetically programmed to fly away and abandon their pool even if it still contains water. Because rainfall is local and sporadic, nearby pools will also go dry. Consequently, the dragonflies from the temporary pool will have to fly a long way to find a suitable home for their progeny. In their wanderings, often 100 miles or more in extent, the lucky ones come upon a place where it recently rained, and there they will lay eggs in newly filled depressions, which their offspring will, in turn, abandon when they become winged adults.

Water striders have varied escape strategies that are adapted to the particular type of habitat occupied by their species. Writing of European water striders, Kari Vepsäläinen noted that the adults of some species are always short-winged and cannot fly, others are always long-winged and capable of flying, and yet others may be either short-winged or long-winged. Species that are always short-winged live in permanent lakes that are so distant from other suitable habitats that a flying individual would be more likely to perish than to reach another lake. Consequently, natural selection favors individuals that stay put. Species that are always long-winged and capable of flying occupy habitats that, as Vepsäläinen put it, "are capricious in time." They are likely to go dry, but that is not reliably predicted by environmental cues. These long-winged water striders are always ready to flee with short notice. Finally, species that have both short- and long-winged forms live in bodies of water that are impermanent, but whose drying up is predicted by environmental cues. The flightless short-winged form generally predominates. Natural selection favors them, because they have more energy and resources to devote to reproduction than do long-winged individuals, mostly because they expend no resources to produce large wing muscles. But if an environmental cue, such as a heat wave, predicts that the pool will soon go dry, the short-winged individuals produce long-winged offspring that fly to safety.

The most famous of the migrating dragonflies is the large and handsome green darner, beloved of the rapidly growing group of amateur naturalists who watch dragonflies through binoculars. This species is particularly interesting because, as we have seen, it exhibits both the sit-tight and migratory strategies. In a pond near Toronto, Ontario, Robert Trottier found two distinct populations of green darners, a "winter population" that survives the winter by sitting tight in the water as half-grown nymphs in diapause and a "summer population" that molts to the adult stage and seeks a more benevolent climate by migrating south. Winter nymphs are present from July of one year to June of the next year. They feed and grow during the late summer and fall and during the following spring. In the winter they lie buried in the mud at the bottom of the pond, do not feed, and do not grow. They become adults in June and July and then mate and lay eggs. Migrants from the south return to the pond in the early spring, and in May lay eggs that become adults, which emerge from the water about 3 months later—in September, more than a month after the emergence of the adults of the winter group—and then fly south.

Some aquatic insects, among them the winter stoneflies, cope with the heat of summer or their habitat's going dry by staying put and estivating, going into a summer diapause.

Some stream-dwelling caddisflies, noted Hynes, estivate as mature larvae sealed up in their pupal cases. He says of another caddisfly, "Unlike many other caddis-worms which go into diapause where they will finally pupate, [the] full-grown larvae burrow down into the gravel where they remain [in diapause] from February to September (in Michigan); then they come up again to pupate at the surface [of the bottom] and emerge in the fall." Some mayflies, he noted, spend the warm summer months as small, presumably estivating, nymphs and do not grow until the temperature drops.

Referring to winter stoneflies, P. P. Harper and Hynes wrote that the adults emerge in the late winter or very early spring, and feed, mate, and lay their eggs about 1 month after emergence. In some species the eggs enter a prolonged estival diapause, and in others they hatch immediately, and it is the nymphs that go into an estival diapause. Accordingly, the summer is spent as a newly hatched nymph in diapause or an egg containing an embryo in diapause. Nymphal feeding and growth starts or resumes the following fall and is completed during the winter. According to Hynes, a winter stonefly of intermittent streams in eastern North America—unlike most stoneflies and other aquatic insects—gives live birth to nymphs that quickly burrow into the bottom. Hynes suggests that bypassing the egg stage is advantageous because a nymph, which can actively seek out a good place to hide, has "a better chance of survival than an egg which must stay where it falls."

There is no doubt in my mind that the larvae of a midge, *Polypedilum vanderplanki*, have the most amazing adaptation—almost unbelievable—of those that aquatic insects have developed for surviving droughts. It is not much of an exaggeration to say that when their habitat goes dry, they die, and that when it refills with water, they are resurrected. These West African insects live in temporary pools in shallow depressions in rock outcrops, including depressions made by native people for grinding grain. The depressions are, reported H. E. Hinton, only 5 to 9 inches deep, exposed to the beating sun, and during the rainy season may fill and dry several times. The larvae live in mud at the bottom of the depression, and, according to Hinton, when the pools dry, they stay in their tunnels, dry out with the mud, enter diapause, and are inert until it rains again.

They dry out almost completely, shrivel up, and show not the slightest sign of life. The water content of their bodies is much less than the usual 75 percent or more. It may be as low as 1 percent but is usually about 8 percent—about the same as a well-seasoned piece of wood in a piece of furniture, a far greater water loss than can be tolerated by other insects. The larvae of several beetles, a caterpillar, and a true bug, noted Wigglesworth, die when the water content of their bodies falls from its usual 75 percent to 60 percent, and a termite dies when it falls to 68 percent from its usual 74 to 80 percent. The eggs of a grasshopper, *Locustana pardalina,* are exceptional in that they can survive a decrease of their water content from 85 percent to 40 percent.

When a dehydrated and apparently dead *Polypedilum* larva is placed in water, it immediately begins to swell up as it absorbs water, and in about an hour it resumes feeding. In the laboratory, Hinton found, larvae survived several repeated cycles of dehydration and resurrection, as they do in nature.

Dehydrated larvae are amazingly tolerant of stress. Hinton

found that larvae stored in dry mud for 3 years and 3 months at room temperature and humidity produced normal adults when placed in tap water. When larvae were similarly stored for 7 or 10 years, a few revived in water and showed feeble signs of life but none survived. Dry larvae were not killed when subjected to temperatures so low that they would instantly solidify and kill other animals and plants. Hinton dropped larvae into liquid air ($-310°F$) and kept them there for 77 hours. All grew normally when afterward placed in water. Even after immersion in liquid helium ($-454°F$) for 5 minutes, dehydrated larvae recovered and grew normally when placed in water. The temperature of liquid helium is only 6°F above absolute zero, the temperature at which all molecular motion stops. Hinton noted that some larvae that had been treated with liquid air or liquid helium later metamorphosed to the adult stage.

While some insects can cope with the drying up of their habitat, others cannot. The research of Jonathan Chase and Tiffany Knight, discussed in the journal *Nature* by Jocelyn Kaiser, showed that this difference can have significant ecological repercussions, in particular on the survival of mosquito larvae. In permanent ponds that do not dry up, mosquito larvae are scarce, because fish, predaceous diving beetles, and other predators are always numerous. Mosquito larvae are also scarce in temporary ponds that dry up every year; they are permanently inhabited by mosquito-eating predators, mainly insects, that have become adapted to survive the regularly occurring dry spells. But predators in ponds that seldom dry up are not adapted to survive the rare dry spells. When these ponds refill after a drought, they will—at least in the first year—have been repopulated by few predators, and mosquito larvae will flourish.

🪰 Are aquatic insects important to people? The answer, as we will soon see, is a resounding yes. Among other things, they give us pleasure. The Japanese write poems about dragonflies, women wear dragonfly jewelry, and many enjoy watching these beautiful creatures swoop over ponds. But aquatic insects are also of great practical importance. They are usually indispensable members of their ecosystems. From a practical point of view, they are food for most of the freshwater fish we eat and play an important role in maintaining the purity and ecological health of the lakes and streams that, as a source of drinking water, are essential to our survival. But they—most notably mosquitoes—also cause more human discomfort, illness, and death than any other group of insects.

Our Friends and Enemies

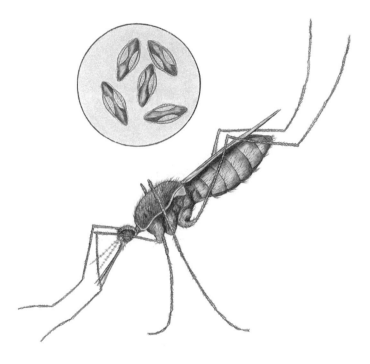

A malaria mosquito feeds in this characteristic position;
it overwinters as an adult and lays its eggs, which
have flotation bladders, on the water's surface

In the spring, black fly season in Ontario's Algonquin Provincial Park, a friend and I stood near a dead maple with a hole that, according to the bird watchers' grapevine, housed a nesting pair of black-backed woodpeckers. Although hundreds of fiercely annoying black flies swarmed around us, we waited and watched for the woodpeckers to appear. Neither of us had ever seen this species. As birders say, it was a "lifer." After we got good views of the female and the golden-capped male entering and leaving the hole, we fled to our car to escape the maddening black flies.

My friend, an avid birder but ecologically untutored, asked, "Why do black flies even exist? What good are they?" I went into my professorial mode and explained that they are an important link in the food chains of the north woods. The adults are food for dragonflies and damselflies and for flycatchers, warblers, and other nesting birds. The larvae, nourished by plankton and bits of detritus they filter from streams, are eaten by stonefly larvae, which, in turn, are eaten by trout that may become food for ospreys, playful otters, or people.

Aquatic insects—black flies, mayflies, stoneflies, true bugs, beetles, caddisflies—are the main food of most freshwater fish and at least a minor part of the diet of almost all others. In Canada, reported Michael Healey, 144 of the 180 species of freshwater fish eat mainly insects, and in Britain and Europe

143 of the 215 species feed mainly on insects. This is to be expected because, as P. J. Gullan and P. S. Cranston reported, aquatic insects are the dominant animals in most freshwater environments. Not only are they very numerous, but their biomass, the summed weights of all individuals, is usually greater than that of any other group of animals in the water—even the much larger and more noticeable fish.

If aquatic insects are scarce or altogether absent, there will be few or perhaps no fish, and the few species that survive will most likely be of little or no value to sport or commercial fisheries. According to Healey, the world's sport fisheries may take as much as 3 million tons of freshwater fish per year, and the total yearly harvest by commercial and sport fishers combined may be as much as 22 million tons. This is, of course, an important contribution to our supply of protein-rich food.

Aquatic insects can be useful "biomonitors" of water pollution, as are mayflies in the Great Lakes, according to Lynda Corkum, and, as Calvin Fremling has shown, in the upper Mississippi River. A declining mayfly population in western Lake Erie was a warning—too long ignored—of increasing pollution by sewage spilled into the lake by the Maumee, Detroit, and other rivers. From 1930 to 1961, John Carr and Jaarl Hiltunen found, the number of large burrowing mayfly nymphs per square yard of lake bottom dropped from an average of 116 to less than 2. At the same time, skyrocketing populations of bottom-dwelling worms and insects that thrive on organic pollutants echoed that warning: the average number of sludge worms per square yard soared from 217 to over 7,500, and that of blood "worms" and other filth-loving midge larvae from 70 to

300. Western Lake Erie, "dead" in the 1960s, revived after pollution was controlled and is now safe for swimming and again abounds with perch, walleye, and other fish.

Although aquatic insects are important and often essential members of aquatic ecosystems, they also have a significant ecological impact on land-dwelling insects, birds, and other animals. But also the geological effects of streams, ponds, lakes, and wetlands—the ways in which these waters shape the face of the land—have profound and far-reaching effects on both aquatic and terrestrial organisms. Ponds, lakes, and wetlands such as swamps, marshes, and bogs serve as retention basins that delay and moderate what, without them, would be a destructive, eroding rush of rainwater back to the seas. Sediments that would otherwise be flushed away by rivers settle to the bottom of ponds and lakes and are trapped in the dense vegetation of wetlands. In this way, William Cunningham and Barbara Saigo wrote, these retention basins "both clarify surface waters and contribute to the formation of fertile land."

Given enough time, ponds, lakes, and wetlands fill with silt and organic debris and become dry land. Peat bogs and the fertile "muck soils" of Wisconsin were once lakes. On their way to becoming dry land, they became bogs covered with a mat of floating vegetation—including sphagnum moss and tamarack trees—that ultimately filled in the lake as this vegetation died and fell to the bottom. As we flew over the Connecticut River Valley in his Piper Cub, Sanborn Partridge, a geologist at Amherst College, and I looked down on the water of oxbow lakes that had been cut off from the river as it meandered and twisted back on itself. Scattered in the valley's crop fields were signs of ancient lakes that had long before filled with silt, oxbow shapes of brighter green growing on ground more fertile than the surrounding soil.

Ponds, lakes, and wetlands are not just retention basins, and streams and rivers are more than mere conduits to the sea. An ecosystem with a healthy community of plants and insects and other animals purifies water. These organisms "eat" organic pollutants such as sewage, which is, after all, a source of nutrients for them. For example, H. B. N. Hynes wrote that a river can "repurify" itself of organic pollutants if the fouling is not too serious. Pollutants, according to Hynes, may be detectable for only a mile or two downstream of their source if the "pollutant load" is light. But as the pollutant load increases, pollutants become detectable farther and farther downstream. Furthermore, as Cunningham and Saigo noted, chemical interactions in the ecosystems of wetlands and other waters neutralize and detoxify poisonous substances in the water. These interactions take place mainly within the bodies of the ecosystem's community of organisms.

Detoxification renders some toxins harmless to all or most organisms. But other toxins may be altered so as to be harmless to the detoxifying organisms but still toxic to others. For example, my friend and colleague Jim Sternburg long ago discovered that insects resistant to the insecticide DDT (a welcome acronym for dichloro-diphenyl-trichloroethane) produce an enzyme that converts DDT to DDE (dichloro-diphenyl-ethylene), which is not toxic to them, but is toxic to birds.

Insecticides applied to crops contaminate aquatic ecosystems and, as happened in Clear Lake with DDD, are concentrated as they are passed up the food chain from plankton to filter-feeding insects, to predaceous insects, to insect-eating fish, to fish-eating fish, and finally to fish-eating birds. By this route, fish-eating birds, notably bald eagles throughout the lower 48 states, ingested toxic concentrations of DDE, which interferes with enzymes involved in the deposition of calcium in egg shells. The eagles' eggs broke when the birds tried to incubate them and the bald eagle population plummeted and was on the verge of being extirpated. After 1972, when the use of DDT was banned in the United States, the eagle population began to recover and today the many that winter along the Illinois and Mississippi rivers delight birders and people who just like to watch eagles.

In virtually all ecosystems, predators and parasites have the indispensable role of preventing population explosions—maintaining the "balance of nature"—by eliminating the excess offspring that all animals produce, more than are required to replace themselves and thereby keep their population stable. Mosquitoes, for example, help to maintain the "balance of nature" by transmitting deadly diseases of birds. But they also transmit diseases of humans. Our population is indeed exploding, but we all hope that it will be controlled by means of our choosing, rather than by epidemic disease.

Most of the 2,500 known species of mosquitoes do not suck blood from humans or other animals, but the few that do—only females—can be a nuisance that makes camping miserable or takes the joy out of a backyard barbecue. But a few species are much more than an annoyance—they are dangerous. Their bites transmit tiny nematode worms and microorganisms—viruses, bacteria, and the amoeba-like protozoans—that cause many of the most debilitating and deadly diseases of humans.

The role of mosquitoes—or any other insects—in transmitting disease-causing organisms was not known until Patrick Manson, an English parasitologist, demonstrated in 1878 that the tiny nematode worm—round worm—that causes human filariasis (a disease named for the nematodes that cause it) is transmitted by a mosquito. Similar discoveries followed, and by the end of the nineteenth century the skeptical medical community was convinced that blood-sucking insects transmit disease-causing organisms. Mosquitoes are by far the most important of them, but there are others that we will come to later.

In 1999, the virus that causes the sometimes deadly West Nile fever made its first appearance in the Western Hemisphere in New York City, and it has since spread throughout the country. The virus is transmitted from birds to people by mosquitoes. More deadly to birds than to people, the first sign of it is usually dead birds, particularly crows, lying on the ground. Similar indigenous diseases, eastern, St. Louis, and western encephalitis, are also transmitted from birds to humans by mosquitoes. As with West Nile fever, most people make good recoveries from these diseases, but in the very young and the elderly the viruses may attack the central nervous system and cause brain damage or death.

In the eighteenth and nineteenth centuries, residents of port cities along the coast from New Orleans to Boston were periodically panicked by raging epidemics of yellow fever, a disease brought to the New World from Africa by slaves and slave traders in the seventeenth century. The virus that causes this frequently deadly disease was often carried north by infected sailors on ships sailing from ports in tropical South America. There forest-dwelling mosquitoes of the genus *Haemagogus* transmit the virus from monkey to monkey and sometimes from monkey to humans such as woodcutters. When an infected woodcutter brought his logs to a South American port, the virus was transmitted to sailors, many of whom sailed to ports in the United States. In the coastal cities of both South America and the United States, the virus was transmitted from person to person by a different mosquito, *Aedes aegypti,* also known as the yellow fever mosquito. It was abundant in cities because of its habit of breeding in water-filled artificial containers such as water barrels, bird baths, and discarded containers. Yellow fever occurred in the United States until the beginning of the twentieth century, but is now limited to tropical Africa and Latin America, where there may be 200,000 cases and 30,000 deaths per year.

As we have seen, Patrick Manson's brilliant research showed that the microscopic nematode worm that causes human filariasis is transmitted from person to person by mosquitoes of the genera *Culex* and *Anopheles.* People suffer from this disease in Asia, the East Indies, and subsaharan Africa. About 120 million are infected and about 40 million of them are incapacitated. Some people show no symptoms. Many have chills and fever as well as swollen lymph nodes. In the later stages of the disease, the lymph nodes in the armpits, groin, and elsewhere may become greatly enlarged, which blocks the flow of lymphatic fluid and causes a swelling known as elephantiasis, enormous enlargements of the arms, legs, the scrotum of men, and the breasts and genitalia of women.

Malaria is certainly one of the worst of the infectious diseases of humans. It is caused by microscopic protozoans of the genus *Plasmodium* that are transmitted from person to person by about 60 mosquitoes of the genus *Anopheles*. Malaria can cause fever, chills, vomiting, exhaustion, anemia, and death. It was formerly common in Europe and the United States but is now virtually absent there. In the mid-nineteenth century, when Illinois was first being settled and the marshy prairies had yet to be drained, it was considered to be a death trap because of the prevalence of malaria. According to a 2002 "news feature" in *Science* by Stephen Budiansky, today this disease occurs in more than 100 countries in southeast Asia, the East Indies, sub-Saharan Africa, and parts of Central America and northern South America. In 2002, there were 300 million cases and over 1 million deaths per year. A more recent article (2004) by Brian Greenwood also estimates over 1 million deaths per year and also reports 500,000 "attacks of acute illness" each year.

There are currently two ways to control malaria: preventing *Anopheles* mosquitoes from biting people or treating people with drugs that kill the malaria-causing plasmodia. Window screens dramatically decrease the malaria transmission rate, but most people in the countries hardest hit by this disease are too poor to screen their homes. Bed nets treated with a pyrethroid, an insecticide, have been effective, but they are expensive and mosquitoes are becoming resistant to this insecticide. *Anopheles* mosquitoes have been killed by DDT sprayed on the inner walls of houses, where the mosquitoes often rest, but they have become resistant to DDT in many areas. Some resistant populations have reverted to being susceptible, but if they are exposed to DDT they will become resistant again, but far more rapidly than they did the first time. Chloroquine has for decades been the drug of choice for treating malaria, but plasmodia resistant to it appeared in southeast Asia and South America in the 1950s, and since then resistance has been spreading. There is now, as Thomas Wellems pointed out, an urgent need to find safe and effective antimalarial drugs to replace chloroquine.

Mosquitoes also transmit the causal agents of other less prevalent or less publicized diseases. Among them is dengue, or break-bone fever, a painful and occasionally fatal disease caused by a virus that is transmitted from person to person by *Aedes aegypti* and a few closely related mosquitoes. In the Old and New World tropics there are about 50 million cases of dengue every year. This disease is "knocking on our door" and has already become established in the southernmost part of Texas near the mouth of the Rio Grande and the border city of Brownsville.

Other aquatic insects—the black flies—transmit the causal agents of other diseases. Anyone who has been in the north woods of the United States and Canada in the spring knows that blood-sucking black flies can be an unbearable nuisance. Fortunately, our North American black flies do not transmit diseases of humans, but in tropical parts of Africa and Central and South America other species, especially the aptly named *Simulium damnosum,* transmit the nematode worm, *Onchocerca volvulus,* that causes onchocerciasis, also known as river blindness. Adult worms may be several inches long, and the tiny larvae they bear occur in large, nodular tumors beneath the skin. But the most serious problem by far is caused by larvae that migrate through the body and happen to enter the eyes, often causing complete blindness in, according to Robert Harwood and Maurice James, from 10 to 15 percent of the people infected with this worm.

The great majority of aquatic insects are neither annoying nor transmitters of disease. To the contrary, they are beneficial to us—most of all because of their essential roles in freshwater ecosystems—but also because we find some of them to be aesthetically pleasing, because they are a source of ideas for developing new technologies, and because some are important foods for many people of non-Western societies.

At a cocktail party given by a group of fellow entomologists, I was greeted at the door by one of my hosts holding a large bowl of deep-fried caterpillars—the big, fat kind you sometimes find chomping on kernels at the tip of an ear of sweet corn. Entering guests were dared to eat at least one. I had never eaten an insect and was repulsed by the thought of it. I really didn't want to eat one of those caterpillars. But—what the heck—I popped one into my mouth. It was crispy and delicious! I came back for more, as did other guests. The crunchy caterpillars were as addictive as potato chips.

Like other members of Western cultures, I had been imbued with a deep-seated prejudice against eating insects, although we do eat shrimps and lobsters, seagoing relatives of the insects. But we Westerners are a minority of perhaps 1.5 billion in a world population of over 6 billion. In virtually all other cultures, there is no such prejudice.

People regularly consume insects in many parts of the world, sometimes as delicacies that are eaten only in small quantities and sometimes as an important part of the diet. Most of these insects are terrestrial species such as grasshoppers, cicadas, beetle grubs, moth caterpillars and pupae, and wasp larvae and pupae. In Africa, roasted termites are a great delicacy. Fried bees with stomachs full of honey are served in fine restaurants in Tokyo. But aquatic insects are also well represented. For example, Professor Tetsuo Inukai told Charles Remington that while some terrestrial insects are poisonous, in Japan all insects found in fresh water are edible and delicious. Swarms of phantom midges, so immense that these tiny flies can be profitably harvested for food, form over Lakes Victoria and Nyasa in Africa. In China, swarming mayflies are collected, pounded, and mixed with honey before being served to people. Predaceous diving beetles and water scavenger beetles, known as *lung shih* (literally dragon lice) in Canton, are boiled or fried. They are also eaten in other parts of China, southeast Asia, and Japan. In Laos dragonfly nymphs are boiled and said to taste like crayfish.

In Mexico, the eggs of water boatmen—just one of the more than 200 insects eaten in that country—are regularly sold in the markets of modern Mexico City. In the lakes around Mexico City, noted W. E. China, certain water boatmen are so astronomically abundant that they are collected and exported to Europe by the ton as food for poultry and caged birds. A ton contains about 250 million of these little bugs. The Mexicans eat the bugs themselves but also collect and eat their eggs. The bugs are prodigious layers and their eggs can be collected in huge quantities with little effort.

According to Friedrich Bodenheimer, when bundles of rushes are placed in shallow water, water boatmen immediately begin to lay eggs on them. About a month later, the bundles—each encrusted with thousands of eggs—are taken out of the water and dried. Then they are beaten on a cloth to knock off the dried eggs, which, according to China, are known as *axayactal* (water face). He wrote that they "are either cooked alone, when they are called *ahuauhtli* (water wheat); or mixed with meal and made into cakes which are eaten with green chilies."

Snipe flies of the genus *Atherix* are different from other members of their family (Rhagionidae) because they are aquatic in the larval stage and, as Harold Oldroyd wrote, they "practise a communal egg-laying that is spectacular. They lay their eggs in masses on leaves overhanging a running stream, and each female remains clinging to the leaf, while others come and cluster on top of her." In the nineteenth century, according to Bodenheimer, the Modoc and Pitt River Indians of California reaped a bountiful harvest of these flies and prepared from them a food known as *kooh-chah-bie*. In the early summer, they floated a chain of linked logs from bank to bank in the Pitt River. Then they went upstream to shake the flies off the willow bushes that lined the banks. Flies that fell onto the water floated downstream and piled up against the log barrier. As many as 100 bushels could be gathered in this way in a single day. The flies were cooked as a mass in a pit lined with hot rocks and green rushes. When cooled, the mass of flies "had about the consistency of head cheese . . . and could be cut into slices with a knife."

A giant water bug about 2 inches long is considered to be a great delicacy in the countries of southeastern Asia and in southern China and Hong Kong. In Vietnam, these bugs, called *con-bo cap unoc,* are roasted and eaten with *nouc-mam,* the famous fermented fish sauce that many American soldiers learned to relish. "It comes to the tables of princes in Bangkok," noted W. S. Bristowe in an article on the eating of insects by the people of Siam (now Thailand). The bugs may be steamed, soaked in shrimp sauce, and picked to pieces as is a blue crab on the Maryland shore, or used as an ingredient in sauces. Bristowe found their flavor to be strong and reminiscent of gorgonzola cheese. In 1986, the entomologist Robert Pemberton was surprised to find giant waterbugs for sale in a Thai food shop in Berkeley, California. Preserved by boiling in salt water and imported from Thailand, the bugs, called *mangda* in Thai, were priced at $1.50 per bug. They are an ingredient in a condiment Thais use as a vegetable dip and a topping for rice. Known as *nam-prik mangda*, it is a combination of whole bugs, salt, sugar, garlic, shallots, *nouc-mam*, lime juice, and hot peppers mashed with a mortar and pestle.

What we learn about insects, even the most seemingly obscure facts, may eventually—perhaps far down the line— prove to have practical applications. To some people, much of the research done by entomologists and other biologists seems to be a search for inconsequential answers to arcane questions: What enables insects to maintain their equilibrium in flight? How do the ectothermic insects survive subfreezing winter temperatures? How is it possible for a tiny midge to beat its wings 1,000 times per second? The answers to these questions are important just because they add to our understanding of nature, the context of our lives. But on a more mundane level, they are important in very practical ways.

As Javaan Chahl and several coauthors have pointed out,

bioinspired engineering of exploration systems (BEES) is a new field that exploits "nature-tested mechanisms of specific crucial functions that are hard to accomplish by conventional methods, but are accomplished rather deftly in nature by biological organisms."

Resilin, which—as we have seen—helps a tiny gnat beat its wings 1,000 times per second, has attracted the attention of nanoengineers, who construct infinitesimal devices composed of individual molecules and atoms. And with good reason—resilin, a protein that also occurs in fleas, grasshoppers, and other insects is probably the most elastic substance known. Its "elastic efficiency" may be as great as 97 percent, with only 3 percent of the energy stored by stretching it lost as heat. Nanoengineers hope to manipulate the genes that control the production of resilin to form new and different elastic substances useful in various nanostructures.

We have seen that insects which spend the winter in diapause survive subfreezing temperatures by permeating their bodies with internally secreted alcohols that lower their freezing point or with certain proteins that prevent the formation of sharp, pointed ice crystals that would burst their cells. People have been taking advantage of the low freezing point of alcohol for a long time. That is old stuff. We have been putting alcohol in car radiators for almost a century. From a down east acquaintance in Maine, I learned how New Englanders have for centuries relied on the low freezing point of alcohol to "distill" applejack (apple brandy) from hard cider. They put the cider outside in freezing weather and later decant the still liquid alcohol, leaving behind the frozen water.

Although the proteins I mentioned have protected insects

from the damaging effects of freezing for millennia, they have come to the attention of scientists only recently. One of their remarkable properties is that they change the shape of ice crystals as they form. Instead of becoming sharp, spiky needles that can burst cell walls, they become smooth, hexagonal disks that do far less damage to cells. These proteins may have practical applications. The deterioration of tissues and organs for transplant could be slowed by holding them at a subfreezing temperature if they are treated with this protein to prevent cell damage from ice crystals. A less vital but still important use for them might be to prevent the formation of ice crystals that alter the texture and flavor of ice cream.

Exploration of the planet Mars would, Chahl and his coauthors think, progress more rapidly if a Mars rover could extend its "range of exploration," inspect a greater area, by sending out "assistants," miniature flyers. Chahl and his group developed a miniature "horizon detector" capable of stabilizing the flight of a miniature flyer. Their device is a mechanical version of a dragonfly's visual horizon detector, which, as Gert Stange and Jonathon Ward have shown, maintains the flying insect's stability by monitoring its movements relative to the horizon.

Dragonflies, as do many other insects, have small simple eyes (ocelli) on the forehead between the large compound eyes. The compound eyes can resolve images, but the simple eyes can only sense the intensity of light. In most insects they seem to have no other function, but in adult dragonflies they are the horizon detectors. Stange wrote that during "balanced" flight, the lower half of the visual field of each simple eye perceives the darkness of the ground while the upper half perceives the brightness of the sky. If the perception of the left simple eye differs from that of the right one, the dragonfly senses that it is no longer in level flight and can take corrective action.

Some aquatic insects benefit us in practical ways while others cause us great grief. But there are some that we value just because they give us pleasure. Dragonflies and damselflies have aesthetic appeal for people in many parts of the world. Dragonfly jewelry, for example, seems to have become more than usually popular with women. My fiancée, Phyllis Cooper, often wears on her blouse a silver dragonfly with amethyst eyes. And one night I saw another woman wearing an exceptionally beautiful dragonfly pin made by a Navaho artisan. The body was silver, the wings were thin slices of mammoth ivory, and the eyes were turquoise.

Other aquatic insects are also aesthetically pleasing, but we seldom notice the sleekly streamlined diving beetle or the caddisfly case made of a pleasing mosaic of sand grains or tiny pebbles of subtly different colors. Even mosquitoes can be beautiful when seen through a magnifying glass. The legs are long and graceful, the hind pair extended and raised in a fluid sweep. Minute and often colorful scales, much like those that cover a butterfly's wing, line the wing veins and clothe the abdomen and other parts of the body. The name of what I think is our prettiest mosquito, *Uranotaenia sapphirina,* was inspired by the sapphire-blue scales that adorn its wings and thorax.

The Japanese have loved and admired dragonflies and damselflies for thousands of years, and they are to this day revered in Japan. In Nakamura City on the island of Shikoku there is a large museum devoted to dragonflies and damselflies, and in 1987 the national dragonfly society established a dragonfly sanctuary nearby. In its ancient mythology Japan was known as Akitsushima, the island of the dragonfly. In 1910, Lafcadio Hearn wrote in *A Japanese Miscellany* that North Americans and Europeans have almost no traditional common names for their dragonflies, but the Japanese have folk names for many of the 200 species on their islands. Hearn lists many of these names. *Shōryō-tombō*, the Dragon-fly of the Ancestral Spirits; *Yanagi-jorō*, the Lady of the Weeping Willow; *Aka-tombō*, Red Dragon-fly; and *Ta-no-Kami-tombō*, Dragon-fly of the God of Rice-fields. The Japanese, says Hearn, have written haiku about dragonflies that "are almost as numerous as are the dragonflies themselves in the early autumn."

> Aki no hi no
> Sométa iro nari
> Aka-tombō!
> Dyed he is with the color of autumn days
> O the red dragon-fly!
>
> Iné no ho no
> Tombō tomari
> Tarénikéri.
> An ear of rice has bent because a
> dragonfly is perched upon it.

Selected Readings

A First Look

Gullan, P. J., and P. S. Cranston. 2005. *The Insects,* 3rd ed. Malden, MA: Blackwell Publishing.

Hagner-Holler, S., A. Schoen, W. Erker, J. H. Marden, R. Rupprecht, H. Decker, and T. Burmester. 2004. Respiratory hemocyanin from an insect. *Proceedings of the National Academy of Sciences,* 101:871–874.

Marden, J. H. and M. R. Thomas. 2003. Rowing locomotion by a stonefly that possesses the ancestral pterygote condition of co-occurring wings and abdominal gills. *Biological Journal of the Linnean Society,* 79:341–349.

Who's Who in the Water

Anderson, N. H. 1967. Life cycle of a terrestrial caddisfly, *Philocasca demita* (Trichoptera: Limnephilidae), in North America. *Annals of the Entomological Society of America,* 60:320–323.

Bleckmann, H. and T. Lotz. 1987. The vertebrate-catching behaviour of the fishing spider *Dolomedes triton* (Araneae Pisauridae). *Animal Behaviour,* 35:641–651.

Brown, H. P. 1952. The life history of *Climacia areolaris* (Hagen), a neuropterous parasite of freshwater sponges. *American Midland Naturalist,* 47:130–160.

Carr, J. F. and J. K. Hiltunen. 1965. Changes in the bottom fauna of western Lake Erie from 1930 to 1961. *Limnology and Oceanography,* 10:551–569.

Comstock, J. H. 1950. *An Introduction to Entomology.* Ithaca, NY: Comstock Publishing Co.

Corbet, P. S. 1999. *Dragonflies: Behavior and Ecology of Odonata.* Ithaca, NY: Cornell University Press.

Corkum, L. D., J. J. H. Ciborowski, and Z. E. Kovats. 1995. Aquatic insects as

biomonitors of ecosystem health in the Great Lakes areas of concern. In
F. M. Butterworth, L. D. Corkum, and J.Guzman, eds., *Biomonitors and
Biomarkers as Indicators of Environmental Change.* New York: Plenum
Press.

Doyen, J. T. and G. Ulrich. 1978. Aquatic Coleoptera. In R. W. Merrit and
K. W. Cummins, eds, *An Introduction to the Aquatic Insects of North
America.* Dubuque, IA: Kendall/Hunt.

Fremling, C. R. 1989. *Hexagenia* mayflies: biological monitors of water qual-
ity in the upper Mississippi River. *Journal of the Minnesota Academy of
Sciences,* 55:139–143.

Frisch, K. von. 1974. *Animal Architecture.* New York: Harcourt, Brace,
Jovanovich.

Hagen, K. S. 1956. Aquatic Hymenoptera. In R. L. Usinger, ed., *Aquatic Insects of California.* Berkeley: University of California Press.

———— 1978. Aquatic Hymenoptera. In R. W. Merritt and K. W. Cummins,
eds., *An Introduction to the Aquatic Insects of North America.* Dubuque,
IA: Kendall/Hunt.

Hynes, H. B. N. 1976. Biology of Plecoptera. *Annual Review of Entomology,*
21:135–153.

Jewett, S. G., Jr. 1963. A stonefly aquatic in the adult stage. *Science,* 139:484–
485.

Klots, E. B. 1966. *The New Field Book of Freshwater Life.* New York: G. P.
Putnam's Sons.

Lange, W. H. 1978. Aquatic and semiaquatic Lepidoptera. In R. W. Merritt
and K. W. Cummins, eds. *An Introduction to the Aquatic Insects of North
America.* Dubuque, IA: Kendall/Hunt.

Linsenmaier, W. 1972. *Insects of the World,* Trans. L. E. Chadwick. New York:
McGraw-Hill.

Lutz, F. E. 1935. *Field Book of Insects.* New York: G. P. Putnam's Sons.

Mackay, R. J., and G. B. Wiggins. 1979. Ecological diversity in Trichoptera.
Annual Review of Entomology, 24:185–208.

Needham, J. G., and C. Betten. 1901. Aquatic insects in the Adirondacks. *Bulletin of the New York State Museums,* 47:383–612.

O'Farrel, A. F. 1970. Odonata. In D. F. Waterhouse, ed., *The Insects of Australia.* Carlton, Australia: Melbourne University Press.

Oldroyd, H. 1964. *The Natural History of Flies.* New York: W. W. Norton.

Peterson, A. 1951. *Larvae of Insects, Part II*. Ann Arbor, MI: Edwards Brothers.

Preston-Mafham, K., and R. Preston-Mafham. 1996. *The Natural History of Spiders*. Ramsbury, Eng.: The Crowood Press.

Roberts, M. J. 1995. *Spiders of Britain and Northern Europe*. London: Harper Collins.

Stehr, F. W., ed. 1991. *Immature Insects*, vol. 2. Dubuque, IA: Kendall/Hunt.

Teskey, H. J. 1991. Order Diptera. In F. W. Stehr, ed., *Immature Insects*, vol. 2. Dubuque, IA: Kendall/Hunt.

Where They Live

Aldrich, J. M. 1912. The biology of some western species of the dipterous genus *Ephydra*. *Journal of the New York Entomological Society*, 20:77–98.

Andersen, N. M., and J. T. Polhemus. 1976. Water striders (Hemiptera: Gerridae, Veliidae, etc.). In L. Cheng, ed., *Marine Insects*. Amsterdam: North Holland Publishing Co.

Beck, S. D. 1968. *Insect Photoperiodism*. New York: Academic Press.

Beebe, M. B., and C. W. Beebe. 1910. *Our Search for a Wilderness*. New York: Henry Holt.

Brock, T. D., and M. L. Brock. 1968. Life in a hot-water basin. *Natural History*, 77:46–53.

Calvert, P. P. 1923. Studies on Costa Rican odonata. X. *Megaloprepus*, its distribution, variation, habits and food. *Entomological News*, 34:168–174.

Cheng, L. 1974. Notes on the ecology of the oceanic insect *Halobates*. *Marine Fisheries Review*, 36:1–7.

———— 1976. Insects in marine environments. In L. Cheng, ed., *Marine Insects*. Amsterdam: North-Holland.

Clarke, C. M., and R. L. Kitching. 1995. Swimming ants and pitcher plants: a unique ant-plant interaction from Borneo. *Journal of Tropical Ecology*, 11:589–602.

Collins, N. C., R. Mitchell, and R. G. Wiegert. 1976. Functional analysis of a thermal spring ecosystem, with an evaluation of the role of consumers. *Ecology*, 57:1221–1232.

Coquillett, D. W. 1901. Three new species of Culicidae. *The Canadian Entomologist*, 33:258–260.

Emery, R. J., Jr. 1934. Another case of Odonate migration. *Entomological News*, 45:50.

Evans, D. L., and G. P. Waldbauer. 1982. Behavior of adult and naïve birds when presented with a bumblebee and its mimic. *Zeitschrift für Tierpsychologie*, 59:247–259.

Fashing, N. J. 1975. Life history and general biology of *Naiadacarus arboricola* Fashing, a mite inhabiting water-filled tree holes (Acarina: Acaridae). *Journal of Natural History*, 9:413–424.

Fincke, O. M. 1992. Behavioural ecology of the giant damselflies of Barro Colorado Island, Panama. In D. Quintero and A. Aiello, eds., *Insects of Panama and Mesoamerica*. Oxford: Oxford University Press.

———— 1996. Larval behaviour of a giant damselfly: territoriality or size-dependent dominance? *Animal Behaviour*, 51:77–87.

———— 1998. The population ecology of *Megaloprepus coerulatus* and its effect on species assemblages in water-filled tree holes. In J. P. Dempster and I. F. G. McLean, eds., *Insect Populations*. Dordrecht, Netherlands: Kluwer Academic Publishers.

Geijskes, D. C. 1975. The dragonfly wing used as a nose plug ornament. *Odonatologica*, 4:29–30.

Givnish, T. J. 1989. Ecology and evolution of carnivorous plants. In W. G. Abrahamson, ed., *Plant-Animal Interactions*. New York: McGraw-Hill.

Hashimoto, H. 1976. Non-biting midges of marine habitats (Diptera: Chironomidae). In L. Cheng, ed., *Marine Insects*. Amsterdam: North-Holland.

Headlee, T. J. 1945. *The Mosquitoes of New Jersey and Their Control*. New Brunswick, NJ: Rutgers University Press.

Horsfall, W. R. 1955. *Mosquitoes*. New York: Ronald Press.

Kettle, D. S. 1995. *Medical and Veterinary Entomology*. Wallingford, Eng.: Cab International.

Koskinen, R. 1968. Seasonal emergence of *Clunio marinus* Haliday (Dipt., Chironomidae) in western Norway. *Annales Zoologici Fennici*, 5:71–75.

Louton, J., J. Gelhaus, and R. Bouchard. 1996. The aquatic macrofauna of water-filled bamboo (Poaceae: Bambusoidea: *Guada*) internodes in a Peruvian lowland tropical forest. *Biotropica*, 28:228–242.

Maier, C. T. 1978. The immature stages and biology of *Mallota posticata* (Fabricius) (Diptera: Syrphidae). *Proceedings of the Entomological Society of Washington*, 80:424–440.

Maier, C. T., and G. P. Waldbauer. 1979. Dual mate-seeking strategies in male syrphid flies (Diptera: Syrphidae). *Annals of the Entomological Society of America*, 72:54–61.

———— 1979. Diurnal activity patterns of flower flies (Diptera: Syrphidae) in an Illinois sand area. *Annals of the Entomological Society of America*, 72:237–245.

Mitchell, R. 1974. The evolution of thermophily in hot springs. *Quarterly Review of Biology*, 49:229–242.

Murray, M. D. 1976. Insect parasites of marine birds and mammals. In L. Cheng, ed., *Marine Insects*. Amsterdam: North-Holland.

Neumann, D. 1986. Life cycle strategies of an intertidal midge between subtropic and arctic latitudes. In F. Taylor and R. Karban, eds., *The Evolution of Insect Life Cycles*. New York: Springer-Verlag.

Smith, J. B. 1901. Some notes on the larval habits of *Culex pungens*. *Entomological News*, 12:153–157.

Thorpe, W. H. 1930. The biology of the petroleum fly (*Psilopa petroleii*, Coq.). *Transactions of the Entomological Society of London*, 78:331–343.

Usinger, R. L. 1956. *Aquatic Insects of California*. Berkeley: University of California Press.

Watts, D. M., S. Pantuwatana, G. R. DeFoliart, T. M. Yuill, and W. H. Thompson. 1973. Transovarial transmission of LaCrosse virus (California encephalitis group) in the mosquito, *Aedes triseriatus*. *Science*, 182:1140–1141.

Watts, D. M., W. H. Thompson, T. M. Yuill, G. R. DeFoliart, and R. P. Hanson. 1974. Overwintering of LaCrosse virus in *Aedes triseriatus*. *The American Journal of Tropical Medicine and Hygiene*, 23:694–700.

Wirth, W. 1971. The brine flies of the genus *Ephydra* in North America (Diptera: Ephydridae). *Annals of the Entomological Society of America*, 64:357–377.

Young, M. W., and S. A. Kay. 2001. Time zones: a comparative genetics of circadian clocks. *Nature Reviews Genetics*, 2:702–715.

The Breath of Life

Alsterberg, G. 1934. Beiträge zur Kentniss der Anatomie und Biologie der limnophilin Syrphidenlarven (Contributions to the understanding of the anatomy and biology of limnophilid syrphid larvae). *Biologisches Zentralblatt,* 54:1–20.

Chapman, R. F. 1998. *The Insects: Structure and Function,* 4th ed. Cambridge: Cambridge University Press.

Dolley, W. L., Jr., and E. J. Farris. 1929. Unicellular gland in the larvae of *Eristalis tenax. Journal of the New York Entomological Society,* 37:127–134.

Edwards, G. A. 1953. Respiratory mechanisms. In K. D. Roeder, ed., *Insect Physiology.* New York: John Wiley and Sons.

Fraenkel, G. 1932. Untersuchungen über die Koordination von Reflexen und automatisch-nervösen Rhythmen bei Insekten. III Das Problem des gerichteten Atemstromes in den Tracheen der Insekten (Investigations of the coordination and autonomic rhythms in insects. III. The problem of directed air streams in the tracheae of insects). *Zeitschrift für Vergleichende Physiologie,* 16:418–443.

Heckman, D. S., D. M. Geiser, B. R. Eidell, R. L. Stauffer, N. L. Kardos, and S. B. Hedges. 2001. Molecular evidence for the early colonization of land by fungi and plants. *Science,* 293:1129–1133.

Horsfall, W. R. 1955. *Mosquitoes.* New York: Ronald Press.

Hynes, H. B. N. 1984. The relationships between the taxonomy and ecology of aquatic insects. In V. H. Resh and D. M. Rosenberg, eds., *The Ecology of Aquatic Insects.* New York: Praeger.

Miall, L. C. 1934. *The Natural History of Aquatic Insects.* London: MacMillan.

Popham, E. J. 1961. *Some Aspects of Life in Fresh Water.* Cambridge: Harvard University Press.

Walton, G. A. 1943. The water bugs (Rhynchota-Hemiptera) of north Somerset. *Transactions of the Society for British Entomology,* 8:231–290.

Westneat, M. W., O. Betz, R. W. Blob, K. Fezzaa, W. J. Cooper, and Wah-Keat Lee. 2003. Tracheal respiration in insects visualized with synchrotron x-ray imaging. *Science,* 299:558–560.

Whitehead, H. 1945. Notes on the biology of *Agrotypus armatus* (Walk.) *The Naturalist,* 1945:123–126.

Wigglesworth, V. B. 1972. *The Principles of Insect Physiology.* London: Chapman and Hall.

Finding Food and Eating

Balduf, W. V. 1935. *The Bionomics of Entomophagous Coleoptera.* St. Louis: John S. Swift.

Basham, E. H., J. A. Mulrennan, and A. Obermuller. 1947. The biology and distribution of *Megarhinus* Robineau-Desvoidy in Florida. *Mosquito News,* 7 64–66.

Bay, E. C. 1974. Predator-prey relationships among aquatic insects. *Annual Review of Entomology,* 19:441–453.

Borg, A. and W. R. Horsfall. 1953. Eggs of floodwater mosquitoes. II. Hatching stimulus. *Annals of the Entomological Society of America,* 47:355–366.

Clements, A. N. 1963. *The Physiology of Mosquitoes,* vol. 17 of the International Series of Monographs on Pure and Applied Biology. New York: MacMillan.

Comstock, J. H. 1940. *An Introduction to Entomology.* Ithaca, NY: Comstock Publishing Co.

Corbet, P. S. 1999. *Dragonflies: Behavior and Ecology of Odonata.* Ithaca, NY: Cornell University Press.

Edmunds, G. F., Jr., S. L. Jensen, and L. Berner. 1976. *The Mayflies of North and Central America.* Minneapolis: University of Minnesota Press.

Erman, N. A. 1981. Terrestrial feeding, migration, and life history of the stream-dwelling caddisfly, *Desmona bethula* (Trichoptera: Limnephilidae). *Canadian Journal of Zoology,* 59:1658–1665.

Farqharson, C. O. 1918. *Harpagomyia* and other Diptera fed by *Crematogaster* ants in S. Nigeria. *Transactions of the Entomological Society of London,* 1918:xxix–xxxix.

Griffith, M. E. 1945. The environment, life history, and structure of the water boatman, *Rhamphocorixa accuminata* (Uhler) (Hemiptera, Corixidae). *The University of Kansas Science Bulletin,* 30:241–365.

Horsfall, W. R. 1955. *Mosquitoes.* New York: Ronald Press.

Klots, E. B. 1966. *The New Field Book of Freshwater Life.* New York: G. P. Putnam's Sons.

Knutson, L. V., and C. O. Berg. 1963. Biology and immature stages of a snail-killing fly, *Hydromya dorsalis* (Fabricus) (Diptera: Scyomyzidae). *Proceedings of the Royal Entomological Society of London* A, 38:45–58.

Lutz, F. E. 1935. *Field Book of Insects*. New York: G. P. Putnam's Sons.

Metcalf, C. L. 1932. *Black Flies and Other Biting Flies of the Adirondacks*. New York State Museum Bulletin 289.

Oldroyd, H. 1964. *The Natural History of Flies*. New York: W. W. Norton.

Poisson, R. 1924. Etude des hemiptères aquatique (Studies of aquatic Hemiptera). *Bulletin Biologique France et Belgique*, 58:49–305.

Price, P. W. 1997. *Insect Ecology*, 3rd ed. New York: John Wiley and Sons.

Resh, V. H. 1976. Life histories of coexisting species of *Ceraclea* caddisflies (Trichoptera: Leptoceridae): the operation of independent functional units in a stream ecosystem. *The Canadian Entomologist*, 108:1303–1318.

Roberts, M. J. 1970. The structure of the mouthparts of syrphid larvae (Diptera) in relation to feeding habits. *Acta Zoologica*, 51:43–65.

Schmidt, J. O. 1982. Biochemistry of insect venoms. *Annual Review of Entomology*, 27:339–368.

Usinger, R. L., ed. 1956. *Aquatic Insects of California*. Berkeley: University of California Press.

Wallace, J. B., and R. W. Merritt. 1980. Filter-feeding ecology of aquatic insects. *Annual Review of Entomology*, 25:103–132.

Wallace, J. B., and F. F. Sherberger. 1975. The larval dwelling and feeding structure of *Macronema transversum* (Walker) (Trichoptera: Hydropsychidae). *Animal Behaviour*, 23:592–596.

Walton, G. A. 1943. The water bugs (Rhynchota-Hemiptera) of north Somerset. *Transactions of the Society for British Entomology*, 8:231–290.

Wigglesworth, V. B. 1972. *The Principles of Insect Physiology*. London: Chapman and Hall.

Going Places

Balduf, W. V. 1935. *The Bionomics of Entomophagous Coleoptera*. St. Louis: John S. Swift.

Bond, C. E. 1979. *Biology of Fishes*. Philadelphia: W. B. Saunders.

Borror, D. J. 1953. A migratory flight of dragonflies. *Entomological News*, 64:204–205.

Brittain, J. E., and T. J. Eikeland. 1988. Invertebrate drift: a review. *Hydrobiologia*, 166:77–93.

Butler, T., J. E. Peterson, and P. S. Corbet. 1975. An exceptionally early and informative arrival of adult *Anax junius* in Ontario (Odonata: Aeshnidae). *Canadian Entomologist,* 107:1253–1254.

Chapman, R. F. 1998. *The Insects,* 4th ed. Cambridge: Cambridge University Press.

Corbet, P. S. 1999. *Dragonflies: Behavior and Ecology of Odonata.* Ithaca, NY: Cornell University Press.

Dunkle, S. W. 2000. *Dragonflies through Binoculars.* New York: Oxford University Press.

Eggers, F. 1926. Die mutmassliche Funktion des Johnstonschen Sinnesorgans bei Gyrinus (The probable function of Johnston's sense organ in Gyrinus). *Zoologischer Anzeiger,* 68:184–192.

Farb, P. 1962. *The Insects.* New York: Time, Inc.

Horsfall, W. R. 1954. A migration of *Aedes vexans* Meigen. *Journal of Economic Entomology,* 47:544.

Klots, E. B. 1966. *The New Field Book of Freshwater Life.* New York: G. P. Putnam's Sons.

Johnson, C. G. 1969. *Migration and Dispersal of Insects by Flight.* London: Methuen.

Linsenmaier, K. E. and R. Jander. 1963. Das "Entspannungsschwimmen" von Velia und Stenus (Expansion swimming by *Velia* and *Stenus*). *Die Naturwissenschaften,* 50:231.

Macan, T. T. 1974. *Freshwater Ecology,* 2nd ed.New York: John Wiley and Sons.

Maier, C. T. 1977. The behavior of *Hydrometra championiana* (Hemiptera: Hydrometridae) and resource partitioning with *Tenagogonus quadrilineatus* (Hemiptera: Gerridae). *Journal of the Kansas Entomological Society,* 50:263–271.

McIntosh, A. R., B. L. Peckarsky, and B. W. Taylor. 2002. The influence of predatory fish on mayfly drift: extrapolating from experiments to nature. *Freshwater Biology,* 47:1497–1513.

Nachtigall, W. 1965. Locomotion: swimming (Hydrodynamics) of aquatic insects. In M. Rockstein, ed., *The Physiology of Insecta,* vol. 2. New York: Academic Press.

Root, F. M. 1912. Dragon flies collected at Point Pelee and Pelee Island, Ontario, in the summers of 1910 and 1911. *Canadian Entomologist,* 44:208–209.

Sheldon, A. L. 1984. Colonization dynamics of aquatic insects. In V. H. Resh and D. M. Rosenberg, eds., *The Ecology of Aquatic Insects*. New York: Praeger.

Taylor, L. R. 1986. The four kinds of migration. In W. Danthanarayana, ed., *Insect Flight*. Berlin: Springer-Verlag.

Tucker, V. A. 1969. Wave-making by whirligig beetles (Gyrinidae). *Science,* 166:897–899.

Usinger, R. L. 1956. Aquatic Hemiptera. In R. L. Usinger, ed., *Aquatic Insects of California*. Berkeley: University of California Press.

Walton, G. A. 1943. The water bugs (Rhynchota-Hemiptera) of north Somerset. *Transactions of the Society for British Entomology,* 8:231–290.

Wolf, W. W., A. N. Sparks, S. D. Pair, J. K. Westbrook, and F. M. Truesdale. 1986. 16 radar observations and collections of insects in the Gulf of Mexico. In W. Danthanarayana, ed., *Insect Flight*. Berlin: Springer-Verlag.

The Next Generation

Alexander, R. M. 1995. Springs for Wings. *Science,* 268:50–51.

Arnquist, G., T. M. Jones, and M. A. Elgar. 2003. Reversal of sex roles in nuptial feeding. *Nature,* 424:387.

Butler, E. A. 1886. *Pond Life: Insects*. London: Swan, Sonnenschein, Lowrey, and Co.

Corbet, P. S. 1999. *Dragonflies: Behavior and Ecology of Odonata*. Ithaca, NY: Cornell University Press.

Craig, G. B., Jr. 1967. Mosquitoes: female monogamy induced by male accessory gland substance. *Science,* 156:1499–1501.

Davies, N. B. 1983. Polyandry, cloaca-pecking, and sperm competition in dunnock. *Nature,* 1983:334–336.

Dickinson, M. H., and J. R. B. Lighton. 1995. Muscle efficiency and elastic storage in the flight motor of *Drosophila*. *Science,* 268:87–90.

Dimmock, G. 1886. *Belostomidae and Other Fish-destroying Bugs*. Annual Report of the Fish and Game Commission of Massachusetts.

Dohan, M. H. 1975. *Our Own Words*. Baltimore: Penguin Books.

Downes, J. A. 1955. Observations on the swarming flight and mating of *Culicoides* (Diptera: Ceratopogonidae). *Transactions of the Royal Entomological Society of London,* 106:213–236.

—— 1969. The swarming and mating flight of Diptera. *Annual Review of Entomology,* 14:271–298.

Edmunds, G. F., Jr., S. L. Jensen, and L. Berner. 1976. *The Mayflies of North and Central America.* Minneapolis: University of Minnesota Press.

Fincke, O. M. 1982. Lifetime mating success in a natural population of the damselfly, *Enallagma hageni* (Walsh) (Odonata: Coenagrionidae). *Behavioral Ecology and Sociobiology,* 10:293–302.

—— 1986. Lifetime reproductive success and the opportunity for selection in a nonterritorial damselfly (Odonata: Coenagrionidae). *Evolution,* 40:791–803.

—— 1992. Behavioral ecology of the giant damselflies of Barro Colorado Island, Panama (Odonata: Zygoptera: Pseudostigmatidae). In D. Quintero and A. Aiello, eds., *Insects of Panama and Mesoamerica.* New York: Oxford University Press.

Griffith, M. E. 1945. The environment, life history, and structure of the water boatman, *Ramphocorixa acuminata* (Uhler) (Hemiptera: Corixidae). *The University of Kansas Science Bulletin,* 30:241–365.

Hassage, R. L., K. W. Stewart, and D. D. Zeigler. 1988. Female response to computer-simulated male drumming call variation in *Pteronarcella badia* (Plecoptera: Pteronarcydiae). *Annals of the Entomological Society of America,* 81:528–531.

Hynes, H. B. N. 1976. Biology of Plecoptera. *Annual Review of Entomology,* 21:135–153.

Klots, E. B. 1966. *The New Field Book of Freshwater Life.* New York: G. P. Putnam's Sons.

Knab, F. 1906. The swarming of *Culex pipiens. Psyche,* 13:123–133.

Maketon, M., and K. W. Stewart. 1988. Patterns and evolution of drumming behavior in the stonefly families Perlidae and Peltoperlidae. *Aquatic Insects,* 10:77–97.

Roth, L. M. 1948. A study of mosquito behavior: an experimental laboratory study of the sexual behavior of *Aedes aegypti* (Linnaeus). *American Midland Naturalist,* 40:265–352.

Slater, F. W. 1899. The egg-carrying habit of *Zaitha. The American Naturalist,* 33:931–933.

Smith, R. L. 1976. Brooding behavior of a male water bug, *Belostoma flumineum* (Hemiptera: Belostomatidae). *Journal of the Kansas Entomological Society,* 49:333–343.

———— 1976. Male brooding behavior of the water bug *Abedus herberti* (Hemiptera: Belostomatidae). *Annals of the Entomological Society of America,* 69:740–747.

———— 1979. Repeated copulation and sperm precedence: paternity assurance for a male brooding water bug. *Science,* 205:1029–1031.

Snodgrass, R. E. 1935. *Principles of Insect Morphology.* New York: McGraw-Hill.

Stewart, K. W., J. C. Abbott, R. F. Kirchner, and S. R. Moulton II. 1995. New descriptions of North American euholognathan stonefly drumming (Plecoptera) and first Nemouridae ancestral call discovered in *Soydina carolinensis* (Plecoptera: Nemouridae). *Annals of the Entomological Society of America,* 88:234–239.

Stewart, K. W., and M. Maketon. 1991. Structures used by Nearctic stoneflies (Plecoptera) for drumming, and their relationship to behavioral pattern diversity. *Aquatic Insects,* 13:33–53.

Thornhill, R., and J. Alcock. 1983. *The Evolution of Insect Mating Systems.* Cambridge: Harvard University Press.

Torre-Bueno, J. R. de la. 1906. Life-histories of North-American water bugs. *The Canadian Entomologist,* 38:189–195.

Waage, J. K. 1979. Dual function of the damselfly's penis: sperm removal and transfer. *Science,* 203:916–918.

Wilcox, R. S. 1979. Sex discrimination in *Gerris remigis:* role of a surface wave signal. *Science,* 206:1325–1327.

———— 1984. Male copulatory guarding enhances female foraging in a water strider. *Behavioral and Ecological Sociobiology,* 15:171–174.

Wilson, A. B., I. Ahnesjö, A. C. Vincent, and A. Meyer. 2003. The dynamics of male brooding, mating patterns, and sex roles in pipefishes and seahorses (Family Syngnathidae). *Evolution,* 57:1374–1386.

On Being Eaten

Anderson, N. L., D. L. Woodward, and A. E. Colwell. 1986. Pestiferous species and two recently introduced aquatic species at Clear Lake. *Proceedings and Papers of the Fifty-fourth Annual Conference of the California Mosquito and Vector Control Association, Inc.*

Askew, R. R. 1971. *Parasitic Insects.* New York: American Elsevier.

Bent, A. C. 1923. *Life Histories of North American Wild Fowl.* Washington, DC: U.S. Government Printing Office.

———— 1948. *Life Histories of North American Nuthatches, Wrens, Thrashers, and Their Allies.* Washington, DC: U.S. Government Printing Office.

Bond, C. E. 1979. *Biology of Fishes.* Philadelphia: W. B. Saunders.

Brown, H. P. 1951. *Climacea areolaris* (Hagen) parasitized by a new pteromalid (Hymenoptera: Chalcidoidea). *Annals of the Entomological Society of America,* 44:103–110.

———— 1952. The life history of *Climacea areolaris* (Hagen), a neuropterous "parasite" of fresh water sponges. *The American Midland Naturalist,* 47:130–160.

Cameron, K. M., K. J. Wurdack, and R. W. Jobson. 2002. Molecular evidence for the common origin of snap-traps among carnivorous plants. *American Journal of Botany,* 89:1503–1509.

Cook, S. F. 1981. The Clear Lake example: an ecological approach to pest management. *Environment,* 23:25–30.

Corbet, P. S. 1999. *Dragonflies: Behavior and Ecology of Odonata.* Ithaca, NY: Cornell University Press.

Fincke, O. M. 1992. Behavioral ecology of the giant damselflies of Barro Colorado Island, Panama (Odonata: Zygoptera: Pseudostigmatidae). In D. Quintero and A. Aiello, eds., *Insects of Panama and Mesoamerica.* New York: Oxford University Press.

———— 1999. Organization of predator assemblages in Neotropical tree holes: effects of abiotic factors and priority. *Ecological Entomology,* 24:13–23.

Fincke, O. M., S. P. Yanoviak, and R. D. Hanschu. 1997. Predation by odonates depresses mosquito abundance in water-filled tree holes in Panama. *Oecologia,* 112:244–253.

Finger, T. E. 1986. Electroreception in catfish: behavior, anatomy, and electrophysiology. In T. H. Bullock and W. Heiligenberg, eds., *Electroreception.* New York: John Wiley and Sons.

Flint, M. L., and R. van den Bosch. 1981. *Introduction to Integrated Pest Management.* New York: Plenum Press.

Givnish, T. J. 1989. Ecology and evolution of carnivorous plants. In W. G. Abrahamson, ed., *Plant-Animal Interactions.* New York: McGraw-Hill.

Gossard, H. A. 1909. Relation of insects to human welfare. *Journal of Economic Entomology,* 2:313–332.

Grzimek, B., ed. 1974. *Grzimek's Animal Life Encyclopedia*, vol. 5. New York: Van Nostrand and Reinhold.

Kalmijn, A. J. 1974. The detection of electric fields from inanimate and animate sources other than electric organs. In A. Fessard, ed., *Electroreceptors and Other Specialized Receptors in Lower Vertebrates. Handbook of Sensory Physiology*, vol. 3, sect. 3. New York: Springer-Verlag.

Lagler, K. F., J. E. Bardach, R. R. Miller, and D. R. M. Passino. 1977. *Ichthyology*, 2nd ed. New York: John Wiley and Sons.

Lloyd, J. T. 1919. An aquatic dipterous parasite, *Ginglymyia acrirostris* Towns., and additional notes on its lepidopterous host, *Elophila fulicalis. Journal of the New York Entomological Society*, 27:263–265.

Malthus, T. 1817. *An Essay on the Principle of Population*, 5th ed. London: John Murray.

Marshall, N. B. 1966. *The Life of Fishes*. Cleveland: World Publishing Co.

Morin, P. 1984. The impact of fish exclusion on the abundance and species composition of larval odonates: results of short-term experiments in a North Carolina farm pond. *Ecology*, 65:53–60.

Needham, J. G., J. R. Traver, and Y-c Hsu. 1935. *The Biology of Mayflies*. Ithaca, NY: Comstock Publishing Co..

Oldroyd, H. 1964. *The Natural History of Flies*. New York: W. W. Norton.

Oliver, J. A. 1955. *The Natural History of North American Amphibians and Reptiles*. Princeton: D. van Nostrand.

Ormerod, S. 1996. Dippers, *Cinclus cinclus*, as predators in upland streams. In S. P. R. Greenstreet and W. L. Taskes, eds., *Aquatic Predators and Their Prey*. Oxford: Blackwell.

Peckarsky, B. L., and S. I. Dodson, 1980. Do stonefly predators influence benthic distributions in streams? *Ecology*, 61:1275–1282.

Peters, R. C., and F. Bretschneider. 1972. Electric phenomena in the habitat of the catfish *Ictalurus nebulosus* Les. *Journal of Comparative Physiology*, 81:345–362.

Power, M. E. 1992. Habitat heterogeneity and functional significance of fish in river food webs. *Ecology*, 73:1675–1688.

Prosser, C. L. 1973. *Comparative Animal Physiology*. Philadelphia: W. B. Saunders.

Reinhardt, K. 1996. Negative effects of *Arrenurus* water mites on the flight distances of the damselfly *Nehallennia speciosa* (Odonata: Coenagrionidae). *Aquatic Insects,* 18:233–240.

Salt, G. 1937. The egg-parasite of *Sialis lutaria:* a study of the influence of the host upon a dimorphic parasite. *Parasitology,* 29:539–553.

Schober, W. 1984. *The Lives of Bats,* trans. Sylvia Furness. London: Croom Helm.

Smith, B. P. 1989. Impact of parasitism by larval *Limnochares aquatica* (Acari: Hydrachnidia; Limnocharidae) on juvenile *Gerris comatus, Gerris alacris,* and *Gerris buenoi* (Insecta: Hemiptera; Gerridae). *Canadian Journal of Zoology,* 67:2238–2243.

Treat, A. E. 1975. *Mites of Moths and Butterflies.* Ithaca, NY: Cornell University Press.

Wheeler, A. 1985. *The World Encyclopedia of Fishes.* London: Macdonald and Co.

Willis, O. R. 1971. A mermithid nematode in naiads of damselflies (Odonata: Coenagrionidae). *The Florida Entomologist,* 54:321–324.

Zug, G. R. 1993. *Herpetology.* San Diego: Academic Press.

How Not to Be Eaten

Arnett, H. R., Jr., and M. C. Thomas. 2001. *American Beetles,* vol 1. Baton Rouge: Chemical Rubber Company Press.

Bateson, W. 1889–90. Notes on the senses and habits of some crustacea. *Journal of the Marine Biological Station of the United Kingdom,* 1:211–214.

Benedict, M. Q., and J. A. Seawright. 1987. Changes in pigmentation in mosquitoes (Diptera: Culicidae) in response to color of the environment. *Annals of the Entomological Society of America,* 80:55–61.

Benfield, E. F. 1972. A defensive secretion of *Dineutes discolor* (Coleoptera: Gyrinidae). *Annals of the Entomological Society of America,* 65:1324–1327.

Brower, L. P. 1969. Ecological chemistry. *Scientific American,* 220:22–30.

Brown, H. P. 1987. Biology of riffle beetles. *Annual Review of Entomology,* 32:253–273.

Clark, H. 1866. Catalogue of the Dytiscidae and Gyrinidae of Australasia, with descriptions of new species. *Journal of Entomology,* 2:214–219.

Cott, H. B. 1957. *Adaptive Coloration in Animals.* London: Methuen.

Darwin, C. 1871. *The Descent of Man, and Selection in Relation to Sex.* The Works of Charles Darwin, vol. 22. New York: New York University Press.

Dettner, K. 1987. Chemosystematics and evolution of beetle chemical defenses. *Annual Review of Entomology,* 32:17–48.

Edmunds, M. 1974. *Defence in Animals.* New York: Longmans.

Eisner, T. 1970. Chemical defense against predation in arthropods. In E. Sondheimer and J. B. Simeone, eds., *Chemical Ecology.* New York: Academic Press.

——— 1972. Chemical ecology: on arthropods and how they live as chemists. *Verhandlungsbericht der Deutschen Zoologischen Gesellschaft, 65. Jahresversammlung,* 1972:123–137.

Elton, C. S. 1922. On the colours of water-mites. *Proceedings of the Zoological Society of London* 1922:1231–1239.

Evans, D. L., and G. P. Waldbauer. 1982. Behavior of adult and naïve birds when presented with a bumblebee and its mimic. *Zeitschrift für Tierpsychologie,* 59:247–259.

Feltmate, B. W., and D. D. Williams. 1989. A test of crypsis and predator avoidance in the stonefly *Paragnetina media* (Plecoptera: Perlidae). *Animal Behaviour,* 37:992–999.

Foster, W. A., and J. E. Treherne. 1981. Evidence for the dilution effect in the selfish herd from fish predation on a marine insect. *Nature,* 293:466–467.

Hamilton, W. D. 1971. Geometry of the selfish herd. *Journal of Theoretical Biology,* 31:295–311.

Hutchinson, G. E. 1981. Thoughts on aquatic insects. *BioScience,* 31:495–500.

Hynes, H. B. N., and M. E. Hynes. 1975. The life histories of many of the stoneflies (Plecoptera) of south-eastern mainland Australia. *Australian Journal of Marine and Freshwater Research,* 26:113–153.

Illies, J. 1963. Revision der Südamerikanischen Griptoterygidae (Plecoptera) (Revision of the South American Griptoterygidae (Plecoptera). *Mitteilungen der Schweizerischen Entomologischen Gesellschaft,* 36:145–245.

Johansson, A., and F. Johansson. 1992. Effects of two different caddisfly case structures on predation by a dragonfly larva. *Aquatic Insects,* 14:85–92.

Johnson, D. M., and P. H. Crowley. 1980. Odonate "hide and seek": habitat specific rules? In W. C. Kerfoot, ed., *Evolution and Ecology of Zooplankton Communities.* Hanover, NH: University Press of New England.

Kerfoot, W. C. 1982. A question of taste: crypsis and warning coloration in freshwater zooplankton communities. *Ecology,* 63:538–554.

Nielsen, A. 1942. Über die Entwicklung und Biologie der Trichopteren mit besondere Berücksichtigung der Quelltrichopteren Himmerlands (On the development and biology of Trichoptera with particular consideration of the Trichoptera of springs in Himmerland). *Archiv für Hydrobiologie,* Supplement 17:255–631.

Otto, C., and B. S. Svensson. 1980. The significance of case material selection for the survival of caddis larvae. *Journal of Animal Ecology,* 49: 855–865.

Peckarsky, B. L. 1984. Predator-prey interactions among aquatic insects. In V. H. Resh and D. M. Rosenberg, eds., *The Ecology of Aquatic Insects.* New York: Praeger.

Peterson, R. T. 1969. *A Field Guide to the Western Birds.* Boston: Houghton Mifflin.

Popham, E. J. 1942. The variation in the colour of certain species of *Arctocorisa* (Hemiptera: Corixidae) and its significance. *Proceedings of the Zoological Society of London* A, 111:135–159.

Scrimgeour, G. J., and J. M. Culp. 1994. Foraging and evading predators: the effect of predator species on a behavioural trade-off by a lotic mayfly. *Oikos,* 69:71–79.

Scrimshaw, S., and W. C. Kerfoot. 1987. Chemical defense of freshwater organisms: beetles and bugs. In W. C. Kerfoot and A. Sih, eds., *Predation: Direct and Indirect Impacts on Aquatic Communities.* Hanover, NH: University Press of New England.

Shelford, R. W. C. 1916. *A Naturalist in Borneo.* London: T. Fisher Unwin.

Sih, A. 1982. Foraging strategies and the avoidance of predation by an aquatic insect, *Notonecta hoffmanni. Ecology,* 63:786–796.

Stenson, J. A. E. 1980. Predation pressure from fish on two *Chaoborus* species related to their visibility. In W. C. Kerfoot, ed., *Evolution and Ecology of Zooplankton Communities.* Hanover: NH: University Press of New England.

Sweeney, B. W., and R. L. Vannote. 1982. Population synchrony in mayflies: a predator satiation hypothesis. *Evolution,* 36:810–821.

Treherne, J. E., and W. A. Foster. 1982. Group size and anti-predator strategies in a marine insect. *Animal Behaviour,* 32:536–542.

von Ende, C. N. 1979. Fish predation, interspecific predation, and the distribution of two *Chaoborus* species. *Ecology,* 60:119–128.

Wallace, A. R. 1866. [No title.] *Journal of Proceedings of the Entomological Society of London,* 1866 (in *Transactions of the Entomological Society of London*), 5:1xxx–1xxxi.

White, D. S. 1989. Defense mechanisms in riffle beetles (Coleoptera: Dryopidae). *Annals of the Entomological Society of America,* 82:237–241.

Coping with the Climate

Borg, A., and W. R. Horsfall. 1953. Eggs of floodwater mosquitoes. II. Hatching stimulus. *Annals of the Entomological Society of America,* 47:355–366.

Bradshaw, W. E. 1973. Homeostasis and polymorphism in vernal development of *Chaoborous americanus. Ecology,* 54:1247–1259.

Campbell, M. D., and W. E. Bradshaw. 1992. Genetic coordination of diapause in the pitcherplant mosquito, *Wyeomyia smithii* (Diptera: Culicidae). *Annals of the Entomological Society of America,* 85:445–451.

Conover, D. O., and S. W. Heins. 1987. Adaptive variation in environmental and genetic sex determination in a fish. *Nature,* 326:496–498.

Coquillett, D. W. 1901. Three new species of culicidae. *The Canadian Entomologist,* 33:258–260.

Corbet, P. S. 1999. *Dragonflies: Behavior and Ecology of Odonata.* Ithaca, NY: Cornell University Press.

Fredeen, F. J. H. 1959. Collection, extraction, sterilization, and low temperature storage of black-fly eggs (Diptera: Simuliidae). *The Canadian Entomologist,* 91:450–453.

Harper, P. P., and H. B. N. Hynes. 1969. Life-histories of Capniidae and Taeneopterygidae (Plecoptera) in Southern Ontario. *American Midland Naturalist,* 82:284–312.

Healey, M. 1984. Fish predation on aquatic insects. In. V. H. Resh and D. M. Rosenberg, eds., *The Ecology of Aquatic Insects.* New York: Praeger.

Heinrich, B. 1996. *The Thermal Warriors.* Cambridge: Harvard University Press.

Hinton, H. E. 1960. Cryptobiosis in the larva of *Polypedilum vanderplanki* Hint. (Chironomidae). *Journal of Insect Physiology,* 5:286–300.

——— 1960. A fly larva that tolerates dehydration and temperatures of −270° to +102°C. *Nature,* 188:336–337.

Horsfall, W. R. 1955. *Mosquitoes*. New York: Ronald Press.

Horsfall, W. R., and J. F. Anderson. 1961. Suppression of male characteristics of mosquitoes by thermal means. *Science,* 133:1830–1831.

——— 1964. Thermal stress and anomalous development of mosquitoes (Diptera: Culicidae). II. Effects of alternating temperatures on dimorphism of adults of *Aedes stimulans. Journal of Experimental Zoology,* 156:61–90.

Huffaker, C. B. 1942. Observations on the over-wintering of mosquitoes near Fort DuPont, Delaware. *Mosquito News,* 2, no. 2:37–40.

Hungerford, H. B. 1919. The biology and ecology of aquatic and semiaquatic Hemiptera. *The Kansas University Science Bulletin,* 11:3–265.

Hynes, H. B. N. 1970. *The Ecology of Running Waters.* Toronto: University of Toronto Press.

——— 1976. Biology of Plecoptera. *Annual Review of Entomology,* 21:135–153.

Jennings, P. J. 1935. *A Book of Trout Flies.* New York: Crown Publishers.

Kaiser, J. 2003. Drought portends mosquito misery. *Nature,* 301:904.

Kavaliers, M. 1980. Rhythmic thermoregulation in a larval cranefly (Diptera: Tipulidae). *Canadian Journal of Zoology,* 59:555–558.

Klots, E. B. 1966. *The New Field Book of Freshwater Life.* New York: G. P. Putnam's Sons.

Krishnara, R., and G. Pritchard. 1995. The influence of larval size, temperature, and components of the functional response to prey density on growth rates of the dragonflies *Lestes disjunctus* and *Coenagrion resolutum* (Insecta: Odonata). *Canadian Journal of Zoology,* 73:1672–1680.

Mowat, F. 1952. *People of the Deer.* Boston: Little, Brown.

Prosser, C. L., ed. 1973. *Comparative Animal Physiology,* 3rd ed. Philadelphia: W. B. Saunders.

Ross, H. H., C. A. Ross, and J. R. P. Ross. 1982. *A Textbook of Entomology.* New York: John Wiley and Sons.

Shelford, V. E. 1963. *The Ecology of North America.* Urbana: University of Illinois Press.

Shine, R., M. J. Elphick, and S. Donnellan. 2002. Co-occurrence of multiple, supposedly incompatible modes of sex determination in a lizard population. *Ecology Letters,* 5:486–489.

Smith, J. B. 1901. Some notes on the larval habits of *Culex pungens*. *Entomological News*, 12:153–157.

Southwood, T. R. E. 1975. The dynamics of insect populations. In D. Pimental, ed., *Insects, Science, and Society*. New York: Academic Press.

Spence, J. R., D. Hughes Spence, and G. G. E. Scudder. 1980. Submergence behavior in Gerris: underwater basking. *American Midland Naturalist*, 103:385–391.

Spielman, A., and M. D'Antonio. 2001. *Mosquito*. New York: Hyperion.

Tozer, W. 1979. Underwater behavioural thermoregulation in the adult stonefly, *Zapada cinctipes*. *Nature*, 281:566–567.

Trottier, R. 1971. Effect of temperature on the life cycle of *Anax junius* (Odonata: Aeshnidae) in Canada. *The Canadian Entomologist*, 103:1671–1683.

Vepsäläinen, K. 1978. Wing dimorphism and diapause in *Gerris*: determination and adaptive significance. In H. Dingle, ed., *Evolution of Insect Migration and Diapause*. New York: Springer-Verlag.

Waldbauer, G. P. 1978. Phenological adaptation and the polymodal emergence patterns of insects. In H. Dingle, ed., *Evolution of Insect Migration and Diapause*. New York: Springer-Verlag.

Wigglesworth, V. B. 1972. *The Principles of Insect Physiology*, 7th ed. London: Chapman and Hall.

Williams, D. D. 1984. The hyporheic zone as a habitat for insects and associated arthropods. In V. H. Resh and D. M. Rosenberg, eds., *The Ecology of Aquatic Insects*. New York: Praeger.

Our Friends and Enemies

Bodenheimer, F. S. 1951. *Insects as Human Food*. The Hague: W. Junk.

Bristowe, W. S. 1932. Insects and other invertebrates for human consumption in Siam. *Transactions of the Entomological Society of London*, 80:387–404.

Budiansky, S. 2002. Creatures of our own making. *Science*, 298:80–86.

Carr, J. F., and J. K. Hiltunen. 1965. Changes in the bottom fauna of western Lake Erie from 1930 to 1961. *Limnology and Oceanography*, 10:551–569.

Chahl, J., S. Thakoor, N. Le Bouffant, G. Stange, M. V. Srinivasan, B. Hine, and S. Zornetzer. 2003. Bioinspired engineering of exploration systems: a horizon sensor/attitude reference system based on the dragonfly ocelli for Mars exploration applications. *Journal of Robotic Systems*, 20:35–42.

China, W. E. 1931. An interesting relationship between a crayfish and a water bug. *Natural History Magazine,* 3:57–62.

Corkum, L. D., J. J. H. Ciborowski, and Z. E. Koovats. 1995. Aquatic insects as biomonitors of ecosystem health in the Great Lakes areas of concern. In F. M. Bjutterworth, L. D. Corkum, and J. Guzman, eds., *Biomonitors and Biomarkers as Indicators of Environmental Change.* New York: Plenum Press.

Cunningham, W. P., and B. W. Saigo. 2001. *Environmental Science,* 6th ed. Boston: McGraw-Hill.

Greenwood, B. 2004. Between hope and a hard place. *Nature,* 430:926–927.

Gullan, P. J., and P. S. Cranston. 1994. *The Insects: An Outline of Entomology.* London: Chapman and Hall.

Harwood, R. F., and M. T. James. 1979. *Entomology in Human and Animal Health.* New York: Macmillan.

Healey, M. 1984. Fish predation on aquatic insects. In. V. H. Resh and D. M. Rosenberg, eds., *The Ecology of Aquatic Insects.* New York: Praeger.

Hearn, L. 1910. *A Japanese Miscellany.* Boston: Little, Brown.

Hynes, H. B. N. 1963. *The Biology of Polluted Waters.* Liverpool: Liverpool University Press.

Keen, F. P. 1952. Bark beetles in forests. In F. C. Bishop, ed., *Insects: The Yearbook of Agriculture, 1952.* Washington, DC: U.S. Department of Agriculture.

Klots, E. B. 1966. *The New Field Book of Freshwater Life.* New York: G. P. Putnam's Sons.

Manson, P. 1878. On the development of *Filaria sanguinis hominis* and on the mosquito considered as a nurse. *Journal of the Linnaean Society of London, Zoology,* 14:304–311.

Oldroyd, H. 1964. *The Natural History of Flies.* New York: W. W. Norton.

Pemberton, R. W. 1988. The use of the Thai giant water bug, *Lethocerus indicus* (Hemiptera: Belostomatidae), as human food in California. *Pan-Pacific Entomologist,* 64:81–82.

Remington, C. L. 1946. Insects as food in Japan. *Entomological News,* 58:119–121.

Stange, G. 1981. The ocellar component of flight equilibrium control in dragonflies. *Journal of Comparative Physiology,* 141:335–347.

Stange, G., and J. Howard. 1979. An ocellar dorsal light response in a dragonfly. *Journal of Experimental Biology,* 83:351–355.

Sternburg, J. G., E. B. Vinson, and C. W. Kearns. 1953. Enzymatic dehydrochlorination of DDT by resistant flies. *Journal of Economic Entomology,* 46:513–515.

Wellems, T. E. 2002. *Plasmodium* chloroquine resistance and the search for a replacement antimalarial drug. *Science,* 298 124–126.

Acknowledgments

I am greatly indebted to the many friends and colleagues whose expertise and support made this book considerably more than it would have been without their help. Outstanding among many are May Berenbaum, John Bouseman, Sydney Cameron, Susan Fahrbach, Norman Fashing, Jeffrey Heilveil, Hugo James, Richard Lampman, James Nardi, Robert Novak, James Sternburg, and James Whitfield. I am particularly indebted to Phyllis Cooper for her constructive criticism of much of the manuscript. Ann Downer-Hazell's guidance in the early stages of the book's development was invaluable. Nancy Clemente was as brilliant as ever in making me look good by editing my manuscript. Marianne Perlak is to be congratulated for designing a truly beautiful book. And for her lovely illustrations, I am grateful to Meredith Waterstraat.

Index

Damselflies, 15, 25; aesthetic appeal of, 246; body temperature, 212; climate and, 210; feeding habits, 79, 80; "giant," 32, 36–38, 41; habitats of, 36–38, 41; locomotion, 107; as "mosquito hawks," 161; parasites of, 155; predators of, 172, 175, 178; protection from predators, 184; reproduction, 141–147; respiration, *57*, 71; wind migrations of, 117

D'Antonio, Michael, 209

Danube River, 117

Dart poison frogs, 170–171

Darwin, Charles, 153, 198

Davies, Nick, 146

DDD insecticide, 169–170, 234

DDE (dichloro-diphenyl-ethylene), 234, 235

DDT insecticide, 169, 234, 235, 238–239

Death-watch beetles, 139

Dengue, 162, 239

Dettner, Konrad, 199

Diapause, 34, 35, 215–225, 244

Diatoms, 83

Dickinson, Michael, 137

Digestion process, 94

Diptera, order. *See* Flies; Mosquitoes

Diseases, insect-borne, 34, 35–36, 162, *229*, 235–240

Dobsonflies, 13, 18–19, 92, 149, 200, 215

Dodson, Stanley, 161, 167

Dohan, Mary, 131

Dolley, William, Jr., 64

Donacia beetles, 64–65, 82, 148

Downer-Hazell, Ann, 47

Downes, John, 134

Downes, William, 46, 174

Dragonflies, *1*, 3, 6, 15, 116–117; as aerial predators, 185; aesthetic appeal of, 246–247; body temperature, 212, 213; climate and, 215; eyes, 80, 245–246; habitats of, 32; Japanese haiku about, 228, 247; metamorphosis of, 12; migrations of, 117, 118–119, 119–123, 222–223; as "mosquito hawks," 161, 174; myths about, 141; natural selection and, 188–189; predators of, 167; reproduction, 141–147; in salt marshes, 46; "wheel" formation, in copulation, 143–144. *See also* Green darner

Dragonfly nymphs, 4, 37; caddisfly cases and, 197; coloration of, 200; feeding habits, *75*, 77–78, 79–80; as food for humans, 241; locomotion, 105–107, 113; parasites of, 156; predators of, 172; protection from predators, 184, 187; respiration, 59, 60, 71; water temperatures and, 208

Drift, as locomotion, 113–115

Drone flies, 24, 61, 88. *See also* Rat-tailed maggots

Droughts, 153–154, 203, 221, 222–223, 224

Drumming, 137–139

Ducks, 173–174

Duckweeds, 81

Dunkle, Sidney, 119

Ear mites, 160–161

Earthworms, 78

Eastern tree hole mosquito, 35

Echolocation, 112

Ecological niches, 42, 49

Ecosystems, 6, 228, 240; food chains